FIRE
FROM THE
SKY

FIRE
FROM THE
SKY

Seawolf Gunships
in the Mekong Delta

RICHARD C. KNOTT

Naval Institute Press
Annapolis, Maryland

Naval Institute Press
291 Wood Road
Annapolis, MD 21402

ISBN 1-59114-447-7

Printed in the United States of America

*This book is dedicated to all of the Seawolves
and to their spectacular courage in combat
in the Mekong Delta.*

Contents

List of Ranks and Ratings

U.S. Navy officer rank abbreviations mentioned in the text:

Adm.	Admiral
Capt.	Captain
Cdr.	Commander
Ens.	Ensign
Lt.	Lieutenant
Lt. Cdr.	Lieutenant Commander
Lt. (jg)	Lieutenant (junior grade)
Rear Adm.	Rear Admiral
Vice Adm.	Vice Admiral

U.S. Navy enlisted personnel specialty rating abbreviations mentioned in the text:

ADJ	Aviation Machinists Mate (Jet Engine Mechanic)
AE	Aviation Electrician's Mate
AMH	Aviation Structural Mechanic (Hydraulics)
AMS	Aviation Structural Mechanic (Structures)
AN	Airman (non-rated)

AO	Aviation Ordnanceman
AT	Aviation Electronics Technician
ATN	Aviation Electronics Technician (Radio & Radio Navigation Equipment)
AX	Aviation Antisubmarine Warfare Technician
CS	Commissaryman

U.S. Army officer rank abbreviations mentioned in the text:

Capt.	Captain
1st Lt.	First Lieutenant
Gen.	General
WO	Warrant Officer

Note: A number following the rating abbreviation indicates the individual's petty officer rank. For example, an AO1 is an Aviation Ordnanceman 1st Class.

Acknowledgments

This book was begun as a Ramsey Fellowship project at the National Air and Space Museum (NASM), Smithsonian Institution, Washington, D.C. As an Adjunct Ramsey Fellow, I was able to make use of the research facilities of NASM and to call upon the museum staff for advice and assistance. I am grateful to them and to other Fellows at NASM for their camaraderie and encouragement.

Of special help in providing material for this book were naval aviation historian Roy Grossnick and his staff at the Aviation Branch of the Naval Historical Center at the Washington Navy Yard, and Sandra Russell, Managing Editor of *Naval Aviation News* magazine. Thanks also go to my good friend Peter Nguyen for his counsel on Vietnamese culture and language.

I am indebted to Rick Burgess of the Navy League's *Sea Power* magazine, U.S. Naval Institute photo archivist Tim Wooldridge, Seawolf Webmaster Ed Pietzuch, author/historian Peter Mersky, and several individual Seawolves for their help in assembling the photographs that illustrate this work.

The official histories of U.S. Navy Helicopter Attack (Light) Squadron Three—abbreviated HA(L)-3—provided me with solid outlines for much of the story, including dates, places, basic descriptions of operations, significant events, and the names of squadron members involved. They also contained a wealth of data on aircraft assigned, detachment locations, weapons developments, ordnance expended, casualty figures, and citations and awards.

Information from the Seawolf Association Web site filled in many blank spaces. Association President Frank Gale, who served in that capacity during 2003–2004, helped to facilitate interviews, while Association Historian Don Thomson was particularly agile in coming up with illusive bits of information and leading me to those who had firsthand experiences in specific areas. Gordon Peterson, then-Senior Editor of *Sea Power* magazine and himself a Seawolf, shared his many contacts and provided me with productive leads. Tom Phillips graciously allowed me to use quotations from his work on the activities of Detachment 9, titled *SCRAMBLE SEAWOLVES!*

Capt. Duane Brofer, U.S. Army, contributed a glimpse of the largely unknown Army Sea Wolves, as did Brig. Gen. Larry Gillespie, who gave an insight into an army pilot's unusual experience of flying from a ship. Navy Seawolves Frank Foster, Frank Koch, and Al Banford each supplied recollections of his participation in operations of the HC-1 detachments, while Michael Peters contributed colorful accounts of his experiences with HC-1 Detachment 21, known as Rowell's Rats.

Conrad Jaburg, the first executive officer of HA(L)-3, arranged meetings with Seawolves of the early squadron period at his home and at the National Museum of Naval Aviation in Pensacola. Bob Spencer, first commanding officer (CO) and an attendee at one of these meetings, provided a good description of what it was like to put a squadron together "in country" with tired old aircraft and extremely little in the way of material resources and support. Several other participants at these meetings were generous in offering other useful information and documentary material on the beginnings of HA(L)-3 as a squadron. I am especially grateful to Jack Bolton for his insights into initial pilot training of Seawolves, as well as early Detachment 2 operations in the infamous Rung Sat Zone.

In addition to Bob Spencer, I was later able to contact and interview subsequent COs individually. Art Munson, Reynolds Beckwith, Charlie Borgstrom (who passed on before this work was completed), and Bill Mulcahy each recalled little-known details and provided a CO's perception of day-to-day activities and significant events during his year of command. Capt. Marty Twite had passed on by the time I began this book, but others came forward to fill in the details of his year of command. These contributions were essential to linking it all together.

Most important were the many other interviews I conducted with pilots and door gunners who served one or more tours. These talks uncovered many gritty, sometimes hair-raising, accounts of combat experiences. I have used these, where appropriate, to give substance and a human dimension to incidents recorded only formally in official histories and other documents.

My heartfelt thanks go out to all of the Seawolves who contributed to this effort. I regret that it was impossible to include many other stories and recollections that were provided to me. In choosing the accounts that I have used in this book, I have attempted to present the reader with a representative look at an extraordinary group of warriors, an accurate account of what they did, and, perhaps most importantly, a gut feel for what the Seawolves were all about. In so doing, I have tried to make this every Seawolf's story.

FIRE
FROM THE
SKY

Introduction

Scramble the Seawolves

It is night, and, as is often the case in this part of the world at this time of year, the moon and stars are obscured by a thick overcast, having a ceiling at about four hundred feet. An occasional light can be seen from a fire ashore, but for the most part, there is only blackness. The water, the land, and the sky seem as one.

Aboard the landing ship tank (LST) anchored in the Bassac River, it is eerily quiet except for the low hum of the ship's generators and the sound of cooling water being pumped over the side. The monsoon season is just beginning, and with nightfall, the temperature has dropped into the high eighties. Moisture from the saturated warm air clings in droplets to the upright structures. It rained less than an hour earlier, and water has pooled in low spots on the steel deck.

A sailor stationed in the bow with a rifle is keeping a sharp lookout for floating clumps of debris. He will shoot at any he spots because it may well contain a satchel charge, fashioned into a makeshift mine and floated downriver in an attempt to sink or damage the ship. This rather primitive form of mine warfare holds little likelihood of success. Still, it has worked before, and the enemy is patient and persistent. The possibility of a mine strike adds to an underlying sense of danger lurking in the darkness. There is a kind of unreality about the whole scene, a feeling of being suspended in a black void as the ship rocks gently in the river current.

Two olive-brown Bell "Huey" helicopter gunships rest on the tiny helipad amidships. Fueled and armed, they are ready to fly at a moment's notice. The duty crews are likewise awaiting the familiar order to launch.

Alongside the ship, several small patrol boats—called PBRs—are tethered to the ship's boat booms. Other PBRs are off somewhere in the darkness, searching for sampans and river junks moving arms, ammunition, men, and supplies to waiting Viet Cong units hidden in the jungle along the riverbanks. Because the enemy uses the darkness to conceal these clandestine waterborne operations, many armed confrontations take place at night. These nocturnal encounters are attended by dramatic pyrotechnic displays, punctuated by fear, courage, heroism, and death!

On this night, two patrolling PBRs have come upon a pair of motorized sampans moving slowly, stealthily and close to shore along a narrow tributary. A shouted "Ngung Lai," the Vietnamese order to heave-to, is met with silence, as the sampans hastily make for the riverbank. The .50-caliber twin mount in the bow of the lead PBR barks a warning to stop that goes unheeded. The PBRs close in, and the jungle suddenly erupts with fire, as Viet Cong guerrillas ashore attempt to rescue the sampans and their contraband cargoes. The PBRs simultaneously return fire, and radio for air support.

Back aboard the LST, the night is shattered by the 1-MC, which blares, "SCRAMBLE THE SEAWOLVES. SCRAMBLE THE SEAWOLVES." The well-choreographed response is immediate and impressive. The two crews, adrenaline pumping, are on deck within seconds. Engines turn over; the fire team leader is on the radio; crewmen have untied the main rotor blades; and the man holding the line on the fire team leader's aircraft is waiting for the signal to let go so the engine can engage the blades. Because just one helo can turn its main rotor at a time on the tiny platform, only after the first gunship is airborne can the other begin the sequence. Still, the evolution is accomplished quickly, with a kind of casual precision.

It is raining again, but no one seems to notice. The lead helicopter lifts off and literally falls over the side of the ship as it loses ground effect. The rotor blades claw for slices of the warm, moisture-soaked air as the Huey transitions to forward flight a few feet above the water's surface. Training, technique, and a good set of nerves are especially critical because merely twenty-two feet lie between the flight deck and the muddy, fast-flowing river. The pilots accomplish this hair-raising maneuver routinely, but always with tightened sphincter muscles. Moreover, flying at night over water, when there is no visible horizon and depth perception is unreliable, is a classic invitation to vertigo. But these are U.S. Navy pilots, accustomed to flying from ships even in high seas and in all kinds of weather. They are highly skilled and well practiced.

The fire team leader recovers a few feet from the surface of the water and begins a climb to a more comfortable altitude of about fifty feet. The pilot of the trail ship follows close behind, also negotiating the hairy takeoff with apparent ease.

Incredibly, less than two minutes after the call to scramble, both helicopters are in the air, hightailing it for the hot spot. Flying low, within another few minutes the pilots can see in the distance tracers from the firefight, green from the enemy ashore, orange-red from the PBRs.

The pilot of the lead aircraft makes radio contact with the boats. As the helos bore in at fifty feet, much of the enemy fire suddenly shifts to them.

The fire team leader squeezes off a couple of rockets at the source of the green tracer fire, being careful to ensure that the aircraft is in balanced flight. Otherwise, the rockets will not wind up where he wants them to go, but will careen in crazy directions, maybe even hitting a "friendly." The copilot, meanwhile, is aiming and firing the M-60 flex guns mounted on each side of the aircraft. He attempts to walk his shots right up to a point on the ground from which the green tracers are being spewed. He is rewarded with a split second of satisfaction when the oncoming stream abruptly ceases. Maybe he has scored a hit, maybe not. In any case, this is just one source of fire from the enemy hornet's nest.

The second helo follows close behind the first. The enemy is ready for it, and bullets penetrate the underside of the aircraft. A couple of rounds strike the armor plating beneath the pilots' seats and are deflected harmlessly. Others penetrate the right side of the helo as it begins its turn to follow the lead aircraft now circling the hot area. Miraculously, no one is hit. The assault from aircraft and PBRs, as well as return fire from the jungle, is intense. The PBRs report that several Viet Cong guerrillas are dug into the riverbank. The helos concentrate a rocket barrage on the suspect location, which one of the PBRs marks with orange-red tracers. The door gunners hang outside on their safety straps, keeping up a steady chatter with their M-60 machine guns. They keep the enemy under almost continuous fire. One of the gunners removes the red-hot barrel of his gun with an asbestos glove and quickly inserts a spare so the barrel will not burn out and jam the gun. Gun barrels are expendable during such encounters, and in only a few seconds, he is firing again.

As abruptly as it had begun, the firefight ceases. One of the sampans is dead in the water, and the PBRs report that it is awash, with no sign of life. The other has been beached; it is afire and burning fiercely. Suddenly, it is blown apart by an explosion that testifies to the nature of its cargo. It disintegrates in a shower of flaming debris that momentarily lights the sky like a fireworks display. With a few halfhearted parting shots, the Viet Cong on the riverbank fade into the jungle. Both the boats and the helos head back to the ship.

Thus ends a routine night engagement involving river patrol boats of the "brown-water" navy and helicopter gunships of Helicopter Attack (Light) Squadron Three, known as HA(L)-3, or the Seawolves.

The river patrol was specifically designed to halt, or reduce to a trickle, the Viet Cong's previously unfettered use of the Delta waterways for the movement of men and supplies into and throughout the Mekong Delta. The HA(L)-3 Seawolf squadron, the U.S. Navy's first and only rapid-reaction helicopter gunship squadron of the Vietnam War, was hurriedly put together and thrown into the fray to provide up close and deadly air support to the boat crews. Such support was critical because immediate, aggressive response to an enemy attack was often the difference between life and death for those below.

Quickly gaining a reputation for rapid-reaction reliability, effectiveness, and great personal courage, the crews found themselves increasingly called upon by other friendly forces operating in the Delta. They inserted navy sea, air, land (SEAL) teams into enemy-held territory and extracted them when their work was done. They rescued Americans and other allied personnel from hot areas in the face of determined enemy opposition. They conducted medical evacuations of the wounded when army "Dust-off" helicopters were not immediately available. Their self-imposed watchwords quickly became, "No one left behind." Under no circumstances would they allow friendly personnel, on the water or on the ground, to be killed or captured by the enemy if they could possibly do anything to prevent it.

As the first and only U.S. Navy helicopter gunship crews to fly combat missions in the Vietnam War, the Seawolves had little to guide them in this nontraditional effort. Rather, they were given considerable discretion to improvise as necessary to get the job done. Given such flexibility, they adapted quickly to their exotic and treacherous environment. The result is one of the great success stories of the Vietnam War.

This is the story of the HA(L)-3 Seawolves, the most decorated U.S. Navy squadron of that conflict.

The Mekong Delta. *Charles Cooney*

1

The Mekong Delta

THE MEKONG DELTA OF VIETNAM IS A GREAT, SOGGY ALLUVIAL mass: part rice paddies, part swamp, part marsh grass, part waist-deep mud, and part dense jungle growth that defies penetration. It is fed by the twenty-six-hundred-mile-long Mekong River, known to the Vietnamese as Cuu Long Giang, or the River of Nine Dragons, and by several other names as it wends its way through six countries. From its source in the highlands of eastern Tibet, it flows through South China, forms a border between parts of Burma and Laos, as well as between Laos and Thailand, and continues south through Cambodia, where it splits in two at Phnom Penh before crossing the border into Vietnam. As it moves farther down the Delta, one branch divides into three. By the time the Mekong empties into the South China Sea, it has become four major rivers: from northernmost to southernmost, the My Tho, the Ham Luong, the Co Chien and the Hau Giang (also known to Americans as the Bassac River, a name given it by the French during the colonial period).

These major rivers feed a maze of smaller waterways, which in turn feed hundreds of channels and canals, some natural, some man-made. Together, they make up several thousand miles of liquid highways and byways, the color of which has been described by one Seawolf as "coffee with cream, dark like cappuccino."[1] These waterways are the essential lines of communication and commerce for the inhabitants of this flat, green-brown, almost completely roadless landscape.

From the air, the Delta seems a living, pulsing thing—a great sprawling creature sustained by an incredible web of arteries, veins, and capillaries. The larger arteries and veins easily accommodate full-sized ships, and such vessels routinely navigate through the Delta from the South China Sea all the way to Phnom Penh in Cambodia. Somewhat smaller arteries and veins can handle smaller ships and such large watercraft as barges and heavy motorized junks. Still smaller veins and capillaries are usable by fair-sized, shallow-draft boats and sampans, while others have silted in and can be negotiated only by diminutive sampans and canoes. Some waterways are partially or totally obstructed by fish weirs or other impediments, both man-made and natural. All offer challenges of one sort or another to watercraft operators.

To make matters even more confusing, many inland streams and rivulets that are no more than wide ditches in the dry season become navigable waterways during the monsoon. From roughly April through November, torrential rains cause the waters of the Delta to rise dramatically as they make their way toward the sea. During this period, as large areas become completely submerged, tree stumps and brush lurking just beneath the surface pose unseen hazards to the unwary boatman.

In the dry season, the landscape changes again. Deep in the Mekong Delta, thousands of acres of sodden real estate emerge like apparitions from their watery respite to again become part of the world of light and air. In other parts of the Delta, as the amount of freshwater provided by the monsoon rains abruptly and significantly decreases, tidal salt water from the South China Sea invades the waterways, reversing current flow and raising water levels by as much as twelve feet in some places.

On the one hand, during the war the Viet Cong found even the smaller, silted-in byways useful. On the other hand, the challenges that the river network presented to watercraft posed a special problem for the Americans, who were initially unfamiliar with the vagaries of the river complexes.

Another land/water complex that is part of this story, but not part of the Mekong River system, encompasses an area to the southeast of what, in the 1960s, was the South Vietnamese capital city of Saigon.[2] The Rung Sat, a tangled labyrinth of mangrove-lined waterways and low-lying, heavily canopied islands, marks the northeastern limits of the Delta. Historically the lair of pirates, thieves, and an assortment of other notorious criminal types, the Vietnamese knew it as the "Forest of the Assassins." Gen. William C.

Westmoreland, U.S. Army, called it, "One of the most savage pieces of terrain in the world."[3] Americans who fought there will testify to the truth of that statement.

The Rung Sat was a made-to-order sanctuary for the Viet Cong and a hotbed of insurgent activity. Indeed, in the early stages of the Vietnam War, Viet Cong guerrillas functioned there with virtual impunity, using the area for training, staging antigovernment operations, and storing caches of military supplies. But the Rung Sat was of great strategic importance because it bordered the Long Tau River, Saigon's primary lifeline to the South China Sea.

During the war, the Viet Cong made a number of command-mine and rocket attacks on ships navigating this waterway. They hoped to block the channel with a sunken ship, or at least give shipping and insurance companies second thoughts about committing their vessels to supply Saigon. Although the Viet Cong did succeed in sinking and damaging a few ships, they were never able to block the channel completely or to seriously disrupt shipping on the Long Tau.

During the war, almost half the population of South Vietnam lived in the Mekong Delta. Some people lived on boats that were both the family home and the means of making a living. Rice farmers, and even villagers, built their houses on earth hummocks or on stilts to keep them from being inundated during wet cycles. Houses were connected by earthen dikes or raised walkways. Small boats provided the sole means of communication for many inhabitants. Regardless of the season, the Delta was, and still is, a perennial water world, its rivers and canals its lifeblood, and the myriad watercraft that ply its waters the vehicles of commerce and social contact that make life in this unique environment possible.

2

An Enemy Called Charlie

RICH SOIL, RENEWED ANNUALLY WITH SILT WASHED DOWNSTREAM by the monsoons, makes the Mekong Delta extremely productive agriculturally, earning it the nickname, "the rice bowl of Vietnam." In the 1960s, it was not only a prize of considerable economic import, but also one of great political and military significance. This fact turned what might otherwise have been a bucolic Southeast Asian landscape into a harsh, treacherous battlefield. To be sure, it was not the classic battlefield where great armies clashed. Rather, it was one where relatively small, highly elusive guerrilla units conducted violent antigovernment activities and terrorized any civilian inhabitants who did not share the guerrillas' revolutionary zeal or accede to their harsh demands.

Like most guerrilla operations, these were extremely difficult to deal with. As quickly as Viet Cong units materialized for a foray against a recalcitrant village or government outpost, they faded into the jungle or mangrove swamps without a trace. Being indistinguishable from the local citizenry gave the insurgents an enormous advantage. Hardworking farmers, woodcutters, boatmen, and villagers by day, they transformed themselves into terrorists and assassins by night. The Viet Cong even recruited women and children, and some of those children, barely teenagers, became accomplished killers. It was virtually impossible to tell the good guys from the bad.

The Delta had long been a haven for Vietnamese insurgents. Known as Viet Minh during their struggle with the French,[1] by the 1960s they were being called Viet Cong, for Vietnamese Communists.[2] The Americans, given their penchant for abbreviation, shortened this to VC, in phonetic alphabet code, "Victor Charlie." They then dropped "Victor" and referred to the enemy, whether singly or collectively, as "Charlie."

At the war's beginning, the insurgents of the Mekong Delta were largely, but not entirely, indigenous to the region. A cadre of North Vietnamese who had fought against the French remained in the area, even after the Geneva Agreement of 1954 divided the country in two at the 17th parallel. During the 1960s, more North Vietnamese infiltrated the Delta to bolster the organized Communist presence and to provide political and military leadership, as well as increased tactical coordination of guerrilla activities. Because the Americans often found it impossible to differentiate between North Vietnamese Army (NVA) personnel and the VC, they also called the regulars "Charlie."

The Delta was extremely important to the South Vietnamese government because it comprised a significant portion of the country's geography and its population. It was no less important to the Communist insurgents. For one thing, it offered a pool of young men who could be recruited, voluntarily or otherwise, to augment Viet Cong forces. For another, this rich agricultural area provided a large and reliable source of food to sustain them. The Viet Cong required Vietnamese farmers, regardless of their political orientation or lack thereof, to donate some of their harvest to support the Communist cause. They also established tax stations on well-traveled waterways, stopping boatmen bound for the marketplace and forcing them to pay levies in cash or to give up a portion of their cargoes.

The swamps, marsh grass, mud, and thick jungle growth of the Delta furnished the VC with ready-made sanctuaries in which to hide and to protect them from sporadic penetrations by the Army of the Republic of Vietnam (ARVN). Absolutely essential to Viet Cong operations, however, was the incredible network of waterways that formed the logistic lifelines for the movements of arms, ammunition, and military supplies from the north.

Many inhabitants of the Delta were unquestionably sympathetic to the Communists, or at least to the idea of independence from foreign control. They were willing participants in insurgent activities. Many others, however, were apolitical farmers who wanted nothing more than to grow rice, engage in simple commerce, raise their families, and live in peace.

This was not to be. Those who protested recruitment of young men, or resisted demands for food, taxes, material aid, and other support, did so at great personal risk. Often, the Viet Cong physically abused or summarily executed them. The guerrillas burned to the ground whole villages that had ties to the government. They dealt brutally with noncompliant village chiefs and government officials in particular, so that other Delta inhabitants would be understandably reluctant to throw in their lot with the South Vietnamese government, lest they meet a similar fate.

By 1965, it had become increasingly clear that the Viet Cong controlled much of the Delta and that the government was continuing to lose ground. Delta inhabitants had learned from bitter experience that Saigon could not begin to guarantee their safety. This state of affairs brought into question the survivability of the government of President Ngo Dinh Diem[3] and his Western-oriented regime. Halting the spread of Viet Cong control in the Delta required timely action, and this in turn required substantially limiting their use of the country's internal waterways.

River warfare was not new to the Delta. The French navy had operated a fleet of river craft that were manned by Vietnamese crews, but commanded by French officers and petty officers. These were known as the Divisions *Navales d'Assaut*, or *Dinassauts* for short. The primary purpose of these river forces was to move troops to otherwise inaccessible areas in order to deal with insurgents, but they also interdicted contraband to a limited extent. Although they were moderately successful, they operated at a decided disadvantage because they had no effective air cover. Frequently ambushed, they had no one they could call upon for immediate assistance.[4]

With the final French departure in 1956, these assets were reorganized into River Assault Groups, manned completely by the Vietnamese but supplied by the Americans, who, in their efforts to contain communism in Asia, were beginning to assume an increasingly active role in the defense of South Vietnam. The primary function of the South Vietnamese River Assault Groups, however, was not to interdict enemy water traffic, but to provide a measure of mobility and logistic support to ARVN troops in the Delta, much as they had under the French.

In the late 1950s, American military advisors strongly suspected that the Viet Cong were being supplied with large quantities of military material by sea.[5] Because of these deep concerns, a plan was approved in 1961 to train and equip a force of Vietnamese junks to interdict Communist supply vessels operating along the South Vietnamese coast. Shortly thereafter, this plan was expanded to include the training and support of river patrol and interdiction forces as part of an overall expansion of the South Vietnamese Navy (VNN).

Even as these initiatives were being taken, dramatic political changes were occurring both in Vietnam and the United States. President Diem was killed in a coup on November 1, 1963, and U.S. President John F. Kennedy died from an assassin's bullet on the twenty-second of that same month, to be succeeded by Vice President Lyndon B. Johnson.

The war moved into a new and more dangerous phase when, on August 4, 1964, North Vietnamese torpedo boats attacked USS *Maddox* (DD-731) and USS *Turner Joy* (DD-951). The U.S. Congress responded by passing the Tonkin Gulf Resolution, which gave President Johnson a free hand to use American forces to conduct operations against North Vietnam and the Viet Cong. The United States suddenly became a full-fledged participant in a war that would become increasingly controversial and would divide Americans for decades to come.

By the mid-1960s, it had become apparent that the movement of supplies and men (including some NVA personnel) into the south—both by sea and by the inland waterway system—was continuing unabated. It was also clear that VNN units set up to deal with such things were unable to cope with the growing problem.[6]

An incident that occurred in March 1965 forced a decision on what to do about it. On the third of that month, 1st Lt. James S. Bowers, an alert U.S. Army helicopter pilot flying along the coast of South Vietnam, spotted a heavily camouflaged steel-hulled vessel bent on delivering contraband to the Viet Cong. Pounded unmercifully from the air, the vessel was disabled and sunk. The ARVN captured large quantities of arms, ammunition, medical supplies, and other military material that had made it to shore. More importantly, the previously debatable proposition that the North Vietnamese were providing major logistic support to the Viet Cong by sea was no longer speculation. It was now a fact beyond dispute.

The Vung Ro incident, as it was called, led to the establishment of "Operation Market Time," an initiative that involved intensive sea-air patrols along the South Vietnamese coastline. Assets devoted to Market Time included U.S. Navy destroyers, destroyer escorts, minesweepers, patrol motor gunboats, patrol craft, U.S. Coast Guard eighty-two-foot cutters, and a number of new patrol craft fast (PCFs), more commonly referred to as Swift Boats.[7]

Carrier-based A-1 Skyraider aircraft were also originally assigned to the Market Time operation, but they were quickly replaced by SP-2 Neptunes,

This 120-foot steel-hulled trawler was intercepted by Operation Market Time forces in 1966. Beached and captured, it was found to be loaded with arms and supplies for the Viet Cong. *U.S. Naval Institute Photo Archive*

SP-5 Marlin flying boats, and P-3 Orion turboprops. All of these replacements were large patrol aircraft that had much better electronics and communications capabilities and could spend many hours on station. The newly created U.S. Navy Coastal Surveillance Force (Task Force 115), which was dedicated to the job of classifying coastal traffic, boarding suspicious vessels, and apprehending or destroying those trafficking in contraband, coordinated this effort.

Market Time dealt strictly with coastal infiltration and supply, but in the late summer of 1965, an order was given to create a new organization called the River Patrol Force. This force was created specifically for the purpose of interdicting Viet Cong lines of communication and logistic activity in the inland waterways of the Mekong Delta.

The first U.S. Navy vessels to serve in this capacity began patrolling the waterways southeast of Saigon in the fall of 1965, under the command of

U.S. Navy Lt. Kenneth Logan MacLeod III. MacLeod's assets were two old and tired thirty-six-foot steel-hulled landing craft patrol large (LCPL-4s) upon which radar, searchlights, machine guns, and grenade launchers were mounted. The two makeshift gunboats, each having a maximum speed of about thirteen knots, conducted operations, mostly at night, in and around the infamous Rung Sat. These nocturnal forays were relatively modest in scope, but they signaled the coming of a much larger effort, using more modern and capable equipment specifically adapted to the inland waterway environment.[8]

3

The First Sea Wolves

On December 18, 1965, Operation Game Warden began with the formal establishment of the U.S. Navy's River Patrol Force, designated Task Force (TF) 116. The mission of Game Warden was to interdict contraband traffic while keeping the waterways open to innocent commerce and communication. To prosecute this task, the navy introduced in March 1966 the first of a new class of navy patrol boats adapted from a pleasure boat design. They were designated PBR, the acronym for patrol boat river.

The first of these craft were PBR-1s, fast, highly maneuverable, and especially suitable for operations in the Mekong Delta waterways. They were made of fiberglass, were 31-feet long, and had a 10-1/2-foot beam. They had a draft of only nine inches at full speed, and about two feet at slow speed or at rest. Driven by a pair of 220-hp diesels that, in turn, drove two Jacuzzi water-jet pumps, these craft were capable of speeds up to twenty-five knots.[1] So agile were these PBRs that reversal of the water jets at full speed reportedly allowed them to stop in their own length.

Each of the PBRs had a four-man crew and was armed with three .50-caliber machine guns, a power-operated twin mount in an open gun tub forward, and a single gun mounted on a pedestal aft. Each boat also carried a vari-

A PBR-1 patrols a Delta inlet in June 1966. *U.S. Naval Institute Photo Archive*

ety of other weapons, including 7.62-mm machine guns, either hand-held or mounted on each side of the boat, and 40-mm grenade launchers.

While this may sound like impressive armament, the Viet Cong boasted some lethal weapons of their own. These included so-called .51-caliber machine guns, 57-mm and 75-mm recoilless rifles, RPG-2 and RPG-7 shoulder-fired, rocket grenade launchers, and a variety of small arms.[2] When confronted with this kind of weaponry, the PBRs often found themselves at a considerable disadvantage. One knowledgeable observer who frequently rode the PBRs into "Indian country" opined that, against such firepower, the PBRs were "not much more than plastic coffins with guns."[3] Lightly armored, their main defense was speed and maneuverability.

As with most innovations, the PBR-1s had some initial problems, particularly fouling of the water-jet pumps by grass and other aquatic debris. Improved PBR-2s and retrofitted PBR-1s, however, proved enormously effective throughout the Delta and in the Rung Sat Special Zone.[4] They operated from land bases along the waterways and from ships, barges, and other floating platforms anchored in the rivers and streams. They worked in pairs for mutual support, stopping and inspecting suspicious motorized junks and sampans, especially those found operating in free-fire zones or violating the nightly curfew. They also provided fire support for allied personnel ashore and protected innocent water traffic from Viet Cong predators.

The sailors who manned these feisty little boats spoke highly of them. Despite their vulnerability to enemy fire, these boats were employed aggressively and effectively. In fact, there are those who will swear that the acronym PBR really stands for proud, brave, and reliable. Those words certainly apply to the men who bet their lives on them.

As might be expected, Charlie took vigorous exception to the PBR incursions into his sanctuaries and to the limitations they imposed on his unfettered use of the Delta waterways and to his heretofore growing control of the Delta itself. He returned fire from the contraband-carrying boats and laid lethal ambushes from the mangrove swamps and dense growth along the narrow waterways.

When an unwary PBR skipper found his boat trapped in a channel that was too narrow in which to maneuver, his only option was to stand and fight. Unfortunately, immobility was tantamount to a death sentence. For the PBR crews, Game Warden operations proved to be very hazardous indeed. Hours of boredom were interspersed with dramatic firefights. PBR personnel quickly learned that keeping alert during long tedious patrols in blistering heat and energy-sapping humidity was synonymous with staying alive. Between 1966 and 1968, one of every three Game Warden PBR sailors was wounded in action.

The Viet Cong had some creative tactical tricks to spring on American boat crews. One was to string a cable across a narrow waterway. If the PBR skipper failed to see it in time, it could decapitate a crew member or do significant damage to the boat. If he spotted the cable and slowed down or stopped, the boat was taken under deadly fire from shore, sometimes from both sides of a narrow waterway. Another of Charlie's innovative ideas was to close off a canal with a bamboo barricade or log boom and then drop a ready-cut tree behind a boat to trap and immobilize it before taking it under fire.

Sometimes the enemy would try to disable a boat with small, homemade mines strung across a waterway and then finish it off with a fusillade of gunfire. All too frequently, the PBRs encountered an unusually large enemy force ashore whose firepower was overwhelming. In any of these circumstances,

Two PBRs patrol a narrow waterway lined with thick vegetation. *U.S. Naval Institute Photo Archive*

they often needed help within minutes in order to survive. Those who planned the Game Warden operation anticipated the savage enemy response to the PBR challenge and knew that rapid-reaction, close air support would be essential to its success.

The U.S. Army had been involved in helicopter gunship operations in Vietnam since 1962. The 197th Armed Helicopter Company had developed the concept into an effective weapon against the Viet Cong, employing the Bell UH-1B Iroquois helicopter, more often referred to as the Huey. Several thousand of these aircraft, originally designed for utility use, had been adapted for combat, and the Huey quickly became the best-known symbol of the Vietnam War. Since the U.S. Navy had neither helicopter gunships nor helicopter pilots trained in such operations, the army seemed, at first, the logical choice for the job. On the other hand, Game Warden was a navy operation, and most people agreed that an all-navy team could best undertake the operation.

Although the army was hard-pressed to meet its own commitments, it nevertheless agreed to provide some of its assets to temporarily support Operation Game Warden. The initial army unit consisted of two fire teams, each comprised of four pilots, four door gunners, and four helicopter gunships. Army crews then operating out of Tan Son Nhut, Saigon's international airport, and out of the U.S. Air Force Base at Bien Hoa, about twenty miles north of Saigon, became the first fire teams. The army unit commander was Capt. Duane R. Brofer.

Captain Brofer, informed of his offbeat assignment in January 1966, began planning for the deployment immediately. Army gunship units traditionally took on such nicknames as Mavericks, Mad Dogs, Playboys, etc., because it was good for morale. This new unit was no exception. Brofer and WO David Anderson, who was also going to be part of the army's new "seagoing" outfit, gave some serious thought to a nickname one afternoon at the bar in the officers' "villa" just outside Saigon's Tan Son Nhut airport.

The two men were in agreement that the name ought to project an aggressive fighting image, some sort of animal, a predator perhaps, one known for its strength and cunning. How about a wolf? That seemed to resonate, but the captain thought the name should also incorporate a reference to the unique aspect of shipboard operations. From there it was a no-brainer. They would call themselves the Sea Wolves (two words). It had a nice ring to it, and Brofer declared it official. Thus, the U.S. Army Sea Wolves were born to the clink of glasses raised in solemn salute.[5]

In March 1966, two of the army Hueys and one fire team began operating from the landing ship dock (LSD-2) USS *Belle Grove,* which was also home to a number of PBRs and their crews. Lt. K. H. Kingston, a naval aviator, was temporarily assigned to the ship to help the army gunship crews get established in their unfamiliar surroundings and to handle any unforeseen problems that they might encounter. The ship's commanding officer, Captain Brofer hit it off from the beginning, and the fire team settled in smoothly.

The other fire team and its two aircraft went to Vung Tau, where there was an army helicopter maintenance unit.[6] The teams switched off periodically between ship and shore.

Aboard *Belle Grove,* the newly created army unit took on its strange assignment with admirable can-do spirit. Within hours of their arrival, the crews were in the air, getting used to flying from a ship. By March 29 they were deeply immersed in a combat mode, supporting Operation Jackstay, a major amphibious assault on the Rung Sat Special Zone by U.S. and South Vietnamese Marines. This operation was especially designed to clear the Viet Cong from the area along the Long Tau River. Although no one thought the

A U.S. Army Sea Wolf gunship lands on the LSD *Belle Grove* during Operation Jackstay. *U.S. Naval Institute Photo Archive*

expulsion would be complete or permanent, the command nevertheless hoped that it would, at least temporarily, reduce the threat to ships heading to or from Saigon and serve notice to the VC that their uninhibited use of the area had ended.

After Jackstay was completed, the army Sea Wolves concentrated their efforts on supporting the PBRs that were engaged in Game Warden operations on and around the Long Tau. The crews flew regular patrols and responded to calls for assistance from the PBRs and others.

Duane Brofer recalls that the PBRs would typically set off upriver for some distance at sundown, shut down their engines after dark, and drift silently with the current, hoping to catch enemy sampans or junks laden with contraband cargo. During these early months, the operation presented a learning experience for everyone involved—the PBR sailors, the helicopter crews, and the ship's company.

When the USS *Tortuga* (LSD-26) relieved the *Belle Grove* on April 10, the embarked gunship team transferred to its new floating home. 1st Lt. Lawrence

"Larry" Gillespie was a member of the army contingent that operated from both the *Belle Grove* and the *Tortuga*. He was ordered in from an army gunship unit known as the Firebirds that was stationed at Bien Hoa.

Gillespie remembers well the completely new experience of flying from a ship. He also remembers operating over the Rung Sat, looking down through the trees at the flooded landscape interspersed with soggy patches of land. He never ceased to be amazed when he received fire from a place that seemed totally inhospitable to humans. How could any military unit survive there, much less fight a war? It was just this kind of environment, however, that suited Charlie and his modus operandi to a T.

The army pilots and crew had to overcome obstacles that were unfamiliar to them. For one thing, they often flew night missions hampered by lack of visual reference. At least in the early months of the operation, the LSDs operated mostly in the vicinity of Vung Tau, and the pilots could use the lights from both the town and distant Saigon for reference.

Gillespie remembers that "on takeoff, the aircraft lost RPM every time it transitioned to forward flight and settled toward the water. The pilot lowered the collective, went on instruments, and waited somewhat apprehensively for the copilot to call out when a positive rate of climb was established. Takeoffs were hairy, and landings were not much better. At night, the flight deck was only semi-lighted, and you had to keep your wits about you."[7]

Weight limitations suddenly became critically important. The chin-mounted 40-mm grenade launchers—standard armament on army gunships working from bases ashore—had to be removed for shipboard operations.

At the end of May, a new army contingent, commanded by Capt. Charles R. Williams, relieved Brofer, Gillespie, and company. On June 12, the ship moved downriver to operate just off the coast in the South China Sea, where takeoffs and landings became even more difficult in the rolling ocean.

In July, two army helicopters were lost near the mouth of the Co Chien River during launches from the *Tortuga*. Early on the morning of the ninth, a Huey flown by 1st Lt. Arvid J. Shearer and WO James R. Ellis crashed on takeoff. The pilots and crewmen were all picked up unhurt. A second, more serious accident occurred on the night of the twelfth. There were no lights from shore for reference, and this time the accident may have involved a deadly case of vertigo. The aircraft took off at 11:06 PM on a night-familiarization flight, flew into the water, and rolled over and sank. Because it was a training flight, only the two pilots were aboard. The copilot, Capt. Richard

Antross, was rescued by the ship's motor whaleboat, but the pilot, who was unit commander Williams, went down with the aircraft.[8]

Despite such difficulties, TF 116 and Game Warden had gotten off to a quick start: its first PBRs were now in operation and had a small, combat-experienced contingent of army helicopter gunships to support them.

SEALs had been in Vietnam since 1962 to train Vietnamese naval commandos. By 1966 they were integrated into the Game Warden effort and operated effectively in the Rung Sat Special Zone in teams of varying size. The SEALs were silent partners, so to speak. Delivered to, and retrieved from, their mission sites by both boat and helicopter, they moved stealthily, mostly at night, along the waterways and through the thick, swampy jungle areas of this treacherous landscape to engage the enemy in his own style on his own turf.[9] The Sea Wolves provided air support whenever called upon.

4

Gunships for the Navy

In the spring of 1966, things were really beginning to heat up in Vietnam, and the U.S. Navy presence "in country" was growing by leaps and bounds. Rear Adm. Norvell G. "Bub" Ward, who had arrived as Chief Naval Advisory Group Vietnam (CHNAVADVGRU) and still held that title, had just been given a much larger and more encompassing job as the first Commander Naval Forces Vietnam (COMNAVFORV). His responsibilities now expanded explosively, and he was obliged to move quickly to confront myriad problems.

On this particular night, he was entertaining some distinguished guests for dinner at his quarters in Saigon. Among them were Gen. William C. Westmoreland, Commander U.S. Military Assistance Command (USMACV), and Adm. David L. McDonald, Chief of Naval Operations (CNO), as well as members of the admiral's staff, who were on a fact-finding tour from Washington. While this was ostensibly a social gathering, Ward knew that the conversation would quickly turn to business. He intended to make some of his more vexing problems known and, hopefully, break down some bureaucratic roadblocks that had plagued his efforts to get Game Warden off to a running start.

One of his chief concerns at that moment was the pressing matter of close air support for his river patrol forces.[1] Army helicopter pilots were doing a fine job responding to calls for assistance from recently arrived PBR contingents, but it had been understood from the beginning that the army's participation was a temporary arrangement and that the navy would ultimately be required to take over the mission. In any case, Ward and others believed that it was more appropriate for navy helicopter pilots and crews to fly from navy ships in support of navy boat crews in the Mekong Delta.

The arrival of increasing numbers of PBRs and their crews created a new sense of urgency. Rapid-reaction helicopter support would have to be expanded quickly to keep pace with the stepped-up tempo of river patrol operations. Admiral Ward knew that the army would not be willing to continue its role much longer and certainly would not be able to provide the additional assets needed. Somehow he had to come up with the wherewithal.

"I had been mulling over for a long time how to get navy helicopters to replace what we had. The navy had told me they didn't have any available and couldn't do anything to help me. So I talked to Chris Cagle, the OP-05 member accompanying Admiral McDonald."[2] (At that time, OP-05 was the abbreviation for the Office of the Deputy Chief of Naval Operations [Air Warfare]. Captain Cagle was Director, Aviation Programs.)

Acknowledging that the navy simply had no helicopter gunships in its inventory, Ward asked Captain Cagle if OP-05 could somehow break loose some navy helicopter pilots if Ward could provide the gunships for them to fly. Cagle thought that he could.

Ward knew that he would never have a better opportunity to sew this thing up. Excusing himself, he made his way over to General Westmoreland and informed him that the navy would provide pilots for Game Warden operations if the general could arrange for a loan of army helicopter gunships.

Westmoreland knew that the army's armed helicopter units in Vietnam were in the process of replacing their old battle-scarred UH-1B gunships with newer UH-1Cs. There was no good reason why some of the older types that were about to be retired anyway couldn't be made available to the navy for Game Warden operations. It was, in fact, a good way to get optimum use out of existing, albeit well-worn, material assets while, at the same time, resolving the major problem of air support for the PBRs. The general gave his stamp of approval on the spot.

During a few minutes of social conversation, Ward had solved two vexing problems in which formal procedures had so far failed to make a dent. The Pentagon bureaucracy would have to approve the deal, of course, but at this juncture, Vietnam had become a top priority, and it was unlikely that anyone would oppose the arrangement. The army, as it turned out, was interested in acquiring a couple of the navy's P2V Neptune patrol aircraft, and this helped to grease the machinery of cooperation.

There was, however, a more immediate problem. One could not just wave a magic wand and create a new, full-fledged operational navy squadron overnight. The mere challenge of identifying and training the pilots and crewmen in an already tight personnel environment was daunting in itself. Even if a top priority were assigned, it would be some time before such a squadron could be formed, manned, and established in country.

An interim solution was at hand, however. Captain Cagle understood clearly the urgency of the situation and moved Admiral Ward's request for helicopter pilots to the front burner. Helicopter Combat Support Squadron One (HC-1), based at Ream Field, Imperial Beach, California, was tasked to make personnel for four helicopter gunship detachments available for assignment to Vietnam as soon as possible.

HC-1 normally supplied helicopter detachments to the fleet, primarily for search and rescue (SAR), utility services, and other duties. Some of these SAR helicopter crews, flying from carriers on "Yankee Station," had already been christened under fire as they flew into North Vietnam to make daring rescues of downed pilots. But this assignment was entirely different. Now, for the first time in history, navy helicopter pilots and crews would be flying attack missions in a close-up, and very deadly, combat environment.

The requirement for additional personnel stretched HC-1's already thin pool of helicopter aircrew resources almost to the breaking point, but there was no help for it. Because of the potentially lethal nature of the gunship mission, only volunteers were solicited from both officer and enlisted ranks. To nobody's surprise, the response was enthusiastic. The volunteer list was filled almost immediately and, to the chagrin of other would-be gunship pilots, was temporarily closed.

Pilots who made it under the wire were itching to get a piece of the combat action in Vietnam, and this call was welcome. It was also a chance to do something that was entirely out of the ordinary, something that would test their skill as helicopter pilots, as well as their courage under fire. It was equally exciting for enlisted crewmen, since they rarely got a chance to be hands-on participants in such highly challenging combat adventures.

The eagerness of the volunteers should not be construed to suggest that the dangers involved were taken lightly. Neither pilots nor crewmen had any illusions that gunship operations were going to be a piece of cake. On the other hand, few, if any, could have fully imagined the unique nature or intensity of the engagements in which they were about to participate.

By 1966 most operational navy squadrons that were likely to be deployed, or have detachments deployed, to Southeast Asia had already sent their personnel to one of the survival, evasion, resistance, and escape (SERE) schools. These schools, which had been established in remote parts of the United States, introduced their students in a very realistic way to a grim possibility: they might be shot down in enemy-held territory, pursued, captured, and subjected to some very unpleasant treatment. The words represented by the acronym SERE provide some insight into a tough, even traumatic training experience. Many, if not most, who have participated in one of these SERE courses will tell you the best lesson they learned: Don't let yourself be captured! Most of the HC-1 people chosen for the gunship detachment had already been through the program, and those who had not were quickly subjected to the grueling curriculum.

The volunteers next got some quick self-defense training at Ream Field and some familiarization with personal weapons at the Point Loma, California, Naval Station. Then, after toughening up for a week with the Marines at Camp Pendleton, the first HC-1 detachment (Det. 29) of eight pilots and eight enlisted men, under Lt. Cdr. William A. "Rocky" Rockwell, left for Vietnam, arriving in country on July 4, 1966. There they began checking out in the Huey with an army helicopter transport company based at Tan Son Nhut airport, just outside the South Vietnamese capital of Saigon. Since they were already highly skilled rotary-wing pilots and crewmen, they quickly mastered the Huey and moved on to Bien Hoa for total immersion in on-the-job training with the army's 197th Armed Helicopter Company. There they began flying Huey gunships on regular missions in split crews, half army and half navy.

Lt. (jg) Frank Koch, one of these early HC-1 gunship pilots, remembers the experience well. "There we learned to shoot rockets and machine guns at moving targets."[3] The targets, of course, were firing back and learning, with ever-increasing accuracy, how to shoot down moving helicopters. Army gunship pilot Mike Howell remembers that the navy pilots and crewmen "flew with us, lived with us, and, sadly, were shot down and died with us."[4]

The army employed their Huey gunships in two- and three-plane fire teams. The former, known as light helicopter fire teams (LHFT), employed aircraft known as "frogs." Each of these gunships was equipped with an XM-158 rocket system, having seven 2.75-mm rockets on each side that were fired by the pilot. The copilot wielded and aimed flex-mounted M-60 7.62-mm machine guns, two on each side. Two door gunners with handheld M-60s completed the firepower complement. As mentioned earlier, the army also employed chin-mounted 40-mm grenade launchers on their gunships.

An army heavy-attack helicopter fire team (HHFT) typically consisted of two frogs and a "hog." A hog was the heavy artillery, so to speak: a specially configured Huey, having an XM-3 rocket system that consisted of two rocket pods, which contained twenty-four rockets, as opposed to the fourteen the frogs carried. With a full fuel and ordnance load, this aircraft often had trouble getting airborne. One HC-1 pilot recalled the unique handling qualities of the hog, saying, "It was so heavy you sometimes had to bounce it to get it off the ground."[5]

Army 1st Lt. Larry Gillespie, who had earlier flown from both the *Belle Grove* and the *Tortuga*, was now involved in training some of the first navy gunship pilots. He remembers one mission when the aircraft he was flying with a navy pilot "was hit pretty bad. We took several hits through the cockpit, breaking the windscreen. It was the navy pilot's baptism by fire."[6]

Gillespie was quick to praise the airmanship of these newcomers to the gunship business. Noting that army helicopter pilots had only basic instrument training, he told of one night mission when they "went to the aid of a base that was under attack by the Viet Cong. There were flares in the air, and to make matters worse, we were in the middle of a thunderstorm, with lightning flashes all around. I got vertigo, and the navy pilot, who was instrument-qualified, took over and flew the aircraft."[7]

After a short on-the-job training stint, HC-1 Det. 29 was ready and eager to relieve the army as part of TF 116. On August 14, Rockwell and his men reported aboard the *Tortuga* and began operating with the army in split crews. On September 19 the army unit turned the entire Game Warden helicopter gunship operation over to Rockwell's detachment.

Other pilots have described Rockwell as "quiet and very professional."[8] According to one of his subordinates, he ran his detachment "by the book." For the tactical details of this particular mission, however, the book had not

A Seawolf gunship accompanies two PBRs on patrol. *Charles O. Borgstrom*

yet been written. The army had taught the navy crews the basics of army gunship operations, but because the navy mission was unique, the crews had to develop a whole new set of tactics. They had to learn a lot about what worked and what didn't, and they had to learn quickly. Items in the "didn't work" category carried with them the potential for some severe penalties, but there was no help for it.

Because this was to be, first and foremost, a rapid-reaction force, an important early goal was to demonstrate, in very real terms, that the gunships would always be there to support the PBRs within minutes of a call for help. It was a matter of confidence building, and the Huey crews took on the challenge with startling vigor.

"We called them Rocky Rockwell and his flying squirrels," remembers Capt. Burton B. Witham Jr., Commander TF 116.[9] This was partly because of the energetic cartoon character that was popular at the time, but it was also because the HC-1 crews were so quick to respond that they seemed to be everywhere at once.

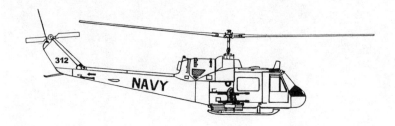

A UH-1B "Huey" gunship. *Charles Cooney*

The *Comstock* (LSD-19) relieved the *Tortuga,* and the *Jennings County* (LST-846) eventually relieved LSD-19. This latter ship, which arrived in Vietnam on November 11, was the first of four old LSTs resurrected from the mothball fleet and refurbished to support Game Warden PBRs and helicopters. These ships were fitted with boat booms for the PBRs and cranes to hoist them aboard and into their tank decks for repairs. Each LST had a tiny helipad for the Hueys, JP-4/JP-5 aviation fuel cells, rocket magazines, and a specially designed combat information center (CIC) for command and control. These LST "mother ships" proved especially suitable to Game Warden operations and, perhaps most importantly, a number of these vessels were available for relatively quick conversion.

The Huey gunships that were loaned to the navy were, for the most part, identical to those used by the army crews during their brief shipboard adventure. They were UH-1Bs, early versions of the Huey, each powered by a T-53, 1,100 shaft-hp turbine engine. The maximum fuel load was twelve hundred pounds, but takeoff from an LST was usually made with no more than six hundred pounds because of weight considerations. The LSTs were even smaller than the LSDs, and their flight decks even closer to the water, leaving less margin for safety.[10]

Rocket loads were often limited to ten, as opposed to a full load of fourteen, and pilots had to keep close tabs on their door gunners to make sure they did not try to take too much extra ammunition. There was a fine line between carrying enough fuel and ordnance to properly execute a mission and keeping the aircraft light enough to prevent it from settling into the water

A heavily loaded gunship loses its air cushion and sinks toward the water. *Seawolf Association*

on takeoff. AMS1 Thurman L. Hicks remembers well the uncomfortable sensation of flying from the deck of an LST, "with the temperature so hot I knew what Hell must feel like. We would lose our air cushion when transitioning from the flight deck to water. As soon as we cleared the ship, we sunk like a rock. More times than I like to talk about, the skids would dip close to the water, and salt spray would wet us; and more than a few times, a box of ammo would go over the side to keep us dry."[11]

The weight problem was not as critical when flying from shore, and the helos could take on a full, or nearly full, fuel and ordnance load. Even so, it was not an uncommon sight to see a door gunner running alongside his aircraft until the overloaded Huey could get a couple of feet off the ground before he scrambled aboard.

Service ceiling for the UH-1B aircraft was, theoretically, twenty-two thousand feet, but no one expected that from one of these Hueys. These old, heavily laden gunships could not possibly have reached such an altitude or anywhere close to it. Nor was there any reason for them to fly that high. Gun runs at treetop level were more the norm, and these were usually accomplished at about eighty-five knots, allowing for reasonably good accuracy for

A door gunner is ready for anything as this gunship checks out a riverside village.
U.S. Naval Institute Photo Archive

both rockets and machine guns. Unfortunately, it also made the helos ideal targets for the enemy on the ground.

Like the army frogs, the navy Hueys had two rocket pods, one on each side. Each pod carried seven 2.75-inch folding-fin aerial rockets (FFAR), which were fired by the pilot. The warheads could be any combination of high explosive (HE), white phosphorous (WP), also known as "Willie Petes," or Fleshette. The HEs were available with either impact or proximity fuses, and the WPs were ideal for starting fires. The Fleshettes each contained twenty-four hundred one-inch-long steel projectiles, which could be highly effective against enemy personnel. The crews called these warheads "Nails."

The aircraft had four electrically controlled, flex-mounted M-60 machine guns, two on each side, which were fired by the copilot. Each pair of these guns could be operated on a horizontal plane from 10 degrees on one side of centerline to 70 degrees on the other, for a total of 80 degrees. The guns could be elevated 10 degrees and depressed 85 degrees.

A gunship bores in on a Viet Cong staging area. Note the rocket and gun sights.
Peter Mersky

Unlike most army Hueys, the Seawolf aircraft had no chin-mounted grenade launchers. Instead, they provided a handheld grenade launcher that could be operated by a gunner from one of the door positions.

The Hueys had both gun and rocket sights, which some pilots used and others did not. As one Seawolf pilot of the latter persuasion observed, "Chewing gum or grease pencil marks, placed on the cockpit windshield, made far less cumbersome and far more accurate gun and rocket sights than those provided by the 'rocket scientists' and bureaucrats in Washington."[12]

In addition to the weapons controlled by the pilots, there was an M-60 machine gun on each side fired by a door gunner. The guns were hung on bungee cords to provide total flexibility, and each gunner was attached to the aircraft by a belt and a strap, having plenty of play to allow him to hang out the aircraft. The longest strap was nine feet long. Macho door gunners called these "sissy belts," but they kept a lot of folks from some very bad falls.

Door gunner Daniel E. Kelly, in his book *Seawolves: First Choice*, describes the belt/strap arrangement. "It was just long enough to let me stand up on the rocket pod, with one foot inside, and still keep the rest of my body outside so I could swing my freehand M-60 around and shoot in all directions. With the belt on, if I slipped or we hit an air pocket, I wouldn't fall to my death. Just get the shit scared out of me."[13] There were also racks that held extra barrels which could be exchanged during a firefight when the one in use glowed red-hot and was in danger of jamming the gun.

These early Hueys were all underpowered, considering what they were asked to carry and what they were expected to do. For the most part, they were tired from hard use. It is a rather large understatement to say that the army, which had its own operational requirements to worry about, did not make a special effort to earmark its best helicopters for the navy. Claude Fourroux, who was an army avionics supervisor at the time, remembers, "We thought that we would get rid of our choice dogs. We loaded the worst avionics, ARC 55, APX44, ARN3, etc., into those birds. It was so bad, I swear you could hear those dogs howling."[14]

One HC-1 pilot would recall: "The Hueys were all beat up from heavy use. We held them together with Band Aids and bubble gum and as far as the army was concerned, they were expendable. But we flew them, made them do the job, and got a lot more out of them than anyone had a right to expect."[15]

The pilots had armored plate under their seats, but that did not protect them from a hit from the side, front, or rear. The door gunner positions had no armor at all, and one pilot later described the Huey as a "Reynolds Wrap tank."[16]

Each pilot and door gunner wore a so-called chicken plate, a Kevlar vest that gave some protection from straight-ahead fire. Door gunners frequently used them as seat cushions to protect themselves from fire from below.

The Huey gunships took incredible abuse—from the enemy, the environment, and the crews that flew them. For aircraft that were not designed for combat, they did some amazing things. Some claimed they could run on empty if they had to, and they routinely brought their crews home despite massive battle damage.

The navy pilots took an immediate liking to these gunships, despite any shortcomings they may have had. They were, after all, the only bona fide combat helicopters in the navy. To this day, most speak fondly of their experiences with the Huey in the down and dirty, fast moving Mekong Delta war.

The original plan called for the LSTs to operate off the mouths of the major rivers, but it was quickly discovered that they were not ideally suited to such locations. The ships, designed for shallow water and beaching, had an unfortunate tendency to roll in the heavy swells, causing serious damage to the PBRs nested alongside. The phenomenon also compounded the hazards of helicopter launch and recovery. Consequently, it was decided to move the ships into the rivers, where the water was quieter. This not only made helicopter operations somewhat safer, but also moved the gunships closer to the PBR patrol areas, where they could respond faster to calls for assistance. Later, as Game Warden forces became increasingly successful and pressed inland, the ships moved with them.

With their shallow drafts of about eleven feet, the LSTs worked well in the rivers and larger tributaries. If one went aground, it was not a major problem because LSTs were designed to do precisely that, and they could be easily refloated.

Although the Mekong Delta river environment offered other kinds of risks, the black-shoe skippers were confident of their ship-handling skills, as well as their ability to deal with enemy threats. The helicopters and the PBRs provided defense for the ships against rocket or gunfire attacks from shore and, of course, the ships had their own limited armament, which included 40-mm guns. Around-the-clock lookouts gave warning of the approach of suspicious vessels or other unusual activity. Even so, in September 1968, Viet Cong soldiers firing recoilless rifles and rockets attacked the *Hunterdon County*. Two men were killed and twenty-five wounded; the ship, as well as one of the PBRs, suffered significant damage.

The possibility of being sunk by a command mine was a continuing concern, as was the possibility of contact with a floating mine released upstream, especially at night. The VC also occasionally employed swimmers who attempted to attach limpet mines to ships or other floating bases. The non-self-propelled repair and maintenance barge (YRBM) number 16 anchored on the Ham Luong River with a number of PBRs attached, was heavily damaged by a swimmer's mine in November 1967.

The crews countered the threat posed by swimmers through the use of concussion grenades, the explosion of which could stun, injure, or even kill a man in the water. Lookouts tossed them overboard at any sign of a disturbance in the water, and also at random intervals. This seems to have engendered an understandable reluctance on the part of VC swimmers to engage in this sort of activity. The explosions from the grenades, which took place without warning, day or night, just outside the hull of the ship, were somewhat disconcerting at first to the people inside, especially those who were trying to sleep. After a time, however, everyone got used to the explosions, and before long, the men barely noticed them. They became just another part of the wartime routine.

Despite the crews' constant vigil and liberal use of concussion grenades, limpet mine threats to ships continued throughout the war. On November 1, 1968, the *Westchester County* (LST-1167) was racked by underwater explosions caused by two limpet mines attached to the hull amidships on the starboard side. The hull was ruptured in an area containing fuel storage tanks and berthing compartments, and twenty-six sailors perished in the explosions.

Such violent occurrences notwithstanding, life aboard ship was reasonably pleasant for the helicopter crews. The food was good, and the sweltering heat and humidity on deck were offset by air-conditioning in the messing and sleeping compartments for officers and enlisted personnel. There were plenty of movies too; good shoot-'em-up westerns were the most popular.

For the PBR and helo crews, of course, there were real shoot-'em-up diversions almost daily. Lt. Frank Koch describes a mission from the *Jennings County* one afternoon in January 1967 that was typical.

Four PBRs had run into heavy fire from both banks of a waterway. As was normal operating policy, we were on the scene within minutes of their call for assistance. Rocky Rockwell was the fire team leader, and I was his wingman. As we came in range of the firefight, you could hear the mortar rounds over the noise of the aircraft's engine and the whap, whap, whap of the rotor blades.

"They're all over the place," announced Rockwell over the radio.

As we bored in, we became the focus of a barrage of antiaircraft fire. Rocky put several rockets into an area that looked promising, and I followed suit, covering him as he made his turn to come around again for another run. As I made our turn, my door gunners were hard at work, one hanging so far out on his strap that he was firing under the aircraft, not an unusual occurrence.

One of the PBRs advised that they were firing grenades at us.

"I doubt they'll hit us with those," Rocky replied, laconically.

The machine-gun fire, though, was quite heavy. One of the PBRs directed our fire at a clump of coconut trees protruding from some thick vegetation, and both aircraft concentrated fire in that area on the next pass. That seemed to do the trick, and several VC were flushed from the thicket and began running across an open area. Lt. (jg) Steve Oftendahl, copilot of the lead aircraft, tried picking them off with carefully aimed fire from an M-16.

Meanwhile, other nests of VC hidden in the dense underbrush were still intact and blazing away at us. We made several more passes, which almost certainly inflicted some serious casualties, before informing the PBRs that we were out of ordnance and would have to return to the ship to reload and refuel.

"We've got enough ordnance for one more pass," said Rockwell.

"Roger," replied the lead PBR. "We're clearing the area."

By the time we returned to resume the fight, the VC had had enough and the jungle had swallowed them.[17]

The river patrol concept was something new to the modern U.S Navy. Captain Witham remembers, "We had no instructions, no NWIPs [Naval Warfare Information Publications] in the beginning for how to go about this mission. We learned as we went along and wrote our own NWIPs."[18]

The first navy helicopter crews were likewise feeling their way. Their primary function was to work hand-in-hand with the PBRs to deny use of the waterways to the enemy. From the very beginning, however, their responsibilities, many self-imposed, took on a much larger scope. They responded to any friendly force in trouble, and their activities in this regard expanded rapidly. The PBR crews, the SEALs, and indeed all "friendlies" in the Delta quickly learned that the navy's rapid-reaction gunships could always be counted upon when things got really hot.

5

In the Thick of It

At night, HC-1 gunners used muzzle-flashes or tracer fire from the ground to pinpoint their targets. As someone observed with wry combat humor, muzzle flashes were especially easy to see when the gun was pointed directly at you! On the water, small boats were relatively easy to spot and engage, but VC units moving through the jungle under cover of darkness were virtually undetectable from the air. In this way, they were able to move men, equipment, and supplies to Viet Cong units throughout the Mekong Delta. Occasionally, an overzealous VC gunner could not resist an opportunity to shoot at a low-flying helicopter silhouetted against a moon- or starlit sky and would give his position away. But for the most part, Charlie was very well disciplined and kept his cool.

The army had equipped some of its gunships with searchlights to ferret out the Viet Cong at night. These gunships were variously called fireflies, lightning bugs, or lightships. One of these aircraft proceeded at relatively safe altitudes, illuminating suspicious areas as it went. A second, darkened aircraft flew low to pounce on any target turned up by the lightship.

Someone in Det. 29 thought the idea might be adapted to the navy mission, and the decision was made to fashion a makeshift lightship, using a discarded landing light from a wrecked aircraft. The HC-1 pilots especially hoped they would be able to illuminate VC junks and sampans taking advantage of the darkness to move contraband. Vessels in free-fire zones were prime targets. The pilots also hoped that illumination in other areas, either on the waterways or ashore, would cause Charlie to open fire on the lightship, thus exposing himself as a bad guy. Then the darkened pounce aircraft would zero in on the target.

It was decided that the lightship would fly above a thousand feet, thereby reducing, but not completely eliminating, the probability of a lethal hit. Unfortunately, when they tried, they discovered that the light from the makeshift searchlight was too diffused at that altitude, and that it could only be focused on a suspicious target by flying much lower. This made Lt. Frank Koch, one of the pilots elected to fly the high visibility bird, somewhat uneasy. But, he thought, "What the Hell! It was worth a try." His fellow pilots assured him, with good humor, that he would make really good bait.

As it turned out, the maneuver was never entirely successful, despite several attempts to make it work. "I think," says Koch, "they heard us coming or saw the light and were able to pull ashore and hide themselves until we left."[1] Whatever the case, the practice was finally abandoned as impractical, but not before a near midair collision between a firefly and a pouncer almost spoiled everyone's night. Follow-on detachments also experimented with the concept, with mixed results, but the navy's Seawolves never used it widely. (Navy personnel liked the army's term Sea Wolves, but they preferred to spell it closed up—Seawolves.)

The next HC-1 detachment to follow Det. 29 was Det. 27, which reported to the Naval Support Activity, Saigon, on July 23, 1966. After a short period of transition to the Huey, the pilots were thrown into the fray with the army, flying from Bien Hoa. Meanwhile, enlisted crewmen got flight experience, as well as maintenance training, with the army at Vung Tau. They came together again, ready to go to work the first part of September.

The officer in charge of Det. 27 was Lt. Cdr. Frank Foster, who had a most unlikely background for this kind of work. In fact, his aviation experience could not have been less suited to either the tropical environment or the Huey aircraft. Only a few months earlier, he had been flying a Douglas R4D Skytrain transport in Kodiak, Alaska. Before that, he had been a flying boat pilot in big Martin PBM Mariners and P5M Marlins. He had never flown a helicopter up to that time, but remembered that he may have once had a ride in one. For some reason, however, he decided that rotary-wing flying looked like fun. "I sort of felt like I was missing something," he said.[2] Since he was

Capt. Burton Witham (CTF-116) congratulates Seawolf pilot Frank Koch during an award ceremony. From left to right are: Seawolves Potter, Koch, Loughmiller, Stevenson, and Oftendahl. *Frank Koch*

due for rotation, he mentioned his new interest to his commanding officer, who called his counterpart at Ream Field to extol Foster's virtues. The next thing Foster knew, he was ordered to HC-1.

Foster was delighted by this turn of events and was soon pursuing his new aviation interest at Ream Field, where he received ten familiarization flights and soloed in a Kaman H-2 Seasprite. As a "bona fide" rotary-wing pilot, he decided to push his luck and volunteered for the new gunship program. "It was a chance," he says, "for some real adventure."[3]

During a brief transition period for training in the Huey, the navy pilots conducted touch-and-go landings at Long Binh, where they were introduced to being shot at by the Viet Cong, who operated boldly on the perimeter of the landing site.

Ultimately, Foster and his detachment found themselves ensconced at the South Vietnamese Naval Base at Nha Be, which supported a variety of watercraft, including minesweepers, MRF vessels, and some of the newly arrived PBRs.

The accommodations at Nha Be were primitive but adequate. At this early stage, the enlisted men slept in tents on wooden platforms, while officers had barracks-type double-decker bunk beds in a decrepit old building. But then, nobody expected the Ritz. The construction battalion (Seabees), however, were working on new facilities that would be ready before the next detachment arrived. Eventually, Nha Be would become one of the largest naval bases in the Delta, with forty or more PBRs and four Seawolf gunships. It would also have some of the better Seawolf accommodations in Vietnam. For now, however, they were pretty marginal.

In a letter to a friend back at Ream Field, Foster described Na Bhe as "a 27-acre sand dune." Sand, it turned out, was a constant problem. It was everywhere, and it was hard on the aircraft, especially the engines. At that time, there was no airfield of any kind at Nha Be, and the helicopters flew from a large flexible rubber mat secured to the ground by steel spikes. One day, one of Foster's helicopters, flown by Lt. Bill Brodie, was hovering over the pad when the spikes pulled out of the sand, and the whole mat came loose. It threatened to envelop the helicopter and pluck it out of the air, but Brodie quickly set the aircraft down, thereby avoiding almost certain disaster.

Foster's flurry of complaints to higher authorities finally resulted in the replacement of the rubber mat by about 250 square feet of steel planking, a series of linked metal planks reminiscent of Marston matting developed in World War II. Detachment personnel jokingly called it Foster Field.

Nha Be was to become the permanent home of the detachment, which would be redesignated Det. 2 when a full-fledged squadron was established in April 1967. Because of the special significance of the Rung Sat, it would be the only detachment that would not move around as the war in the Mekong Delta progressed. "The army called itself the Sea Wolves," Foster remembers. "That seemed an especially appropriate name for a navy helicopter outfit, so we kept it. When HA(L)-3 was formed the following year, the squadron adopted it as well."[4]

Detachment 27's primary responsibilities entailed covering PBR operations and other friendly activity in the Rung Sat Special Zone, as well as guarding the shipping channel to Saigon on the Long Tau River. These assignments kept them busy and provided plenty of combat activity. In addition to supporting the PBRs, Foster's gunships frequently needed to provide protection for ARVN units working in the Rung Sat, as well as for the Vietnamese provincial reconnaissance units, or PRUs—good guys who could be distinguished from the bad guys even from the air by the red bandanas they wore around their necks.[5]

"We were our own bosses," remembers Foster, "completely independent."[6] This flexibility gave the detachment a fairly free hand to develop tactics best suited to the Rung Sat area. As is always the case, there were annoying minor problems, such as navy-type helmets whose earphones and mikes were not compatible with the army Huey communications systems. Then there were the more serious problems, like the lack of radar altimeters. In a letter to the HC-1 commanding officer back at Ream Field, Foster emphasized the dangers involved with helicopter operations at low altitudes at night and strongly advised that radar altimeters be provided for all the navy gunships as soon as possible.[7] For whatever reason, they were not immediately forthcoming.

Like Rockwell's detachment, Foster's experimented with lightships. A report to the HC-1 detachment liaison officer tells of experiments in which the lightship flew at fifty knots and five hundred feet, while the pouncer flew beneath and behind at a hundred feet.[8] A monthly report to TF 116 commander in March 1967 describes the use of the searchlight to detect and destroy two enemy sampans "with probable enemy casualties."[9] Despite such occasional successes, Foster's detachment found the lightship to be largely impractical.

A third HC-1 detachment (Det. 25), under Lt. Cdr. Joseph B. "Joe" Howard, arrived in Vietnam in August and was ultimately stationed at the army airfield at Vinh Long. To the Viet Cong, Howard and his group were further evidence of an expanding incursion into their Delta sanctuary.

Det. 25 was involved in perhaps the earliest major engagement between the Viet Cong and Game Warden forces. It occurred on October 31, 1966. As two patrolling PBRs rounded a bend in the My Tho River, they surprised two sampans loaded with uniformed North Vietnamese troops attempting a crossing. The PBR crews were surprised as well, especially by the appearance of uniformed soldiers.

Having sunk one sampan, the PBRs set out in pursuit of the other. Then came the next surprise, when they suddenly found themselves face to face with a fleet of some forty or fifty small, troop-carrying sampans. Calling for air support, they plowed through the enemy fleet, raking the boats with .50-caliber machine-gun fire. Small arms and light machine-gun fire from the boats, as well as a barrage from heavier weapons ashore, answered the attack. Around another bend in the river, Det. 25 came upon still another concentration of small enemy craft. Altogether, it must have looked like a mini-

Joseph B. Howard (center), officer in charge of Det. 25, during a mission briefing.
U.S. Naval Institute Photo Archive

invasion fleet. The PBRs again charged at full speed, wreaking havoc on the boats, particularly those carrying troops.

As they completed this run, two Det. 25 helicopter gunships arrived on the scene. Together, the helos and the PBRs mounted a coordinated and devastating attack under heavy fire, sinking many of the boats and setting off a few secondary explosions. The helicopters also raked the riverbanks, killing many of the enemy ashore and silencing some of the larger weapons.

There is little doubt that it was a disaster for the Viet Cong. When it was over, the PBRs had accounted for some thirty-five sampans sunk, while the helos claimed another sixteen. There are varying accounts of this engagement and the number of Viet Cong and North Vietnamese killed, but it seems safe to say that enemy casualties numbered in the hundreds.[10]

The My Tho River was the site of another similar setback for the enemy on December 15 of that same year. The PBRs had come upon an enemy attempt at river crossing and called in the Seawolves for support. Arriving on the scene within minutes of that call, the gunships suppressed fire from the shore, putting several rockets into a VC position on the riverbank that turned

A gunship fire team on patrol and looking for trouble. *U.S. Naval Institute Photo Archive*

out to be an ammunition bunker. It went up in an enormous explosion that rocked the area. Some twenty-eight sampans were also destroyed, and many Viet Cong were killed that day during the combined PBR and helicopter effort.

The fourth and last HC-1 detachment (Det. 21) did not arrive in Vietnam until November 1966, but quickly made its presence felt. Coincidentally, the officer in charge of this detachment, Lt. Cdr. George Rowell, also bore the nickname "Rocky," a fact that would later confuse historians trying to chronicle the period. Rowell had an assertive personality and was sometimes at odds with superior authority. Nevertheless, he was well regarded by the men he flew with and commanded. The Det. 21 crews took on the pugnacious character of their colorful leader and were known during their tenure in Vietnam as "Rowell's Rats."

The stateside training for Det. 21 had been somewhat different than that of the earlier detachments. The navy arranged for the later crews to go to the Bell Helicopter Factory in Hurst, Texas, where the Huey was built. Detachment pilot Lt. Alfred J. "Al" Banford Jr. recalled: "Our instructors were the factory test pilots for the Hueys, and they were the best. The instruction was phenomenal, just phenomenal! I was shot down three times during my tour in Vietnam, and I was able to make the best of it because of what they taught me."[11]

Upon arriving in Vietnam, this detachment, like its predecessors, was assigned to the army for on-the-job training. It was split into two groups, one stationed at Soc Trang and the other at Vinh Long. Banford further recalled:

We had some preconceived ideas about how to go about gunship operations. The army pilots said "Better listen to us; we'll keep you alive." We did, and they did!

The army pilots knew their business, and we enjoyed flying with them. I flew some five hundred missions with the army and earned my DFC with them. By the time we went back to being a navy detachment, we were full-fledged combat veterans and pretty knowledgeable about gunship operations and about staying alive.[12]

Lt. (jg) Michael J. Peters was a member of Det. 21 who also won a DFC flying with the army. He vividly remembers one particular day when things went to hell in a hand basket!

Lt. Kenny Lund and I were flying an army gunship as part of an army support mission. We were inserting South Vietnamese troops into Ca Mau, an area on the southern tip of the Mekong Delta. The mission was typical, but the area was one of the worst. It was completely under control of the VC. We had planned on three fire teams (six aircraft) to support the UH-1D troop transports called slicks.

One of the gunships had mechanical difficulties and had to leave the combat site, so our ship was ordered to loiter solo over the drop zone while the other two fire teams covered the troop insertion. Almost immediately, the first troops on the ground encountered heavy fire.

Typically, as they did that day, the slicks would fly single file as they descended into the landing zone [LZ]. They were spaced so that one ship would land, drop troops, and depart the zone, and the following ship would replicate the maneuver on the same spot. The aircraft were on the ground for less than a minute. Meanwhile, the gunships would fly a racetrack pattern on either side of the descending slicks, providing a continuous escort in and out of the LZ. They might lay down some covering fire. When out of the LZ, they would break off and pick up the next group of slicks.

As noted, we were loitering overhead, watching the series of drops in the LZ and monitoring the radio traffic. We heard the ground controller order the incoming slicks to move over about fifty yards, due to enemy fire coming out of the original LZ. Unfortunately, the new LZ was adjacent to a heavily fortified VC position.

The VC opened up as the first slick landed. That aircraft rolled over. The VC brought down the next three or four ships and also took out the four gunships that were trying to cover the downed aircraft. At this point, everything was complete chaos: aircraft going down, and aircraft trying to wave off. A medevac helo tried to get in, but the fire was so intense that it had to wave off, a very unusual event. The guys who flew those helicopters were, without question, the bravest and most admired pilots of the war.

At this point Kenny and I are the only gunship flying, and we dropped down to provide cover for the crews of the downed aircraft."[13]

Lund and Peters made repeated attacks, diving on the VC positions, circling to keep moving, and hitting the enemy again and again from different angles. Peters remembers "a tremendous amount of gunfire going both ways."[14] By the time his helo had exhausted its supply of ammunition, the South Vietnamese troops had been able to regroup and secure the area. The aircraft was riddled with bullet holes, but by some miracle, Lund, Peters, and their door gunners came through without a scratch.

Rocky Rowell's Detachment 21 was still operating with the army by the end of 1966, but they would join the other three navy detachments in the next year. Meanwhile, HC-1 Dets. 29, 27, and 25 had written the first dramatic pages in the history of U.S. Navy helicopter gunship operations. They had pioneered the early tactics and demonstrated the kind of aggressive spirit and reliability that their successors could build on.

6

Navy Again

THE MARKET TIME PATROLS OF TF 115 ALONG THE COAST OF SOUTH Vietnam during 1965 and 1966 had done a thorough job of interrupting the enemy's direct seaborne supply line. Large steel-hulled trawlers, anywhere from 75 to 125 feet in length, once accounted for as much as 70 percent of Viet Cong logistic support. (The larger ones could carry as much as four hundred tons of military equipment and supplies.) These trawlers were discovered and tracked by U.S. air assets, often while they were still far out to sea. When they crossed into RVN territorial waters, they were apprehended or sunk along with their cargoes. A variety of smaller coastal vessels from North Vietnam attempted to blend in with innocent commercial traffic headed south. They were stopped and searched in a well-coordinated air-sea effort. Boats were seized, crews captured, and contraband cargoes confiscated. It was one of the great successes of the Vietnam War. COMUSMACV General Westmoreland would later write that by the end of 1966, enemy seaborne supply "had been reduced to a trickle of less than 10 percent."[1]

In one sense, the Market Time effort may have been too successful, because the focus of enemy seaborne traffic now shifted to Cambodia. By the terms of a 1966 deal between the North Vietnamese and Cambodian Prime Minister Prince Norodom Sihanouk, Chinese and Soviet cargo vessels were now able to unload thousands of tons of war material at the port city of Sihanoukville, on the Gulf of Thailand. Communist vessels no longer had to penetrate the South Vietnamese territorial sea to land their cargoes. Since they could not be stopped in international waters or in Cambodian territorial seas, they were immune to search and seizure. From Sihanoukville, military goods and supplies were transported overland via the so-called Sihanouk Trail to distribution points along the border with South Vietnam and thence into the Mekong Delta via the adjoining network of waterways. There was an immediate quantum increase in interdiction business for Game Warden forces.

In early 1967, TF 117, also known as the Mobile Riverine Force (MRF), was established under Capt. W. C. Wells to provide a river assault capability. With heavily armed and armored watercraft, TF 117 provided transportation and waterborne gunfire support for the Second Brigade of the U.S. Army's Ninth Infantry Division. The troops conducted search and destroy operations, often against large, entrenched and fortified Viet Cong units in the Delta and the Rung Sat Special Zone.

The MRF used a large number of landing craft, mechanized (LCM) that had been modified and adapted to the riverine mission. Some became armored troop carriers (ATCs). Each of these typically embarked a rifle platoon and mounted its own 20-mm cannon and .50-caliber machine guns. Several of these even had tiny helicopter pads, upon which gunships or slicks could barely perch, more than a third of the aircraft hanging over the stern.

Some LCMs became fire support vessels. The most heavily armed and armored were the monitors, each of which had a 40-mm turret-mounted Bofors canon forward plus a 20-mm canon and a couple of .50-caliber machine guns aft. Some monitors mounted one or more flamethrowers, called "Zippos," that were used against enemy bunkers and heavy jungle foliage. The weapons also had an unpleasant psychological effect on enemy personnel. The monitors were floating fortresses, sinister-looking vessels that were not to be trifled with.[2] Army helicopter gunships usually supported the MRFs, but they did not hesitate to call on the Seawolves when they were needed.

All of these elements—the PBRs of TF 116, the MRFs of TF 117, the HC-1 helicopter gunships, and the SEALs—now brought their unique capabilities to bear in a determined effort to bring Viet Cong dominance in the Mekong Delta and the Rung Sat to a timely end.

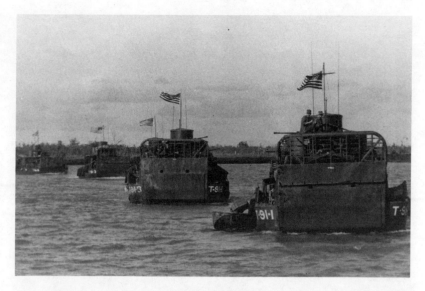

Armored troop carriers (ATCs) of the Mobile Riverine Force move soldiers of the Ninth Infantry Division into position to engage the enemy. *U.S. Navy/PH3 C. B. Hall*

By March 1967 Det. 21, the last of the HC-1 detachments, had left the army with a solid combat record and was back in the navy. Det. 21 was split: two crews and two Hueys were assigned to the *Harnett County* (LST-821), leaving the remaining two crews ashore at the Vinh Long Army Base. They traded off every other week.

Ultimately, four specially configured LSTs—the *Garrett County* (LST-786), *Harnett County* (LST-821), *Hunterdon County* (LST-838), and *Jennings County* (LST-846)—were dedicated to support Game Warden operations in the rivers of the Delta. Each LST was mother ship to ten boats and carried two Huey gunships. Typically, three LSTs were on the line at any one time while one was undergoing scheduled maintenance and crew rest.

Al Banford remembers life aboard ship.

It was crowded, of course, but the chow wasn't bad. Our hosts from the gator [amphibious] navy treated us well, but our relationship with the PBR sailors who, like us, were also based aboard, was especially tight. The PBR sailors were the cream of the crop as far as I'm concerned. Talk about balls!! The ferocity of some of the firefights they were involved in is unbelievable.

Two PBRs head out on patrol from the LST *Harnett County.* The ship is anchored
on the Co Chien River with a Seawolf gunship detachment embarked. *U.S. Naval
Institute Photo Archive*

At Vinh Long, we lived like the army guys, in hootches. It was
pretty good living. There was an O-Club and an EM-Club. There were
no drugs to speak of at that time—maybe a little marijuana, but nothing like in Saigon. The Viet Cong smoked marijuana though. We could
tell when there was going to be a Viet Cong attack on the base, because
we could smell garlic and marijuana wafting in from the outside. They
were eating and smoking their courage.

Vinh Long was a nice little town, but there really wasn't much to
do there, and there was a strict curfew. No one was allowed in town at
night.[3]

Det. 21 was kept busy from the start, whether operating from Vinh Long
or the *Harnett County.* As Michael Peters recalled:

We flew in instrument-weather conditions a good bit of the time, but as
I recall, it did not pose any special problems. All naval aviators are well-
trained instrument pilots, and in any case, we usually flew under the
weather, about fifty feet off the deck.

Even in decent weather we avoided what was known as "the dead man zone." That was between two hundred and twelve hundred feet, where we were sitting ducks for antiaircraft fire. Mostly, we operated under two hundred feet and would pop up once in a while to orient ourselves. It was all contact navigation in the Delta, no electronic nav-aids or instrument approaches. We were very much on our own in that respect.[4]

Like most of the other Seawolf pilots, Peters had good things to say about the Huey gunship.

After awhile it became like your car, and you got to be very familiar with its handling characteristics. You knew what the aircraft would do in any situation, and it sort of became part of you. We operated it in its full envelope and made it do everything it was capable of and some things it wasn't supposed to be capable of.

There were a number of tricks to the trade. To get down fast—and often that was essential and immediate when people were shooting at you—we would just dump the aircraft over on its side to destroy the lift, and it would drop like a rock. Then we would right the aircraft to pull out at just the right moment before hitting the ground. It took a split-second calculation when you were really low, but after awhile it became a matter of routine. We did it when the situation called for it, without thinking much about it.

The vegetation was very dense, and it was often impossible to spot the enemy on the ground, even when you knew they were there. The VC quickly learned not to shoot at the first helo in the fire team, because the second aircraft would see the muzzle flashes and drop a smoke marker on them. Then we would know exactly where they were and concentrate our fire on and around the smoke.

When the enemy held their fire and waited for the second helo, it was a little bit harder to pinpoint them, especially if the second plane was unable to get off a smoke. When this happened, the first helicopter would whip around as quickly as possible and try to put a smoke on them. Then both aircraft would take them under fire and hose down the area.[5]

Gun runs were literally made at treetop level, and it was not uncommon for a Huey to return to ship or base sporting greenery wedged in the skids or the armament package. On one occasion, palm fronds removed from the

Gunship operations were mostly low level. *Association of Naval Aviation*

aircraft Peters flew were jokingly used as a centerpiece on the *Garrett County's* wardroom table.

As previously noted, the gunship pilot fired the rockets and the copilot fired the M-60 flex guns. The door gunners each had a handheld M-60 hung on a bungee cord and routinely hung outside the aircraft to fire them. They got so far out that they could actually shoot underneath the helicopter, and often did so.

Sometimes, in the heat of battle, a door gunner might inadvertently put a few slugs into his own aircraft. During one such incident, Peters took a friendly M-60 round in his hand, but after being patched up, he was soon back in business. A real concern was that errant rounds might disable a tail rotor, with disastrous results. This concern would eventually lead to door guns being mounted on the aircraft to limit their movement.

Occasionally, the intense fire concentrated on a VC position would flush one or more of the enemy out into the open. It was not a smart move on Charlie's part, but when you were taking the kind of fire that a gunship could bring to bear, choices for survival became somewhat limited. A gunner might call out, "I've got one running." A quick, terse, tight-lipped reply from the aircraft commander would likely be, "Get him," and that would be the end of it.

It sounds cold and heartless to shoot a desperate man running for his life, but the helo crews knew that a VC gunner taken out of action today might save an American or South Vietnamese life tomorrow, maybe their own.

7

Ready or Not

WHILE THE HC-1 DETACHMENTS WERE HOLDING THE LINE AND laying the groundwork for an expanded navy effort, things had been moving ahead back in the United States to get a full-fledged gunship squadron up and operating as quickly as possible. OP-5 tasked the Bureau of Personnel (BUPERS) to identify pilots to man the new squadron. The job fell to Lt. Cdr. (now a retired rear admiral) Lee Levenson, who was then a placement officer for the navy's helicopter squadron. As he recalled:

> We took people from every possible source, drawing down on HS heli-
> copter antisubmarine squadrons and HC combat support squadrons as
> well as from the shore establishment, working with the COs to make
> their losses palatable if not painless. Our plan was to assign on the basis
> of a one-to-one ratio; that is to say, we tried to assign one second-tour
> volunteer for each first-tour pilot. We took as many second-tour volun-
> teers as possible, and there were ample numbers of those. For the most
> part, first-tour pilots were just assigned. It was essentially a one-year tour
> for everyone, but we tried to arrange it so that some would leave the
> squadron early and some late, with the ultimate goal of rotating one-
> twelfth of the people every month.[1]

Cdr. Conrad J. "Con" Jaburg, the squadron's first executive officer, aggressively lobbied for the job with BUPERS. He recalls, somewhat disdainfully, that some commanding officers counseled their pilots against volunteering, in the belief that it was a poor career move. It was not very good advice, Jaburg reflects, but no matter, "the warrior blood in our Seawolves said 'volunteer' anyway."[2] And volunteer they did—in large numbers. In the final analysis, being a naval aviator is about being a warrior, and the ultimate test of one's competence in that capacity is combat.

Lt. Cdr. John M. "Jack" Bolton had tried to wangle orders to one of the HC-1 gunship detachments, only to be told the billets had been filled. His detailer at BUPERS made the mistake of telling him, first, that a new navy gunship squadron would eventually replace the detachments and, second, that perhaps he could have a slot. Thereafter, Bolton badgered him almost every day to make sure he was not forgotten. "I was determined that the navy was not going to have a helicopter gunship squadron without me."[3] He became an intolerable pest, and the detailer finally cut him orders to the squadron to get rid of him. Bolton was not alone in his persistence; other Seawolves report using similar tactics to get themselves selected.

Meanwhile, Commander Levenson had been working to set up an initial training program. There were meetings at the Pentagon with OP-05 and BUPERS planners, as well as with army representatives and others, to provide at least minimal preparation of both pilots and aircrew before they were dispatched to Vietnam. And minimal it was!

The problem was that the army's training units were already overcommitted and overworked. They were bulging at the seams, and there was an understandable reluctance on the part of army planners to shortchange their own people's needs to accommodate the navy. Nevertheless, a sense of national purpose and the growing urgency to get the squadron established and engaged as quickly as possible kept things moving toward timely deployment. The very success of Operation Game Warden depended on it, and there was no time to waste.

In the end, a very basic course of instruction for the pilots took place at Fort Benning, Georgia.[4] This involved three weeks of indoctrination in the Huey, only about fifteen hours of which was actual flight time. Some pilots remember that ten hours was more like it. Then there was SERE school at Warner Springs, in the mountains of California, for those who had not had the pleasure of this experience. Next, it was small arms and self-defense training with the Marines at Camp Pendleton, similar to that which the HC-1 people had undergone.

Everyone did his best to get the new gunship personnel ready, cramming as much as possible into a very short period. Of the Huey indoctrination, Jack Bolton said

> The army guys were great folks. Most had already served one tour in Vietnam in Huey guns [gunships], and several had two tours.
>
> My first hour in a Huey included full autorotation to the ground (that's engine at idle), a maneuver that the U.S. Navy prohibited. The second hour was low-leveling up a stream bed at fifty feet and 110 knots. Then back to Lawson Army Airfield for more groundwork, full autos and low-level engine failure practice. It was really a hoot!
>
> At the end, we were taken out to an ordnance area where we shot fourteen 2.75 rockets and one hundred rounds of 7.62 from the four M-60 flex guns. We were now declared UH-1 Huey gunship pilots. By the way, for tactics training, we were given, to the best of my recollection, two handouts, one containing do's and don'ts for gunships and the other a graph depicting probability of being hit by ground fire, depending on altitude and airspeed.[5]

Not all of the early HA(L)-3 pilots had the same training experience in the United States, but they all seem to agree that there was not very much of it. Timing and availability of assets were important factors in determining the scope of training. Some pilots remember having almost no ordnance training, while others leave out the word "almost." Some say that the first time they got to fire rockets was on a combat run in country. Whatever the individual experience, the commitment had been made to get a navy gunship squadron to Vietnam *now*, and that was how it worked out.

Despite the abbreviated training, HA(L)-3 people were confident of their ability and eager to show what they could do. Helicopter Attack (Light) Squadron Three was officially established at Vung Tau on April 1, 1967, even though none of the new squadron people had yet arrived. It turned out to be the only navy squadron to be established in a combat zone during the Vietnam War.

Joe Howard became the acting commanding officer while awaiting the arrival of the new skipper and the first contingent of squadron personnel. It was Howard's thankless task to prepare the HC-1 detachments for a more structured way of doing things. The squadron would still be parceled out in

Gunships on patrol in the Mekong Delta. *U.S. Naval Institute Photo Archive*

detachments, but there would be more of them, and, as might be expected, there would be a new emphasis on administrative and operational control and conformity.

Many of the HC-1 pilots and crewmen who had pioneered navy gunship operations in Vietnam did not entirely welcome the new turn of events. Before, there had been no close squadron-level supervision except, of course, for a few required periodic reports and mostly perfunctory contact with the HC-1 parent command back at Ream Field in California.

Some of the HC-1 people swore that their success in combat was the result, to a great extent, to the autonomy they had enjoyed, which had in turn allowed them freedom to innovate outside customary procedural bounds. Their missions were unquestionably unique, and they had carried them out with imagination and—as some might admit—even a bit of a dramatic flair. One HC-1 pilot described the operation of his detachment as something out of *Terry and the Pirates*, the popular and colorful adventure cartoon strip set in Asia that once appeared in major Sunday newspapers across the United States. The HC-1 detachments were, in effect, mini-squadrons operating with almost complete independence. They were tough, tight little units. Morale was high, and there was a strong sense of esprit de corps among pilots and crewmen alike.

The new, centralized authority grated on some who thought Big Brother would now be looking over their shoulders, dampening spirit, hampering operational flexibility, and reducing combat effectiveness. Despite such concerns, however, most understood that the expansion of rapid-reaction gunship operations was imperative if Game Warden was to succeed. Most also conceded, albeit grudgingly, that expansion brought with it the necessity of organizational change.

In the end, the HC-1 detachment personnel expended every effort to impart to the newcomers the hard lessons the detachments had learned. Those lessons would help the new pilots and door gunners do maximum damage to the enemy, while keeping as many of themselves as possible alive during the months to come. The newcomers, in turn, would carry on what the HC-1 people had begun and maybe even improve on it. The goal was to keep Charlie on the defensive and, in the process, to neutralize or eliminate his influence in the Mekong Delta.

8

All in One Sock

CDR. ROBERT W. "BOB" SPENCER HAD SERVED IN THE KOREAN WAR with a distinguished combat record as an AD Skyraider pilot. He had subsequently been qualified in helicopters and had now been selected as the first commanding officer of HA(L)-3. Along with Con Jaburg, the executive officer, and Cdr. Ron Hipp, the operations officer, Commander Spencer arrived at Tan Son Nhut airport in Saigon at around noon on May 5, 1967. They had already conspired to avoid the customary formal calls on the navy hierarchy in the capital city.

"My orders told me to report to the senior naval officer at Vung Tau," says Spencer. "I allowed as how that was me, so we caught the first available plane out, and I reported to myself."[1] As Jaburg remembers their arrival at Vung Tau, "We found one beat-up building, a desk and two chairs, and decided to call it home. Bob Spencer looked around, pinned his command badge on his shirt, and said, 'Let's go to work.' So we did."[2]

There was no ceremony, and the necessary formalities were accomplished through paperwork alone. The original HC-1 detachments became Detachments 1, 2, 3, and 4 of Helicopter Attack Squadron (Light) Three. Det. 1 was stationed aboard an LST at the mouth of the Bassac River; Det. 2 was at Nha Be; Det. 3 was at the Vinh Long Army Base, where the Co Chien and Ham

Luong rivers split; and Det. 4 was on another LST near the mouth of the Co
Chien River.

The problems of starting a full-fledged squadron in country were formidable and required a substantial amount of imaginative effort. They were
exacerbated by the reality that the squadron had been thrown together so hurriedly that the usual support functions were late catching up. Some say they
never completely materialized. Likewise, there were early problems integrating the newly formed squadron's needs into the local supply system. Added to
this was the fact that the Seawolves were flying borrowed helicopters and
depended on the army for major maintenance and parts. The navy squadron
was not at the top of the army's priority list.

Spencer remembers that they "had very little in the way of material support in those early days. I hate to say it, but much of what we had to work
with we acquired in very unorthodox ways. Bluntly said, we had to fight for
everything we got through customary channels and steal everything else."[3]

One example was the lack of even the most basic ground transportation.
There wasn't so much as a bicycle. Then suddenly, as if by magic, the maintenance officer, Lt. Tom Driver, presented the CO with a nice, shiny jeep. Ominously, there was also a shiny spot on the engine block where the
identification numbers had been filed off. The squadron needed the vehicle
desperately, so Spencer decided not to ask any questions.

The following day, however, he was taken aback when he learned that
someone had had the audacity to steal the jeep assigned to the Air Force
inspector general, who was visiting the area. That was a bit much. Spencer
reluctantly returned the vehicle to the general with his apologies and offered
to have it repainted with air force markings. "He was very good about it,"
Spencer recalled with tongue in cheek.[4]

As the Seawolves became more sophisticated in their interservice "transactions," they learned to trade cases of steaks, lobster tails, and beer, acquired
through imaginative navy supply procedures, for vehicles, equipment, and
even such things as aircraft parts and ordnance. Even so, midnight acquisitions continued to account for a considerable amount of squadron supplies
and equipment.

Nagging problems remained. One of the more serious was the condition
of the helicopters. The squadron was supposed to have been provided with
completely rehabbed aircraft in top-notch condition, but most were tired old
birds, some with more than twenty-four hundred hard flying hours on the
airframes. Squadron mechanics were somehow able to breathe new life into

Seawolves labor in the blistering heat to keep their aircraft flying. *U.S. Naval Institute Photo Archive*

them. Spencer would later say: "We had a secret weapon on the ground; the magicians who kept those old aircraft in the air."[5]

Like the original aircraft assigned to the HC-1 detachments, and despite repeated requests, those subsequently received by the squadron had no radar altimeters. Neither did they have such basic things as rotor brakes. That meant that the rotor systems could not easily be shut down in a high wind. This problem could be particularly serious aboard the LSTs, where space on the helipad was extremely limited and the second aircraft in a fire team could not land until the main rotor on the first had completely stopped turning. Circling the ship with a low fuel state and nowhere else to go could cause anxious moments.

Sometimes it was even a problem for aircraft operating ashore, despite the fact that there was usually more room to spare. "On one occasion," remembers Spencer, "I couldn't get the rotor to stop, and the helicopter was in danger of rolling over. I ordered the crew to jump and rode the aircraft until I could get it secured."[6]

Like the HC-1 personnel before them, most new HA(L)-3 pilots and door gunners were temporarily farmed out to the army when they arrived in

Space on the flight deck of an LST was severely limited. Here, aboard the LST *Garrett County,* one aircraft has shut down and aligned its rotor blades so the second aircraft can land. *U.S. Navy*

country to get a taste of gunship combat. Spencer remembers that he tried to get them placed in army units close to where they would ultimately be assigned. The plan worked reasonably well, and most were moved into navy detachments a short time later.

Col. Joseph N. Laseau was commanding officer of the army's 336th Assault Helicopter Company, known collectively as the "Warriors," which included a gunship platoon called the "Thunderbirds." He had thirty-two Huey helicopters and not nearly enough pilots. "My unit was never at full strength, yet we flew well over the planned flying hours for a full strength unit. My aircraft commanders were meeting themselves coming and going. What's more, my boss was constantly after me to get more aircraft in the air."[7]

When a naval officer appeared at Laseau's command at Soc Trang offering to send him fifteen navy pilots, he thought he had died and gone to heaven. Of course, he would have to check them out, but he was sure he could do that and come out ahead on the deal. Laseau's operations officer was skeptical, but two days later the navy people arrived and were immediately given copilot's seats. Laseau remembers that, "One day the operations officer came to me and said, 'these pilots are pretty good.'"[8]

The naval aviators had begun to qualify as aircraft commanders and fire team leaders, and soon it was not unusual to see a Huey take off with two navy pilots and army door gunners. "These officers became part of us," says Laseau. "Before long, the first group returned to their own command, and another fifteen arrived to start the process all over again. All too soon, this group went back to the navy and was not replaced. We all hated to see it end."[9]

Flying with the various army units was total-immersion training, encompassing all of the associated hazards of the combat environment. Ens. James F. Burke Jr. was killed on August 1, flying copilot in an army gunship.

Not all early HA(L)-3 pilots did a stint with the army, however. Some went directly to the navy detachments and were plunged into the combat melee without much in the way of introduction. Such was the case with some Det. 1 pilots who launched on a particularly hairy mission not long after reporting aboard the *Garrett County* in June 1967. It was the sixteenth of that month, a rainy night when no one should have even thought of flying. The ship received an urgent call for help from U.S. Army Green Berets operating with South Vietnamese forces upriver. Their outpost was under attack by a large number of Viet Cong and, without immediate air support, would soon be overwhelmed.

Within minutes, a Det. 1 fire team, led by Lt. Tom Greenlee, launched into the weather and quickly made its way to the battle site, which was under heavy mortar fire. The situation was grim, and the Americans on the ground reported that Charlie was about to penetrate the outer defenses of the compound.

Lt. (jg) Matt Gache was the pilot of the trail helo. Having been with the detachment only a few weeks at that point, he remembers that visibility was so bad they had difficulty distinguishing the Viet Cong from the friendlies. The darkness, combined with the heavy rain, made it impossible for the gunships to concentrate their fire without hitting their own people on the ground.

An air force AC-47 gunship, known variably as "Spooky" and "Puff the Magic Dragon," circled helplessly overhead, unable to bring its lethal guns to bear because it could not get below the thick overcast that bottomed out at about five hundred feet, maybe less.[10] Greenlee asked Spooky if he had any parachute flares aboard.

Spooky responded, "I've got 99 big ones."

"Well, start kicking them out," said Greenlee, we'll take it from there."[11]

It was an unusual request to ask that parachute flares be dropped above an overcast, but the air force plane commander understood exactly what the Seawolves had in mind and quickly complied. Within minutes, flares began to descend into the fight below. Their bright light, reflected against the clouds and rain, gave the scene an eerie cast. Now the waiting helicopter gunships pounced on the surprised and exposed enemy, killing several and sending the others into a hasty retreat.

"They're heading for the river," reported the Green Beret on the ground.

"Roger that," replied the fire team leader.

The Seawolves had already expended their rockets and now concentrated machine-gun fire on the Viet Cong's getaway vehicles, a group of sampans on the riverbank. Rolling in, they laid waste to the small fleet of boats, killing more of the VC who were now in total disarray. Gache described the action as "a real turkey shoot."[12]

By this time, Spooky's parachute flares seemed to fill the sky. Many had gone out, making them impossible to see and thus a serious hazard to the low-flying helicopters. "There were so many of those things floating down around us," says Gache, "that it's a miracle we didn't run into one."[13]

The hardest part of the mission, however, was getting back aboard the *Garrett County*. When they arrived at the ship, it was dark as the proverbial "well-digger's ass at midnight" and still raining hard. Visibility could be measured in yards. To make matters worse, the flares had played havoc with the pilots' night vision, turning an already treacherous landing situation into a game of blindman's buff. Despite this, and the understandable "pucker factor" experienced by the pilots, both gunships made it aboard without incident.[14]

MOST SEAWOLF DOOR GUNNERS HAD BEEN SELECTED AND RECEIVED their initial training in the United States. Some, however, were picked up along the way, and this was especially true in the early days of the squadron when Spencer, Jaburg, Hipp, and others were working hard to put it all together. Some were unlikely candidates who just wanted to get in on the action.

Perhaps the most unlikely of all was twenty-two-year-old Anthony M. "Tony" Reynolds-Huntley. Not only was he a noncombatant; he was not even an American. In fact, he was a member of a Royal Australian Air Force contingent who had been assigned to Vung Tau as a baker in 1966. Settling easily into his duties in the mess hall, he soon began to cast about for something a bit more interesting to occupy his time. There must, he thought, be more to the war in Vietnam than bread and biscuits.

The U.S. Navy, he observed, had a few gunships that flew in and out of Vung Tau for maintenance. He found this especially interesting because, at one point in his career, he had qualified as a door gunner with RAAF #9 Squadron and coveted an opportunity to fly with a combat unit. When the Navy squadron formed at Vung Tau in the spring of 1967, he saw his chance.

Taking advantage of the hustle and bustle involved in getting a new squadron up and operating, he managed to talk himself onto a few flights. At first, Spencer was not aware of the Aussie's presence and was completely taken aback when he learned of his activities. What to do with a guy who so passionately wants to be a door gunner?

According to Reynolds-Huntley, "He [Spencer] was very gracious and ultimately approved my participation." The Australian understood fully that Spencer was sticking his neck out. "Had I been wounded or killed," he acknowledges, "there would have been a diplomatic incident for sure."[15] At the very least, Bob Spencer would have had some explaining to do.

Reynolds-Huntley flew more than forty missions, whenever he could get the time off from the mess hall. It was so important to him that he even took leave and gave up his R&R trips to fly with the Seawolves. "They kinda, sorta took me under their wings," he says. "Maybe because I was an Australian, I was something of a novelty to them. I don't know, but what a great bunch of blokes."[16]

When Reynolds-Huntley left to return to Australia, Commander Hipp presented him with a pair of enlisted combat air crew wings, which he still treasures.[17] Today, he is the only Australian who is a full-fledged member of the Seawolf Association.

9

Up Close and Personal

CON JABURG GOT HIS FIRST TASTE OF COMBAT IN VIETNAM WHEN he went as executive officer to Vinh Long to fly with Det. 3 as copilot for detachment officer in charge Rocky Rowell. Shortly after takeoff, they turned up a motorized sampan, hidden in the vegetation along the riverbank in a free-fire zone where it was not supposed to be. After checking with Paddy Control, they were cleared to attack. Both gunships in the fire team let loose with rockets, some of which scored hits on the offending craft. It suddenly blew up, revealing its cargo of explosive ordnance intended for the Viet Cong. Transportation of munitions via the network of waterways was, as might be expected, an enemy priority, and secondary detonations of this nature would not be uncommon.

The fire team continued downriver to the South China Sea and turned south along the coast to check out another free-fire zone. There they found a small craft whose cargo amidships was covered with a tarp. While the fire team leader called for clearance to fire, the boat turned into a narrow over-grown canal in a futile effort to escape. In the end, the Seawolves made short work of it, Jaburg taking out the VC boatman with his flex guns.

Now they rendezvoused with Lt. Al Banford and his fire team from the *Harnett County* to put in a four-plane strike on a known VC position halfway

A Seawolf gunship has just let go with a rocket at a small craft hiding in the vegetation along a narrow waterway. *U.S. Naval Institute Photo Archive*

between the mouths of the Ham Luong and the My Tho rivers. This time, the Viet Cong were ready and put up a barrage of .51-caliber fire. The four helos each made rocket attacks on the site, after which they returned to base to refuel and rearm. Upon landing at Vinh Long, Jaburg "was astounded to learn that we had been gone for only a little over an hour and a half. As much as had happened on the patrol, it seemed like a much longer time."[1] There was not much time to think about it then, because they were soon in the air again hunting for bad guys.

Later, as Jaburg reflected on the day's events, the realization began to sink in that "it was the first time I had knowingly taken another man's life. I didn't see it as a happy occurrence, but I knew that at times it would be necessary, and I could deal with it."[2]

Seawolf crews in the detachments normally worked twenty-four hours on and twenty-four hours off. At Vung Tau, maintenance and other personnel worked twelve on and twelve off. In some locations there were opportunities to spend some time in towns or villages, although stringent restrictions applied at night. Viet Cong and Viet Cong sympathizers were everywhere.

Officers and enlisted men took pleasure where they could find it. Softball and horseshoes were popular, and the base clubs did a steady business. The Seawolves even managed some volunteer civic action projects, supporting local schools and charitable organizations with both money and labor. Sometimes, they ferried medical personnel into areas in the Mekong Delta where basic medical services were sparse to nonexistent. The helicopters fascinated the children, who always treated the crews with awe. There was great potential to foster goodwill, but the Americans had to take great care when in contact with locals. An innocent-looking teenager might well be carrying a hand grenade in a school bag.

Lt. Cdr. William D. Martin, Det. 3's officer in charge, took on one rather unusual civic action project. An accomplished magician, he spent many hours sandwiched between flights and administrative chores trying to bring a positive view of Americans into villages and outposts in his area. PBR sailors would precede him into a carefully selected location along the river and prepare a site for his appearance. Martin would arrive a short time later in his helicopter, stepping out in his signature black top hat to greet a crowd of children and their parents. He also had with him a small table and a variety of tricks. The PBR crews and the rest of the gunship crew provided security for the show. Martin would dazzle his audience with feats of magic, in which he tried to involve as many children as possible, before departing into the sky in his helicopter. It was good fun, and the locals loved it.[3]

Despite such diversions, the business of the Seawolves was war. HA(L)-3 had begun in April with four detachments. By mid-June there were six, and by the end of August, seven. Four were based ashore, one each at Vung Tau, Binh Thuy, Dong Tam, Vinh Long, and Nha Be. Three more flew from LSTs anchored in the rivers: one on the Ham Long, another on the Co Chien, and

Lt. Cdr. Bill Martin, officer in charge of Det. 7, and his fire team put down at a South Vietnamese outpost following a mission against the Viet Cong. *U.S. Naval Institute Photo Archive*

the third on the Bassac. All detachments were operating at full tilt and making the Viet Cong sit up and take notice wherever they were encountered.

COOKS SEEM TO HAVE HAD A THING ABOUT BECOMING DOOR GUN-ners. U.S. Navy CS1 William H. "Charlie" Johnson arrived at Vung Tau in the summer of 1967 and was assigned to the U.S. Army 765th Consolidated Mess. Because he was senior man, he was put in charge, and quickly turned the messing facility into one of the best in the Delta. Having accomplished that task in record time, he turned his attention to setting up a first-rate officers' mess, both feats attracting the attention of Jaburg. The XO didn't know it at the time, but he was about to be sucked in to a carefully calculated plot.

Johnson now called in his chips and asked Jaburg to let him fly on the gunships. Unlike Reynolds-Huntley, he had no experience whatsoever with either gunships or machine guns. What he had was an obsession to become a full-time door gunner.

The XO stifled his amusement and pointed out to Johnson that a gunship crewman should have an aviation rating. He may also have thought that the cook was a bit long in the tooth, but refrained from saying so. Being a door gunner was clearly a young man's job. Besides that, Johnson already had a job, and keeping men fed was critical to any military operation.

Undeterred, Johnson pressed his case. The mess hall was running well, largely through his efforts, and he thought he could get his boss to let him go. "Tell you what," said Jaburg. "I'll let you fly if you can qualify as a crewman."[4] By this time the squadron had some firm rules in place for new crewmen, and they were tough. That was important, because the men in the detachments not only had to know how to fight their aircraft, but how to keep them flying as well.

So much for that, thought the XO, knowing that Johnson would have to learn the mechanical systems of the UH-1B and demonstrate his knowledge to the satisfaction of some very hard-nosed maintenance personnel. Being a Huey crewman and a door gunner was no job for a cook, especially not one who was a doddering old man of thirty-two.

Johnson now persuaded the supply officer for whom he worked to let him pursue his dream. Then he buttonholed the HA(L)-3 maintenance chief and told him what he wanted to do. He remembers that the chief laughed at the idea. Nevertheless, the XO had given his approval, so the chief shrugged and told his people to do what they could to help.

Turning a cook into a helicopter crewman was no easy task, so they worked him hard and drilled him daily on the UH-1B systems. When he thought he had it down pat, he took the test and passed with flying colors. An astonished Con Jaburg kept his word and assigned him to fly on mail and logistic runs. That was not exactly what Johnson had in mind.

One day Lieutenant Banford of Det. 4's somewhat infamous Rowell's Rats limped into Vung Tau with battle damage. While the bird was being patched up, Johnson approached Banford and told him he wanted to be a full-time door gunner. "I guess old 'Dirty Al' must have had some pull somewhere, because he went to Ops [Operations] and came back after a few minutes and said, 'Pack your seabag Johnson; you're going to Det. 4.'"[5]

Johnson may have been a qualified Huey crewman, but he knew nothing about machine guns or gunnery. Confidence and determination, however,

William H. "Charlie" Johnson, "the flying cook," displays his prowess with an M-60. *William H. Johnson*

can sometimes go a long way toward substituting for training and experience. On-the-job training can fill in the rough spots later.

"On the way to the *Garrett County* where Det. 4 was based, Fred Mahana, the crew chief, showed me how to hold the M-60 upside down to keep the empty brass out of the tail rotor. Fred forgot to mention that when firing the M-60 in this manner, you have to have your flak vest closed tight to keep empty brass from getting down behind it and frying a nice little brown spot on your chest before you could get it out."[6] It was a good first lesson. Johnson took it in stride and did reasonably well as a first-timer with the M-60.

"As we neared the ship, our wing aircraft came out to join us, and we did an evening patrol of our sector. Right away, we spotted two sampans where they shouldn't have been and got permission to take them under fire. I offered to give the gun back to Fred, but Dirty Al said, 'No, let's see what you've got Johnson.' I sank both sampans and got a secondary explosion from one of them."[7]

It was an impressive demonstration of natural ability enhanced by a healthy helping of luck. Johnson was ecstatic with his newfound occupation, and it got even better as time went on. "In a few weeks I had gone from cook to bona fide aerial gunner and had started to work on the first of my nineteen air medals. I became the crew chief on old #533 and flew most of my 450 strike flight missions with Lt. Bill Butcher Barnes."[8] Before Johnson returned home in May 1968, he had been shot down twice, survived the rigors of Tet '68, and won a Purple Heart.

It was now late summer 1967. The last of the HC-1 people were now short timers and would soon be going home. Sadly, not everyone would make it. Michael Peters vividly remembers a mission that took place on August 22, 1967.

He had launched as part of a two-plane fire team to check out a large concentration of sampans in an area controlled by Charlie. Arriving on the scene, the Huey pilots quickly confirmed that these were indeed enemy boats, and after receiving clearance to engage, began the task of turning them into splinters. The enemy returned fire with a vengeance.

During one of the runs, the lead aircraft, flown by Lt. Bill Pressey, took a hit that shattered the windscreen, wounding the copilot, Lt. (jg) Thomas E. Gilliam. The two helos hightailed it to the nearest LST, where Pressey landed, picked up a medical corpsman to attend Gilliam, and then headed for the army medical facility at My Tho. Sometimes, however, all deliberate haste is not quite enough. Just as the two helos were about to land, Pressey reported over the air, "Tom's gone!" Both aircraft landed at My Tho, and Gilliam's death was confirmed.

Pressey and one of his crewmen flew back to the base at Vinh Long as passengers in the good aircraft, while Peters and Pressey's crew chief limped home in the damaged helo. "We didn't talk," says Peters. "There must have been the normal radio chatter, but I just remember it as very quiet and surreal. It was near sunset, and that landscape, with the shimmer the intense heat gives off and the reflections you get from the water in the rice paddies, created colors and hues that I remember to this day but cannot quite describe."[9]

Fatalities were not limited to combat. Flying underpowered, overweight Hueys, day or night, in all kinds of weather, from ship and shore, continued

The fire team leader is first off; the trail ship will follow in less than a minute.
Conrad Jaburg

to challenge the navy helicopter pilots who were by training and experience some of the world's best.

On September 1, 1967, Lt. (jg) Tom Anzalone awoke aboard the *Garrett County* on the Co Chien River and was deathly ill. The steamy, tropical climate was a perfect breeding place for all kinds of exotic microorganisms and debilitating diseases. Anzalone had contracted one of those bugs.

Knowing there was no way he could function effectively or safely as copilot on fire team leader Lt. Cdr. Robert D. Johnson's (no relation to CS1 Charlie Johnson) aircraft, he asked Lt. Al Bacanskas to fill in for him. Bacanskas readily agreed. It was no big deal, and there was nothing much to do aboard ship anyway. At least the time passed more quickly when one was flying.

That night, the all-too-familiar call came over the 1-MC: "SCRAMBLE THE SEAWOLVES! SCRAMBLE THE SEAWOLVES!" It was an especially black night, and Johnson became disoriented in the rush to get airborne and flew into the water. The helicopter rolled over and sank immediately. Bacanskas and one of the door gunners were able to extricate themselves and swim free. Johnson and door gunner ADJ1 Edward L. Ott III did not survive the crash. Again, the loss of comrades hit this closely knit detachment hard. At least Bacanskas, who had replaced Anzalone on the flight, had been able to spare his friend a burden of guilt that would have followed him all his life.

Back at Vung Tau, Bob Spencer took time to write to the families of the deceased Seawolves, one of the more difficult and emotionally draining tasks a commanding officer is sometimes called upon to do. In wartime, however, death lurks constantly in the shadows, and an effective commander cannot allow it to distract him from his mission.

Now it was back to the task of molding the pilots, crewmen, and support personnel into a well-oiled and coordinated fighting organization. "Even though we were broken down into detachments," Spencer says, "we were all close enough geographically so that the XO, the Ops. Officer, or I were able to visit the detachments periodically, fly with them, encourage them, check to see if they had any problems, and generally try to engender some squadron cohesiveness. There was some resistance, but I think, for the most part, we were successful."[10]

To be sure, there was still a sizable degree of independence among the detachments and a certain amount of competitive pride in being part of one of these small cohesive units. That would not change, but perhaps without realizing it, detachment personnel had also begun to think of themselves as members of a squadron, one that was fast acquiring a reputation as a formidable combat element.

10

The Whisperer

Lt. Cdr. Jack Bolton was one of those who had not flown with an army unit before he arrived in country. He took over almost immediately from Frank Foster as officer in charge of Det. 2, which was based at Nha Be in June 1967, and received his final on-the-job training from Lt. John "Cotton" Smoot, one of the HC-1 veterans.

The perennial problem with all combat operations in Vietnam was sorting out the good guys from the bad guys. Except for uniformed North Vietnamese personnel, the Viet Cong looked like the farmers, villagers, and fishermen many of them had been and, to some extent, still were. For this reason, the tactical operations center (TOC) in the Rung Sat Special Zone, call-sign Moon River, had one or more South Vietnamese officers assigned at all times to evaluate reports of enemy contact and to clear attacks on river traffic.

From the beginning, Rocky Rockwell had driven home the point that the new pilots should "damn well know who they were shooting at," because, as he put it, "we don't kill 'friendlies' or innocent civilians."[1] The Seawolves did their best to adhere to that principle, even if it sometimes meant a lost opportunity. Even after a fire team leader had been cleared to attack, he often held fire until he had positively identified the target to his own satisfaction. This paid off on a number of occasions, at least in terms of peace of mind. "I had no use for the Viet Cong," recalled Jack Bolton, "and to this day I would have no compunctions about cutting one's balls off, but I remember Rockwell's admonition vividly. It was a good one that I enforced in my detachment. As a result, I slept well at night and still do."[2]

Nha Be was somewhat typical of a midsize Vietnamese town when the first of the Seawolves began to arrive. Having only dirt streets, it was hardly a metropolis, and there were few amenities. Lt. (jg) Richard S. "Dick" Stanger recalls there were several bars just outside the gate to the base that catered to U.S. sailors from the minesweepers, the PBRs, and the Seawolf detachment. To make American clientele feel at home, one was known as the "San Diego Bar." The one next to it was named—what else—"The Bar Next to the San Diego Bar." But the undisputed high-class establishment in the area was the "Lucy Bar." Its five-star rating came from the fact that it was the only one with electricity. This much-coveted upgrade was delivered to the Lucy Bar from a long extension cord that snaked through the fence from some unknown building on the base. Stanger also remembers that "there was a little old lady in the Lucy Bar whose job it was to drain beer bottles left on the tables by departing patrons until she had a full one. Then she capped it and resold it to an unsuspecting customer."[3]

At Nha Be, the Seawolf crews lived in barracks-type buildings, which while hardly luxurious, were an improvement over those initially occupied by Foster's people. During this period, the detachment had two gunships. Later, Det. 2 would be assigned four aircraft for a time, with a corresponding increase in personnel. Still later, this would be reduced to three, providing the detachment with the only permanent heavy-fire team until HA(L)-3 was disbanded. In 1967, however, Det. 2, like the other detachments, had two Hueys, eight pilots, and eight enlisted men making up two light-fire teams.

A ready duty fire team (four pilots and four enlisted door gunners) flew patrols and responded to all scrambles for a twenty-four-hour period (0800-0800) in most detachments. Then, because of the rigors associated with a ready duty period, they had twenty-four hours off, during which they dealt with paperwork or helping to keep the birds ready to fly. Or, it might mean a few hours in town with a stop at one of the watering holes. Other than that, the clubs were the popular spots in the evening for the off-duty crews.

The Nha Be Officers' Club was located in the bachelor officers' quarters (BOQ). Many considered it one of the best in the Mekong Delta, but certainly not because it was very elegant. Made of raw wood, it was rather rustic and

Jack Bolton on patrol in the Rung Sat Special Zone. *Lillian Bolton*

heavily flavored with the ambiance of war. Along with the Seawolf pilots, the PBR and minesweeper officers, members of the attached SEAL team, and others from the ships and units that called Nha Be home frequented the club. Mostly, it was a place to relax and swap hairy combat stories and enjoy a special kind of camaraderie. The stories were dramatic, punctuated with colorful language and, as one pilot put it with a wry smile, "basically true." There were certainly enough of them to fill several issues of more than one true adventure magazine.

The Na Bhe O-Club was run by a savvy chief petty officer, who was said to be "well connected" in Saigon and kept the club well stocked, not only with local Ba Mui Ba (Beer 33), but with a variety of other brands. Most important, the beer was available in bottles that were more prized than the canned versions. The bar was complete with an alcoholic monkey who hung out in the overhead, probably gathering intelligence information. His name, of course, was Charlie!

There is little doubt that the clubs were important for maintaining morale, but because alertness and immediate response were critical to the mission, Commander Bolton changed the timing of duty shifts to 1600-1600 to give oncoming crews more time to fully recover from club activities of the night before.

On average, the ready duty gunships of Det. 2 flew three scheduled patrols during a shift: more often than not, two flights during the day, and one at night. A primary purpose of these flights was to detect any unusual activity in the area that might signal a Viet Cong attack on shipping in the Long Tau River. While these patrols did not eliminate such attacks, they were certainly disruptive to enemy attempts and undoubtedly reduced their frequency.

In 1965 and 1966 mines had damaged several cargo ships, although none was sunk. Small minesweeping boats, or MSBs, whose job it was to keep the river clear, had a particularly bad time of it in 1966 and 1967, some being sunk and others severely damaged.[4] Shipping companies, faced with increased insurance premiums, to say nothing of the possible loss of their vessels and danger to their crews, were becoming increasingly skittish about the transit of their ships through the Long Tau gauntlet.

In addition to guarding this critical waterway with regular patrols, the Seawolves had plenty of other opportunities to tangle with Charlie in response to calls for help from friendly forces operating in the area.

Three weeks after he took over as officer in charge of Det. 2, Bolton and his wingman, Lieutenant Stanger, were on a patrol in the Rung Sat area when he was called by the TOC with a request for assistance in nearby Go Cong Province.

"Seawolf two-six, this is Moon River. We have a man on the ground in close proximity to a small enemy force. If you're lucky, you can get the jump on them."[5] The phrase "close proximity" turned out to be a considerable understatement.

A few minutes before reaching the area, Bolton established contact with the controller on the ground and was surprised to have him return his call in a whisper. Bolton could hardly hear him. It sounded like he had laryngitis, but Bolton immediately understood that the enemy must have been within a stone's throw, lying low in some leafy cover so they would not be spotted by the helicopter. The contact asked Bolton to drop a smoke some distance away in a rice paddy to be used as a reference point for an attack. The fire team leader complied, but the smoke was extinguished by water in the paddy. After the same thing happened to a second smoke, the whisperer said, "Go out to the west, go low level, then reverse course and I'll con you onto the target."[6]

Bolton did as he was told, and as he and Stanger came out of their 180-degree turn, the whisperer was back on the air. "That's good."[7] Silence! The fire team held the heading.

Several seconds later, the whisperer responded, "Come right; that's it; now hold it. Now come left just a little. Right on. They're in that tree line in your twelve o'clock. They're all yours."[8]

At a hundred knots and thirty feet, the tree line was coming up fast, and Bolton knew that the whisperer must be very close to it. He would probably fly right over him. The guy, probably a SEAL, had nerve. For a split second, it made Bolton question what he was about to do. Killing an American with friendly fire was a Seawolf pilot's worst nightmare.

Bolton glanced at the ball of the turn and bank indicator to make sure the aircraft was in perfectly balanced flight. If he was just a little bit off with his shot. . . . He didn't want to think about it. "I had my rocket sight down," he says, "and punched off all fourteen 2.75s into the tree line. The impact was a grand sight."[9]

"Beautiful," said the whisperer, now in a full-throated voice. "Right on!"[10]

It had all happened so fast that the wing helicopter was not able to get off a shot, but it probably would have been overkill anyway. No one in the target area was likely to have survived the rocket barrage.

Det. 2 at Nha Be. Jack Bolton is on the front row, at the extreme left; Dick Stanger is third from the left. *Richard S. Stanger*

The helos circled the spot several times, but there was no sign of life. The enemy had been taken completely by surprise.

"Good shooting, Seawolf," said the whisperer, "and thanks much."[11] This may have been one of the first whispering close-air support missions flown by the Seawolves, but it would not be the last.

Located on the edge of the village of Nha Be, the base itself was vulnerable to periodic Viet Cong attack. One morning, during the wee hours while it was still very dark, a round from a recoilless rifle hit the club. Fortunately, even the off-duty Seawolves had turned in by that time, and no one was killed or injured. Bolton, who was asleep in his room down the passageway, was knocked out of his bunk by the impact. Pulling on a pair of khaki trousers, he ran outside and dove into a bunker, only to be piled upon by several others who had also been rudely awakened.

Suddenly, realizing that he was the ready fire team leader, he untangled himself from the gaggle of bodies and sprinted with bare feet down a gravel road to his chopper. He jumped in just as a mortar round hit only a few yards away. Had it not been a dud, the story of this nocturnal adventure and Jack Bolton's tour in Vietnam would have ended there. As it was, he had the engine started just as the rest of his crew arrived, and they launched into the fray, followed close behind by wingman Dick Stanger.

The radio crackled with chatter. An air force Spooky AC-47 gunship circled the area, dropping parachute flares. A Viet Cong unit was firing from a position across the river, lobbing mortar rounds into the base, a number of them also falling indiscriminately on the town. An army Huey gunship heavy-fire team was making passes over a position where the VC were dug in. Bolton's fire team was told by Moon River to hold off its attack until the army helos had expended their ordnance and Spooky had a chance to hose down the area with its mini-guns. No one wanted any midair collisions in the darkness.

About that time, the army fire team leader reported that one of his door gunners had taken a round in the chest, and he was departing the area. To make matters worse, the pilot of the AC-47 came on the air and reported he was returning to base with one engine out. It was complete chaos.

Bolton was now cleared to attack. He and Stanger went in low, looking for bad guys, but drew no fire and could not acquire any targets in the dark. As was so often the case in this war, the VC had simply vanished.

The TOC now asked if Bolton could make an emergency medical evacuation. He landed at Nha Be and loaded four injured civilians—two women and two children—aboard his aircraft and rushed them to the hospital at Tan Son Nhut in Saigon.

It wasn't until his helo was being refueled there that he noticed people looking at him somewhat strangely. Only then did it occur to him that he was shoeless and half naked, an unlikely looking U.S. naval aviator.

Returning to Nha Be, which was now secure and quiet, he and Stanger walked back to the BOQ, noting how painful it was to negotiate the distance on the sharp gravel in bare feet. He marveled that he did not even notice it on his initial run to the aircraft. Morning was now beginning to filter through the clouds in the eastern sky. Charlie had robbed him of his beauty sleep again, but he was hopeful that there was still enough time to steal an hour or so of shut-eye before the start of the daily routine.

11

Taking on All Comers

By the fall of 1967, the detachments were operating smoothly as a squadron. Combat tactics learned from hard experience were being incorporated into a tactics manual, and standard pilot qualifications were being formalized.

An attack helicopter aircraft commander (AHAC) was required to have at least 500 total pilot hours, 150 of which had to be in rotary-wing aircraft, and 50 in the UH-1B. He was required to complete written and oral exams to determine his knowledge of the aircraft and its systems. Finally, he had to take a check ride to demonstrate not only pilot proficiency but also his ability to operate the rocket and flex-gun systems and to command and train pilots and crew members.

Qualifications for a fire team leader (FTL) were all of the above plus a hundred more pilot hours, a demonstrated knowledge of the rules of engagement (ROE), and a tough FTL flight check ride. Qualification, rather than rank, governed who flew in what position. A lieutenant, junior grade, who had been in the detachment for several months and was a designated FTL might have a newly arrived lieutenant commander, or even a commander, as a copilot.

By this time, the last of the HC-1 personnel were about to head for home. Mike Peters, who had been a member of HC-1, Det. 21, was one of these. He flew his last flights in the Mekong Delta on October 25, 1967.

The day began routinely enough: Peters flew as AHAC in the trail helicopter on a reconnaissance flight out of Vinh Long that was led by Lt. Cdr. Sam Aydolotte. Not long after takeoff, they were dispatched to an area southeast of Vinh Long where Viet Cong forces had engaged an ARVN patrol. After receiving fire from a wooded area, the Seawolves hosed down the spot and proceeded to the LST *Hunterdon County* on the Ham Loung River to replenish.

No sooner had they refueled and rearmed when they were scrambled to assist three PBRs that had been attacked by a large group of VC near the town of Ben Tre. One of the PBRs had been disabled by recoilless rifle fire, and one of its crewmen badly wounded. He required immediate evacuation.

Aydelotte's two gunships were joined by the two *Hunterdon County* Seawolves, which were already in the air, led by fire team leader Lt. Bill Butcher Barnes. Arriving on the scene, Barnes went in to pick up the wounded PBR crewman while the other three helos suppressed fire from Viet Cong positioned in a tree line. After a successful, if somewhat hairy rescue, Barnes headed for the army base at Dong Tam, where there was a medical facility, while the three remaining choppers continued to pound the VC until they expended their ammunition.

Landing at nearby Ben Tre to rearm and refuel, Peters discovered that his main rotor had suffered hits, and he had to depart the fray for repairs at Vinh Long. Meanwhile, Barnes had dropped off the wounded man at Dong Tam and returned to Ben Tre just in time to help repulse a Viet Cong attack on the town itself.

It had been a busy day, but not an especially unusual one for the Seawolves. For Peters, one of the last of the HC-1 pilots, it was the end of a year-long adventure, one in which he had accumulated a Distinguished Flying Cross, a Purple Heart, and thirty-eight air medal awards, among other decorations. And, like many of his HC-1 comrades and others who would come after him, he felt like he had aged several years in only twelve months.

By the end of December 1967, 155 PBRs were operating in the Delta and the Rung Sat. Some flew from bases ashore, some from three LSTs in the rivers, and some from a barracks ship, non-propelled (APL) and a YRBM that had been added as floating bases. There were also six SEAL platoons, three in

A gunship arrives on the scene firing rockets in support of PBRs. *U.S. Navy/PH1 Dan Dodd*

the Rung Sat and three in the Delta, contributing their unique brand of mayhem to areas that had once been exclusive and impenetrable VC preserves.

Essential to the Game Warden mix was the devastating fire from the sky provided by the rapid-reaction fire teams of the HA(L)-3 Seawolves. The squadron now had twenty-two aircraft, deployed in seven detachments. At least fourteen aircraft were maintained in an operational "up" status at all times, leaving no more than eight in various stages of maintenance or for use as spares.

Det. 1 was based aboard the *Jennings County* on the Bassac River. Det. 2 was at Nha Be, covering the Rung Sat Special Zone. Det. 3 was based at Vinh Long. Det. 4 operated from the *Garrett County* on the Co Chien River. Det. 5 made its home aboard the *Harnett County*, which had relieved the *Hunterdon County* on the Ham Loung River. Det. 6 flew from the Dong Tam Army Airfield, which was built on a man-made island in the middle of the My Tho River. Det. 7 operated from the Binh Thuy Naval Base near Can Tho City. At this point, the squadron had 243 enlisted men and 96 officers, 92 of whom were pilots.

In a relatively short time, the PBR crews, the SEALS, and the HA(L)-3 Seawolves of Operation Game Warden had become a deadly and highly effective combination. During 1967 the gunship crews had put almost ten thousand hours on their old Hueys, flying more than seven thousand missions. The HC-1 pioneers had departed, but they had left a superb legacy to build on. In a few short months, the newly formed squadron had become an integral and essential part of TF 116.

It had not come without cost. To date, three pilots and four crewmen had been killed, and fifty Seawolves had been wounded. But Game Warden had taken hold and was now moving into high gear. The Market Time coastal operations of TF 115 and the search-and-destroy tactics of the MRFs convinced Charlie that his dominance of the Rung Sat and his control of large areas of the Delta and its waterways were being seriously contested. Top-level North Vietnamese and Viet Cong leaders knew, however, that an important event, which they hoped would go far toward bringing the war in the south to a quick end on their terms, was about to take place.

12

Tet '68

As the Seawolves' reputation for courage and reliability grew, so did the demands for their services. This was particularly true during the infamous Tet Offensive of 1968, when the navy gunships were continuously called upon to assist in keeping bases, cities, and villages from being overrun and to drive the Viet Cong from towns and enclaves they had succeeded in capturing. The provincial capital of Vinh Long and the adjacent army airfield from which Seawolf Det. 3 operated was the scene of some especially heavy fighting during Tet, and the Seawolves took part both in the air and on the ground.

Tet celebrates the lunar New Year and is the most important holiday period in the Vietnamese culture. Some have characterized it as being equivalent to the American Christmas, Thanksgiving, and Fourth of July rolled into one. Visiting, gift giving, feasting, fireworks, and a celebratory atmosphere accompany it. It should be noted, however, that Tet is more than just a holiday fling. It also has spiritual significance and is a time for families to gather together and pay their respects to each other and their ancestors.

During 1967, the Viet Cong had, for the most part, been stymied in their drive to take over the south. They were losing ground in the Mekong Delta and saw a major push during Tet '68 as an opportunity to regain the momentum they had lost. Vietnamese believe that what happens during Tet sets the pattern for the year to come, so the psychological value of a Viet Cong victory at this time held great promise. Indeed, the enemy hoped it could be turned into a rout during Tet Mau Than, the Year of the Monkey.

The plan involved a North Vietnamese call for a seven-day cease-fire, which the Communists fully intended to violate in an all-out series of attacks by some eighty-four thousand NVA and VC against hamlets, district and provincial capitals, and even Saigon. North Vietnamese Gen. Vo Nguyen Giap, architect of the victory over the French at Dien Bien Phu and commander in chief of the North Vietnamese Army, firmly believed that the South Vietnamese people would rise up during the Tet '68 attacks and join the VC in overthrowing the government and expelling the foreigners from Vietnam once and for all.[1]

From the beginning, it was an ambitious but risky plan in which, for the first time, the enemy would engage in massive military assaults as opposed to the relatively small-scale, hit-and-run guerrilla attacks of the past.

Because Tet was so special to the Vietnamese people, the South Vietnamese government embraced the offer of a cease-fire, apparently believing that neither the North Vietnamese nor the Viet Cong would dare to desecrate the sacred holiday. The truce was agreed to, and ARVN personnel were allowed a liberal leave policy.

The U.S. government, hoping to use the Tet cease-fire to encourage some sort of dialogue with the north, supported the arrangement, although U.S. military officers, including General Westmoreland, were skeptical and would not rule out an enemy deception. Even if the North Vietnamese and the Viet Cong intended to honor the cease-fire agreement, Westmoreland and others knew that it could only benefit the enemy, who would use the lull to move troops and supplies and to prepare for bigger, better, and more lethal attacks.

Lieutenant Anzalone kept a diary of his tour in Vietnam that recalls the period in some detail. On the evening of January 29, he was copilot on fire team leader Lt. Wade Turner's aircraft, flying from LST *Garrett County*. As the two Det. 4 gunships patrolled their area of responsibility, they encountered several Viet Cong units moving openly through the jungle. Some of the VC guerrillas brandished their weapons threateningly at the Seawolves but did not fire, secure in the knowledge that they were safe from attack by virtue of a truce they were about to violate. The gunships flew on, but the military movements were an ominous warning of what was to come. There was an air of defiance among the VC, for they knew something the Americans only suspected.

The LST *Garrett County* anchored in the Co Chien River near Vinh Long. *U.S. Naval Institute Photo Archive*

Between midnight and about 0300 on the morning of January 30, the Viet Cong attacked several towns in the central highlands and along the South Vietnamese coast. The attacks were premature, the probable result of enemy miscommunication. They had originally been ordered for the night of January 29–30, but General Giap imposed a twenty-four-hour delay, an order that apparently was not received in time by some of the Viet Cong units. In a way, it was a lucky turn of events for the Americans and South Vietnamese, because it provided a warning of the enemy deception. The cease-fire was immediately cancelled, and the allies dug in for the anticipated assault, which was not long in coming.

The Tet Offensive erupted in full force in the early hours of January 31, with attacks on the U.S. embassy in Saigon, the presidential palace, MACV headquarters, Tan Son Nhut airport, and a number of provincial and district capitals and towns throughout the South.

Aboard the *Garrett County*, anchored on the Co Chien River, Det. 4 pilots and crewmen were rudely awakened when the call to "SCRAMBLE THE SEAWOLVES" blared over the ship's 1-MC system. It was still dark as the fire team launched and headed for the army airfield at Vinh Long. Det. 3

ADJC Francis Smith (left) and two unidentified men check sandbags and fifty-five-gallon drums filled with water that shield the Seawolf operations trailer at the Vinh Long Army Airfield. *Tom Crull*

was stationed there and already had its hands full. As a provincial capital, the city of Vinh Long, which was adjacent to the base, was a major objective of the Communists. Before the Det. 4 fire team could reach its destination, however, it was diverted to the town of Tra Vinh, which was also under assault and seemed to be more vulnerable at the moment.

In the face of massive attacks throughout South Vietnam, and simultaneous demands for immediate air support, it was hard to know which areas should receive priority. After launching only one strike on the enemy positioned on the edge of Tra Vinh, the gunships were hastily diverted again to the Vinh Long airfield, now under very heavy attack and in immediate danger of being overrun. Refueling and rearming quickly aboard the *Garrett County*, Turner and company took off again and made for the besieged army air base. Arriving shortly thereafter, they discovered that Vinh Long was indeed in extremis. Charlie had breached a section of the perimeter and now held one end of the runway. Anzalone remembers that fighting was heavy, and the situation was serious.

"It was like the Fourth of July at home, only much more so. It was still dark. The air force was dropping flares, and tracers crisscrossed the sky. The field was under attack by mortars and everything else the Viet Cong could throw at it."[2]

Having expended their ammunition, Wade Turner elected to land at the army base rather than take precious time to go back to the ship for replenishment. It was a courageous decision, because by this time the tower was warning him that the Viet Cong had taken the western part of the field. The fire team leader weighed the alternatives and determined that the dire circumstances justified the risk of landing there.

Turner and his two gunships set down on the eastern end of the runway, which was still under U.S. control. Upon touchdown, the door gunners jumped out with their M-60s and took up positions facing the western part of the airfield to protect the two aircraft from attack while they were being refueled and rearmed. Turner instructed the gunners to "shoot anything that moves."

Things were indeed hectic on the ground. The army base commander had been killed in his jeep early in the fighting by an AK-47-toting Charlie, one of several who had breached the perimeter defenses and had made their way as far as the army's aircraft revetments. At one point, several Viet Cong made their way nearly to the command post beside the tower.

Twenty-two Seawolf maintenance personnel under Lt. Cdr. Joseph S. "Joe" Bouchard were involved in the fighting that ultimately halted the enemy attack. Having been forewarned about the cancellation of the ceasefire, the Seawolf contingent was ready.

Joe Bouchard remembered that: "Our fighting bunkers were manned when the Viet Cong made their initial assault. We killed a batch of them. Charlie also had a .50-caliber machine gun mounted in the tower of a nearby Buddhist temple and was firing into the base, shooting up the runway. We put a couple of belts of tracers into that temple with our M-60s and the fifty stopped firing."[3]

An army unit set up artillery across the river to shell the enemy on the edge of town. The VC attacks verged on the suicidal, while the American response was stubborn and unyielding. A tape from a recorder left running in the main Seawolf bunker has preserved some of the sounds of the battle for posterity. There are incoming mortar rounds, outgoing rockets, and the constant chattering of machine guns. A voice is heard shouting, "Get down; take cover; stand by your defenses; they're coming in on the west end!"[4] At this point, the Viet Cong were on the runway about three hundred yards away. Then the sound of helicopter gunships coming in low over the Seawolf bunkers as they made strafing and rocket runs can be heard.

Turner and his two aircraft, having refueled and rearmed, were off again, dispatched back to Tra Vinh that was again in deep trouble.

During repeated strikes there, both gunships were hit, but the crews returned safely to the *Garrett County* to refuel, to assess the damage to their aircraft, and to take time for breakfast and a short breather. Then they flew to Vung Tau for battle damage repair. On the way, they stayed glued to the operational frequency for news of what was happening around the country. They picked up several real-time reports from towns, bases, and outposts that were under heavy and continuous attack. Some were being overrun. The situation was grim. Anzalone remembers thinking: "There's not a safe place in all of South Vietnam for us to land."

That evening, after hasty patch jobs at Vung Tau, the fire team returned to the ship, with time for only a few hours' rest before they would go at it again.

Turner and company were back in action early on the morning of February 1, concentrating most of their efforts at Vinh Long. One apparent enemy objective was the destruction or capture of the PBRs at the U.S. Navy base, which was actually in the town. The Viet Cong now held key positions in the provincial city, and it was clear that the PBR base was not defendable. As the situation worsened, the decision was made to evacuate the boats, and the PBRs moved out into the river, where they were relatively safe for the moment. The Seawolves provided covering fire during the withdrawal. Later, the *Garrett County* would move upstream to serve as mother ship to the orphaned boats, as well as her own. Det. 4 was moved ashore at Vinh Long at this time to make room for the orphaned PBR crews aboard ship.

By daylight, most of the town was under the control of the Viet Cong, and the army airfield was surrounded. Despite this, the Americans repeatedly repelled assaults by the enemy. Things were not going quite as Charlie and his North Vietnamese sponsors had expected, and his attacks on the army facility became desperate.

Anzalone vividly remembers the carnage at the airfield. Viet Cong dead were everywhere, some of them children whom he estimated to be not more than twelve years old. In the city, buildings were on fire and large numbers of civilian refugees were leaving any way they could.

Meanwhile, Commander Bouchard had another problem to deal with. What happened next was clearly beyond the call of duty; indeed, had things not worked out well, Bouchard and others would almost certainly have been subjected to severe criticism, or even court-martial.

The Seawolves had befriended and provided various support to the Good Shepherd Convent, an orphanage for Vietnamese girls located about four hundred yards north of the main gate. The Viet Cong were known to deal harshly with those who involved themselves with, or took assistance from, the Americans, and Bouchard was concerned about the possible fate of the children and the Irish Catholic nuns who cared for them.

On the night of February 1, he took two volunteers, ADJC Francis Smith and AO1 Charles "Chuck" Fields, and made it to the orphanage under cover of darkness. Smith was the Seawolves' maintenance chief and Fields was a door gunner whose aircraft had been disabled and put out of action. Armed with grenades, machine guns, and plenty of ammunition, the three men set up defensive positions on the roof of the convent, from which they covered the compound and held it throughout the night.

The next day, Bouchard was able to enlist the services of army gunship pilot Capt. Robin Miller, who maneuvered his helicopter into the incredibly small compound and, in repeated flights, evacuated 130 terrified little girls and a dozen nuns, ten or twelve at a time, to the comparative safety of the base.[5]

A letter from the Mother Superior attests to the remarkable feat and to the courage of Joe Bouchard and his men.

> We are not likely to forget the terrible night of February 1, nor the heroic action of Commander Bouchard, Chief Smith, and Petty Officer Fields. With complete disregard for their own well-being, these men voluntarily came to our help in the midst of intense enemy fire and terrorism. Only those who have lived through those panic-filled hours, knowing what to expect from the brutality and ruthlessness of the Viet Cong, can fully understand our debt of gratitude towards these heroic and selfless men.[6]

Back at the Vinh Long Army Airfield, the Viet Cong assaults went on for six days, with varying degrees of intensity. Occasionally, the enemy would break through the perimeter, but the Americans were always able to beat them back. At one juncture, Bouchard found himself in command of a mixed pick-up force of army, navy, and Vietnamese personnel, who successfully defended the northern sector of the perimeter for several days while under almost constant attack.[7]

A Seawolf gunship makes a rocket run. *Richard Knott*

Meanwhile, the pilots and door gunners of Det. 3 and Det. 4 continued their strikes against the enemy in the town of Vinh Long. They also flew against the Viet Cong, who were besieging other towns and outposts throughout the area. Lt. (jg) Michael S. "Mike" Louy's logbook shows that he flew some ninety-six hours of combat in a fourteen-day period.[8] He was not alone in what seemed a marathon. There was plenty of combat flight time for everybody, day and night. As someone later quipped, "you just can't buy that kind of experience."

Two Viet Cong battalions concentrated their attack on Chau Doc on the upper Bassac River near the Cambodian border, but they were thwarted in their attempts to take the town, in great part by the timely and persistent efforts of the Seawolves, the PBRs, and the SEALs. Seawolves and PBRs also played a key role in preventing the town of Ben Tre, the capital of Kien Hoa Province, from being overrun during continuous and determined attacks over a thirty-six hour period.

Tet was a busy time in the Delta, and Bob Spencer recalls that virtually every operational aircraft in the squadron suffered some degree of battle damage. A supply statistic for the period provides additional insight into the intensity of operations. The Seawolves burned out 275 M-60 gun barrels and had to borrow more from a U.S. Marine Corps unit stationed at Da Nang.

AX3 Wendell Maxwell recalls, "When it was all over [at Vinh Long], there were dead Viet Cong everywhere. Hundreds of bodies were stacked like cord wood while a bulldozer cut a slit trench more than fifty yards long for a mass grave."[9]

The Tet '68 offensive was, without question, a tactical disaster for the Viet Cong, who lost somewhere between forty and forty-five thousand men. By comparison, U.S. and South Vietnamese losses were eleven hundred and twenty-three hundred, respectively. The Viet Cong never fully recovered from the Tet debacle. The defeat was incomprehensible to the Communists, who had fully expected the citizens of South Vietnam to join them in a mass uprising. Nothing of the kind materialized. It was the enemy's most serious miscalculation to date.

Chuc Mung Nam Moi—Happy New Year Charlie!

13

Of Seabirds and Lawnmowers

Unlike antiwar activists at home, American servicemen prosecuting the war in Vietnam had little time for political or philosophical debate. During Tet '68, the NVA/VC had departed from their strategy of small-scale hit-and-run attacks to launch a direct, massive simultaneous assault upon the United States and its allies. They had come up short.

In the Mekong Delta, the Viet Cong had been so decimated that their ranks were now being filled to the extent possible by regular North Vietnamese troops. The enemy now nursed his wounds and reverted to the tactics of guerrilla warfare. The Seawolves, along with other allied forces that had performed so well during Tet, quickly adapted to the new situation. Combat operations continued across the board, but there were some interesting noncombat incidents as well.

On March 6, Lieutenant Louy of Det. 4 was flying as AHAC on a flight from the *Garrett County* to Vung Tau. At the time, the ship was anchored near Tra Vinh, just downriver from Vinh Long. The Huey had suffered battle damage during a firefight the night before, taking a tracer in the rotor cuff. After careful consideration, it was determined that it could be safely flown to the maintenance facility for repair. The alternative was to wait until it could be lifted out, and that would put the fire team out of action for some time. Nobody wanted to do that.

Lt. Cdr. Arthur R. Clark, the Det. 4 officer in charge, had just completed all the fitness reports on his officers—an important task, but one that was somewhat difficult to accomplish in-between combat missions. He thought this flight would be a good opportunity to deliver them to HA(L)-3 headquarters at Vung Tau. He went along on the flight, riding in the copilot's seat. Because this was not a combat flight, AMSAN Richard Bauske was the only enlisted crewman aboard.

Mike Louy remembers feeling a little torque in the rudder pedals along the way. It gave him some concern, but because they were now about three-quarters of the way to Vung Tau, it was better to keep going then to turn back. A bit farther on, as they began a long, slow descent toward their destination, Louy felt another rudder pedal kick, this one more severe. Suddenly, the RPM began to unwind.

> I had just enough time to turn into the wind before we ditched. When we hit, the aircraft rolled right, as Hueys tend to do in such circumstances. The water rushed in, and the bird began to sink. I was out of my harness instantly, but the boss had become hung up in his straps. Fortunately, I was able to free him and pulled him out of the aircraft. Bauske had already made his exit and was treading water when we surfaced.
>
> We were down in the South China Sea, still several miles from Vung Tau, but within swimming distance of shore. It was hostile country, with lots of bad guys in the area, and not a good place for us to be. A bit further out was a framework of fish stakes with cross pieces and wire mesh sticking out of the water about four or five feet. It required a longer swim across a fairly strong current to get there, but it was a safer bet. We made it, with considerable effort. The whole thing was heavily crusted and white with bird crap, but we climbed up and perched there like three bedraggled old seagulls that had forgotten how to fly.[1]

Now they had to decide what to do next. They could actually see in the distance aircraft taking off and landing at Vung Tau. Surely they would soon be missed and a search started. Since they had flown a standard track from the *Garrett County*, it would be a simple matter for searchers to fly it in reverse, and there they would be. No sweat! The problem was that communications had somehow gone awry. No one at Vung Tau knew they were coming, and so they were not missed. Time went by slowly out on the fish stakes, and nothing happened. Meanwhile, planes and helicopters were flying over, but they paid no attention to them, no matter how hard the men waved. They probably looked like Vietnamese fishermen tending their nets.

"Bauske had a .38-caliber pistol with tracers in it, and we decided to use it to attract attention. With all the aircraft flying about, someone was bound to see it. He fired it into the air several times, and an approaching army Huey answered with a burst of machine-gun fire. The pilot must have thought we were Viet Cong, but he kept on going, probably with more urgent business. We decided not to do that again."[2]

Late in the afternoon, the other Det. 4 gunship flew into Vung Tau, and the pilot, Lt. (jg) Marv Bulson, wanted to know where Louy and company were. No one had seen them, and that set off alarms. Bulson took off immediately and began to fly the standard track back toward the ship, this time searching for a downed Huey along the way. Within minutes, he found the three men on their perch and plucked them off without much difficulty.

"We had been sitting out there, baking in the sun for more than four hours, but were no worse for wear. Our Huey had sunk in twenty-five to thirty feet of water, along with my camera and all the officers' fitness reports. The Huey was not worth recovering and is undoubtedly there to this day."[3]

Meanwhile, combat activity continued at a good clip. Two days after the Det. 4 dunking, a Det. 3 fire team at Vinh Long was scrambled in response to a call from two PBRs out of Sa Dec. Joe Bouchard recalls having the feeling that that call was going to result in a significant engagement. He had his ground crews put together complete rearming packages for the two aircraft in case they returned and had to be rearmed in a hurry.

While they were doing this, Bouchard got a call from the tower, alerting him that a lone Seawolf helicopter was inbound with major damage and with wounded crew members on board. That was bad news in itself, but more ominous was the question, "What had happened to the other aircraft?" Seawolf helicopters always operated in pairs in combat situations and never split up except in extraordinary circumstances.

Crash crews and medical personnel were on hand, prepared for the worst, when the incoming helicopter made a running touchdown and slid to a lurching halt. Bouchard ran to the chopper and found Lt. Hal Guinn, the aircraft commander, slumped over the controls. The door gunner on the right side of the aircraft was wounded in the hand and arm, and he was trying to stem the bleeding with a piece of cloth. The helicopter was badly shot up.

Bouchard remembers yanking open the bullet-pocked door and shouting at Guinn, "Are you alive?"

Then, says Bouchard, "He sat up, surprising me with a sly smile! Yep, he was alive, but blood was all over the cockpit; he had been hit in the legs."[4]

Even so, he was lucky. So was the rest of the crew. While the pilot and the wounded crewman were receiving emergency treatment, Guinn gave Bouchard and Lt. (jg) Thomas Crull a quick account of what had happened.

Two PBRs had been acting as a blocking force for an ARVN battalion out of Cao Lanh that was deployed on a sweep mission a couple of kilometers inland. The South Vietnamese force had clashed unexpectedly with a much larger enemy unit, and a hard-fought battle was in progress when the Seawolves arrived on the scene. The outgunned friendlies were getting the worst of it.

Lt. Cdr. "Wes" Weselesky, the fire team leader, was told that two American Green Beret advisors had received head, chest, and other wounds and were in critical condition.

Weselesky assessed the situation quickly. The ARVN battalion was pinned down with mortar and heavy machine-gun fire. An extraction would be extremely hazardous; some might have called it impossible. Two light, unarmed fixed-wing "Bird Dog"-type aircraft—one army and one air force— were circling overhead. They had made urgent pleas for assistance, but no other gunship assets were immediately available. If the wounded American advisors on the ground were to have a chance, it would be up to the Seawolves to provide it.

Commander Weselesky decided to make the attempt to pick up the Americans and told Lieutenant Guinn to provide covering fire. The Viet Cong on the ground had other plans, which included bringing down one, maybe two, U.S. helicopter gunships.

While Guinn attempted to suppress enemy fire, Weselesky made a fast approach to the landing zone. The air at ground level was literally saturated with machine-gun fire and shrapnel from the Viet Cong mortars. As he started to flare for touchdown, one of the wounded Americans on the ground told him to abort and get the hell out of there. An extraction would be suicidal! The two helicopters complied and retired a safe distance.

Both aircraft had been hit in the brief rescue attempt, but Guinn's had suffered the worst. He and one of his door gunners had been wounded, and the aircraft was not responding properly to the controls. He thought the hydraulic system might have suffered damage. The copilot took control of the aircraft and held it steady while Weselesky flew alongside to check the damage. As nearly as he could tell, the helo looked flyable. Weselesky then asked Guinn if he thought they could make it back to Vinh Long by themselves, and the wounded pilot replied in the affirmative.

Weselesky now considered his alternatives and decided that, as far as he was concerned, there was really only one. There were badly wounded Americans on the ground who would not survive unless he intervened. Contrary to squadron doctrine, he ordered Guinn to proceed home on his own and to call him or the PBR base at Sa Dec if he got into difficulty on the way.

Guinn and company had now made it back, although somewhat the worse for wear. Their tale was sobering, but it was not the end of the day's action by any means. The two wounded men were flown to the U.S. Army field hospital at My Tho, while Bouchard and the others at Vinh Long anxiously awaited news of the other Seawolf helicopter.

Meanwhile, Weselesky had wasted no time getting back to the combat site, and again began an approach to the landing zone. He told his copilot, Lt. (jg) William "Bill" Mackey, to finish the mission and get the wounded men out if he (Weselesky) was hit and disabled. By this time, one of the Bird Dog aircraft had made a chance radio contact with an army AH-1G Cobra gunship that was out on a test flight. It was vectored to the scene to provide some covering fire. That increased the odds a bit, but it was still a very dicey situation.

Incredibly, Weselesky made it into the LZ with his aircraft intact, despite determined efforts by the Viet Cong to bring it down. The door gunners jumped out and quickly loaded the two wounded Americans onto the aircraft. The senior ARVN officer, who was also seriously wounded, was put aboard as well. This sight prompted several of the frightened South Vietnamese soldiers to run for the aircraft and try to claw their way aboard as the door gunners fended them off.

With seven people aboard, the helicopter was now overloaded and sitting in what door gunner Glen L. Wilson describes as "the bottom of a hole" in the jungle.[5] Only a running takeoff would get them out of there, and there was not enough open space for that. What's more, they would have to take off into the wind, where all the Viet Cong were. Even if the helicopter could get past that formidable obstacle, it was obvious that it would not be able to clear the trees beyond.

Weselesky ordered his copilot to start shooting straight ahead with the M-60 flex guns and not to stop until he told him to. "We're going to chop a path through the enemy and right through that green wall," he said.[6]

They flew directly into the Viet Cong, firing as they went and certainly killing many. The enemy, of course, was firing back, determined to bring the helicopter down. Door gunner Wilson recalled, "We were actually experiencing bodily contact with VC and NVA enemy troops as we struggled to gain speed to lift out of there."[7]

Now the treetops loomed, and the guns continued to blaze away straight ahead. It was clear they were not going to make it. At the last minute, Weselesky let loose with all the rockets he had, not only to lighten ship, but hopefully to clear out some of the oncoming vegetation with concentrated firepower. Suddenly, they found themselves thrashing through the greenery like a lawnmower. It seemed like an eternity, but it was only a second or so. Then they were in the clear. The helicopter was shaking badly as they proceeded directly to the army hospital, where the three wounded men were offloaded.

Returning to the base at Vinh Long some two hours after Lieutenant Guinn had landed, they were met by Bouchard, Crull, and others. In a recap, Crull later wrote: "As he [Weselesky] air-taxied into our revetments, it was obvious [the helicopter] had sustained bullet/mortar shrapnel damage; that the windscreens were all but destroyed and had to be replaced and holes in the rotor blades caused them to whistle."[8]

C. J. Roberson, who was the senior combat air crewman of Det. 3, was also on hand when the helicopter landed. As he tells it, "The lead aircraft, commanded by Lieutenant Commander Weselesky, looked like it had been used as a battering ram!"[9]

The action that day generated considerable controversy within the squadron and, indeed, there was even talk of a court-martial. Weselesky had, in fact, violated standing orders by going head-to-head, alone, against a vastly superior force, risking not only his own life, but those of seven other Seawolves as well. Two men on Guinn's aircraft had been wounded, and both Hueys were seriously damaged. On the plus side, all pilots and crewmen had survived, while two American advisors and one South Vietnamese ally had been successfully extracted.

In the end, Weselesky was awarded the Navy Cross for his day's work. It was the first that several Seawolf pilots would receive. Bill Mackey received a Silver Star, while door gunners Wilson and Bolton were each awarded a Distinguished Flying Cross. Moreover, the Seawolf legend, already formidable, had grown in stature.

⚓

Back in the United States, Washington, D.C., had become a political pressure cooker. Many in the media continued to paint Tet '68 as a U.S. military disaster, even after it became increasingly clear that the opposite was true. The Viet Cong had been all but crushed, and the North Vietnamese were reeling from the blow. But the erroneous perception of defeat, combined with dramatic images of Tet '68 carnage, rallied the antiwar activists. With their numbers swelled by many misinformed Americans, their demands for an immediate end to the war became deafening.

On March 31, 1968, President Lyndon B. Johnson appeared on national television and announced a halt of all bombing of North Vietnam. Further, he declared, he would not be a candidate for reelection. The military victory of Tet '68 had been transformed into a resounding political defeat for the president and a psychological disaster for the American people.

14

Keeping the Faith

O<small>N THE NIGHT OF</small> A<small>PRIL</small> 7, 1968, <small>TWO</small> PBR<small>S WERE AMBUSHED ON</small> the Bassac River in a narrow, shallow channel between the shore and the elliptically shaped islands of Cu Lao May and Tan Dinh. Shifting sandbars in the channel, some only an inch or so below the surface, some just breaking water, limited both the speed and maneuvering capability of the boats and made them especially vulnerable to Viet Cong fire. The PBRs were obliged to move slowly and carefully through the area, knowing that a high-speed grounding could immobilize them and make them easy targets for enemy gunners ashore. As they picked their way through the treacherous area, they were hit by devastating fire from both sides of the channel. They fought back as best they could and radioed for help.

The call brought immediate assistance. A Det. 7 Seawolf fire team from Binh Thuy, led by Lt. James R. Walker, arrived on the scene within minutes and engaged the enemy in extremely low-level attacks. Such attacks were always dangerous at night, but the fire team leader deemed them necessary in this case. Aggressive action by Jim Walker's helos considerably diminished enemy fire against the PBRs and allowed them to escape into deep water. It was one of many routine saves by HA(L)-3. To the sailors of the brown-water navy, it had become an article of faith. The Seawolves would always be there for them when they were needed.[1] The promise was as good as gold, something you could take to the bank, so to speak.

On May 5, 1968, the squadron held its first change of command. There was little time for pomp and circumstance, so it was a simple affair at which Capt. Arthur H. Munson relieved Cdr. Bob Spencer. "After the ceremony," Spencer says, "I passed on my Thompson sub-machine gun and headed for Tan Son Nhut. I remember the day very well, because the Tan Son Nhut airfield was under mortar attack when I left."[2] The dirty war in Vietnam continued unabated.

The rapid-reaction air support idea, once only a theory, had been more successful than originally hoped for, and the mission and size of the organization was expanding beyond initial expectations. HA(L)-3 had become an essential element in the Mekong Delta combat equation, and for that reason, it now required increased horsepower at the top to deal with the competing demands for men, material, and upper-level command attention. While most navy squadron COs were commanders, it is testimony to the growing importance of the HA(L)-3 mission that the skipper had now been upgraded to a four-striper.

Captain Munson had just come from a tour as assistant chief of staff, Carrier Division Four. He found his new command to be considerably less formal, but a quick assessment told him he had inherited an organization of dedicated warriors who had been battle tested and had not been found wanting. "I was really impressed with the squadron. These were people who really wanted to fly gunships, and they were very good at what they did."[3] It was true. Their accomplishments during the squadron's short period of existence had been nothing short of extraordinary, and they were all eager to get on with it.

According to Cdr. Otto Gerken, who relieved Con Jaburg as executive officer a short time later, Art Munson was

> a level-headed guy who was easy to work for. One of us would go out to a detachment every month to see how it was doing and to find out what the people needed to do the job. We did our damnedest to provide the wherewithal. Captain Munson was also insistent that each detachment have the best possible balance of newly arrived and experienced pilots and crewmen. Other than that, he relied on the judgment of the officers in charge, letting them run the detachments and make the on-scene decisions. He was a good CO."[4]

Capt. Art Munson did his damnedest to ensure that the detachments had what they needed to do the job. *Arthur Munson*

The results from the detachments seemed to confirm squadron leadership policy. Pilots consistently seized the initiative and made the kind of bold, split-second calls that made the Seawolves some of the most respected warriors in the Delta. A case in point is another incident involving Lieutenant Walker, who in September 1968 was flying with Det. 3 out of Vinh Long.

Slightly before 10:00 AM on September 13, sector control assigned Walker and his fire team a target not far from the base. Walker surprised some VC as they were moving boxes from sampans onto the riverbank. It was a brazen effort, the kind of thing usually confined to the cover of darkness. Walker thought it highly probable that the boxes contained ammunition and supplies. There was only one way to find out.

He decided to make his initial attack against the sampans. In doing so, he came under heavy fire from lethal .51-caliber heavy machine-gun mounts ashore. No question now who they were dealing with. No innocent fishermen or farmers these. The two helos now came in low at an angle across the river and made a sharp turn toward the boats. Suddenly, out of the corner of his eye, Walker caught sight of something he had initially missed, something that looked to him very much like a pair of old-fashioned cellar doors he recalled from his childhood. They were set into the riverbank and were wide open, framing a large black hole in the earth. Knowing what that probably meant, he now focused his attention on the opening.

Ignoring concentrated fire from the .51-calibers and other smaller-caliber guns, Walker led his team around for another attack. This time the helos came in low across a rice paddy on the opposite side of the river, snaking their approach in an attempt to confound ground fire. At the last moment, the helos made a sweeping turn to position themselves so that they were looking directly into the hole in the riverbank. Walker, in the lead aircraft, fired two rockets. He watched, almost transfixed, as one of them streaked within a few feet of a startled VC and entered the hole. A nanosecond later, the whole riverbank erupted in what Walker describes as "an orange-black explosion that billowed a good fifteen hundred feet into the air."[5]

Walker also remembers the shock wave that shook the aircraft and flattened the rice fronds as it moved across the paddy. They had really hit pay dirt. So pronounced were the fireball and smoke that they were seen several miles away by the tower at the Vinh Long base. Jim Walker and his fire team had earned their flight pay and then some.

The next day, the Viet Cong ambushed a U.S. Navy self-propelled fuel barge, also called a lighter, a few miles upstream from Vinh Long. Here, a large elongated island split the river into two channels. The lighter was proceeding northwest between the island and the shore when it was taken under fire from both sides. Working against a strong current at the time of the ambush, its forward speed of no more than a few knots made it an irresistible target for the enemy entrenched along the riverbank. Although Walker and his fire team arrived within minutes of being called, the lighter had already taken a number of heavy hits, and one crewman had been struck in the head by flying shrapnel. He was critically injured and bleeding profusely.

Two PBRs tried valiantly to protect the lighter by dashing close to shore to suppress enemy fire, or at least to get it directed at them. It was tough going because the VC had dug a long, deep trench along one side of the riverbank and were hunkered down inside. Because of the angle, they were almost totally invulnerable to fire from the PBRs.

Walker and his fire team made several frontal attacks without much result, but they at least took some of the pressure off the lighter. They quickly exhausted their ammunition and were about to return to Vinh Long to rearm when the lighter skipper radioed that the wounded man would surely die if he did not have immediate medical attention. While the wing aircraft made threatening passes at the enemy, Walker maneuvered over the lighter and made a steep descent, flaring at just the right moment to place his right skid on the bow of the vessel. "All this time we were taking hits. They were even using mortars to try to sink the lighter, and one round splashed so close it threw muddy water up on our wind screen."[6]

One of the lighter's crewmen was already staggering forward, half carrying, half dragging the wounded man, who had a blood-soaked rag around his head. As he reached the side of the aircraft, the right door gunner reached down and snatched him aboard.

Walker and his wingman now made a mad dash for the air base at nearby Vinh Long. An ambulance and a medical team were waiting to whisk the wounded sailor away. The two helos quickly took on fuel and ammunition in a performance that would have made a pit crew at the Indianapolis 500 proud. Then they were in the air again, heading for the same hot spot.

By this time, the lighter had managed to retire to a safe distance, but the PBRs were still engaging the enemy. As before, the VC were well protected by the long slit trench, and it was clear that a continued frontal assault would be fruitless, as well as extremely hazardous. Walker opted for something a bit different. "This time we approached from the flank, coming in low over some trees and using them for cover. When we got to an open area, we dropped down even lower and flew along the trench line, raking the VC, who were almost completely exposed from that angle. It was an unusually large disposition," says Walker, "and altogether, we must have inflicted at least two hundred casualties.[7]

The damaged lighter was able to make it to Vinh Long, where it was laid up for extensive repairs. It is not known whether the wounded crewman survived, but Walker received a Navy Cross to go with a Distinguished Flying Cross and two Purple Hearts that he had earned earlier.

Back in the Rung Sat Special Zone, Det 2 at Nha Be continued to thwart Viet Cong attacks on ships in the Long Tau River and to support the PBRs and other river craft in their area of responsibility. They also sought out and attacked VC units hiding in the swamps, keeping them constantly on the move and denying them sanctuary. As a result, pacification began to blossom, hamlets slowly became repopulated, and basic forms of commerce were reestablished.

Det. 2 worked closely with the SEALs, making and covering insertions and extractions and responding to calls for assistance. SEAL and Seawolf

Jim Walker receives an air medal and a Purple Heart from the squadron's executive officer, Con Jaburg. *James R. Walker*

units were stationed together at Nha Be and spent much of their off-duty time together at the clubs. Some had become good friends.

On October 11, 1968, a call for immediate assistance came in to the detachment. The Viet Cong had pinned down a small group of SEALs, three of their number wounded. It was night, and the weather was especially bad.

Army gunships were unavailable. Technically, so were the gunships of Det. 2 because one of the detachment's two helicopters was in a down status for mechanical reasons, and firm squadron policy prohibited one helicopter from engaging the enemy alone.

Lt. (jg) Alan J. "Al" Billings, having almost completed his tour, had seen lots of action and was due for rotation the following month. Relatively junior in rank, he was nevertheless a highly qualified fire team leader and one of the most experienced combat pilots in the detachment at the time.

For the SEALs, as well as other friendlies in the Delta, it was a matter of faith that the Seawolves would never let them down. Official policy notwithstanding, Al Billings and his crew launched into the bad weather and were soon on top of the firefight.

Visibility was extremely limited, and as in so many other situations in which Seawolves found themselves, it was hard to distinguish between the SEALs and the enemy. Using a blinking red light to mark his location and to provide a reference point for the helo pilot, the SEAL team leader was able to coach Billings onto the Viet Cong positions, which he attacked with rockets and machine-gun fire. He continued to cover the SEALs until army slick helicopters arrived to get them out and then suppressed enemy fire until they had all been evacuated.

Despite the fact that Billings had ignored squadron policy to make his lone assault, it was decided that he had properly bent the rules under the circumstances. He was awarded the Distinguished Flying Cross for his part in the rescue.[8]

Short timer Billings had one more spectacular rescue to take part in before he left Vietnam. On November 8, 1968, he was flying copilot on the wing aircraft of a two-plane fire team, more or less only along for the ride. The pilot was Lt. (jg) Tim Hayes, a more recent arrival, as was the fire team leader.

Two PBRs had come under a fierce attack from both banks of a small stream. The PBR patrol officer aboard one of the boats had been killed, and two wounded crewmen were in critical condition. One had a serious head wound and was not expected to live unless he could be evacuated immediately.

As the gunships arrived, the seriousness of the situation became evident to the crews. "The whole top of the boat had been blown off by a well-placed rocket," remembers Billings.[9] An army Dust-off helicopter was twenty minutes away, and one of the wounded men couldn't wait that long. To add to the problem, the Viet Cong were still firing at the PBRs, and there was no place ashore for the Dust-off helicopter to land.[10]

Billings, the more experienced of the gunship pilots, took over from Hayes and asked the fire team leader in the other chopper to cover him while he attempted a rescue. "Keep their heads down," he said. "I'm going after him."[11]

Billings remembers, "There was gunfire in all directions: VC shooting from shore, the lead aircraft shooting at the VC, and the other PBR shooting at the VC. Bullets were flying everywhere."[12]

As the helicopter approached, the wash from its rotor pushed the badly damaged boat away, but Billings somehow managed to maneuver the aircraft to put one skid on the bow of the boat and hold it there. In a considerable understatement, Billings recalls, "It was a little tricky to land a 42-foot-long helicopter on the bow of a 31-foot boat."[13]

The wounded PBR crewmen were unable to climb into the helicopter unassisted. One of them was unconscious. Door gunner AN Glen R. Smithen jumped down into the boat and, one by one, dragged each of them to where the other gunner, AMH3 George C. Heady, could grab them and lift them into the aircraft. Then Smithen climbed aboard, and Billings disengaged.

The gunship was still heavy with fuel and ammo, and the two extra men now created a weight problem for the old underpowered Huey. The aircraft was too heavy to gain altitude, and as Billings moved downriver trying to get some forward speed, it began scooping up water through the nose bubble. By this time, Heady and Smithen were throwing things out, allowing Billings to get a few critical feet of altitude. As more armament, ammo, and miscellaneous equipment were jettisoned, water began draining from the aircraft and the margin of safety slowly increased. Because the two wounded crewmen needed attention quickly, they headed for the nearest medical facility.

As George Heady recalled, "One of the wounded PBR sailors had a nasty leg wound with heavy bleeding. That was bad enough, but the other had a bullet hole in his head. There was blood all over the aircraft. I held my hand over the hole, trying to stop the bleeding and to keep his brains from oozing out. We flew directly to the hospital in Saigon. The amazing thing (was), both those guys lived."[14]

Billings and Hayes were awarded the Silver Star for their efforts, while Heady and Smithen each received the Distinguished Flying Cross.[15]

15

Zumwalt, Sealords, and Vietnamization

Vice Adm. Elmo R. Zumwalt Jr. assumed command of U.S. Naval Forces Vietnam on the last day of September 1968, relieving Rear Adm. Kenneth L. Veth. Chosen for the job because of his energy and competence, Zumwalt would also demonstrate an ability to provide some innovative ideas to deal with the problems at hand.[1]

By this time, American and South Vietnamese forces held sway over much of the lower Mekong Delta. TF 116 and TF 117 had, for the most part, succeeded in driving the enemy from the major rivers, eliminating Viet Cong tax collectors and making these main arteries relatively safe for legitimate traffic and commerce. TF 115's Market Time operation had reduced the amount of weapons, ammunition, and supplies previously funneled to the enemy via the South China Sea coastal route to a trickle.

The loss of this latter avenue of supply was a significant problem for the enemy. To compensate, they struck a deal with Cambodian Prime Minister Prince Sihanouk for use of the port of Sihanoukville (later Kompong Som). The VC now shipped large quantities of military material into supposedly neutral Cambodia via this route. From there, they moved the supplies along the Sihanouk Trail to training camps, supply dumps, and staging areas on the Cambodian border. There, an assortment of sampans and other enemy river

Vice Adm. Elmo R. Zumwalt combined and concentrated his forces to sever enemy supply lines and infiltration routes and to destroy enemy camps and bases deep within the Mekong Delta. *U.S. Naval Institute Photo Archive*

craft picked up the goods and transported them across the border, deep into South Vietnam, to points as far away as the southern tip of the Ca Mau Peninsula. Human mules carried them across land segments, but for most of the journey, boats conveyed the supplies through the vast network of small canals and streams that made the Delta such a unique and friendly environment. And, of course, virtually all of this clandestine movement took place at night.

Zumwalt now brought the assets of TF 115, TF 116, and TF 117 together to create TF 194, a combined effort to accomplish the objectives of Operation Sea Lords.[2] His plan was to sever the enemy infiltration and supply routes from Cambodia, or, more realistically, to make it extremely difficult for the NVA/VC to use them without severe consequences. His other major goal was to destroy or disrupt enemy bases, camps, and facilities deep within the Delta, especially on the Ca Mau Peninsula.

Elements of this new task force were deployed to create barriers across the Delta. On November 2, 1968, Operation Search Turn initiated the first barrier, which ran along the canal from Rach Gia to Long Xuyen, cutting across an approximately forty-mile stretch between these two towns.

On November 16, Operation Foul Deck formed a barrier partway along the Cambodian border, from Ha Tien on the Gulf of Thailand, along the Rach Giang Tann and Vinh Te canals, to Chau Doc on the Bassac River.

To the east, Operation Giant Slingshot began on December 6. It covered the Vam Co Dong and the Vam Co Tay rivers, where they bracketed the so-called Parrot's Beak, a border protrusion that poked into South Vietnam from Cambodia.

Finally, on January 2 of the following year, Operation Barrier Reef filled in the gap along the Le Grange–Ong Lon canals, completing a 250-mile chain across the upper Delta from Ha Tien to Tay Ninh. Operation Foul Deck now became a secondary system to interdict infiltrators and contraband that made it through the northern barrier. Perhaps as much as half of PBR assets were moved north to cover these barrier operations, and there was plenty of action for everyone.

PCF Swift Boats of TF 115 now began operations on the rivers and waterways of the Ca Mau Peninsula to the extent that their draft of four feet, ten inches allowed. The deployment of the PCFs into the rivers relieved PBR assets so they could be moved north and deployed along the shallower waterways along the Cambodian border.

HA(L)-3 executive officer, Cdr. Otto Gercken, recalled: "Admiral Zumwalt's policy was to take the action to the enemy. On one occasion in early

Swift boats began raids into the waterways of the lower Ca Mau Peninsula in October 1968. *U.S. Naval Institute Photo Archive*

1969, he even had army helicopters airlift PBRs overland to a canal east of Chau Doc that would otherwise have been inaccessible. To support such deployments, HA(L)-3 detachments moved into a lot of places we had never been before. Living arrangements were often very primitive, but we were a lot freer in the things we could do."[3]

Det. 5 was one of the first to redeploy, moving to Rach Gia on the Gulf of Thailand in the early fall to support Operation Search Turn, while Det. 4 moved to Dong Tam in November to participate in Operation Giant Sling-shot. There would be other moves.

It is difficult to say exactly when the concept of Vietnamization became a priority. As early as October 1968, COMUSMACV had begun to develop a serious program to make the South Vietnamese armed forces self-sufficient and to begin turning over equipment and responsibility for military operations. President-elect Richard M. Nixon made reference to Vietnamization in

Army heavy-lift helicopters moved PBRs to small isolated waterways near the Cambodian border, where rapid reaction by Seawolf gunships was essential to their survival. *U.S. Naval Institute Photo Archive*

a speech on December 31, 1968, and as president, he made it official U.S. policy at the Midway Island Conference on June 8, 1969.

The U.S. Navy's part of the program was called the Accelerated Turnover Plan, or ACTOV for short. Before being relieved by Admiral Zumwalt, Admiral Veth had recommended turnover of two River Assault Squadrons to the South Vietnamese by the fall of 1969. Zumwalt carried it a step further, establishing a plan to turn over the equipment and responsibilities of all surface river forces by the end of June 1970.[4] The Vietnamese would continue to need materiel assistance for a time, but the admiral envisioned that all support activities, including bases, would be turned over by the fall of 1972.

The VNN did not have an air arm, and the Vietnamese air force had neither the pilots nor the aircraft to provide the kind of rapid-reaction, close air support to the brown-water surface forces now furnished by HA(L)-3. The Seawolves would continue to provide that. Further, a new U.S. Navy squadron of fixed-wing gunships, commissioned at North Island, San Diego, on January 3, 1969, was on the way. Light Attack Squadron Four (VAL-4) would arrive in March and be fully operational in the Delta by April 19. Equipped with North American OV-10A Broncos and some heavy ordnance capabilities, the VAL-4 Black Ponies would be a welcome addition to the Sea Lords program.[5]

Meanwhile, the U.S. Navy began integrating Vietnamese personnel into riverine combat units almost immediately. It was done on a one-for-one basis. A VNN sailor would come aboard a boat to be trained by his American counterpart, who would depart as soon as his charge became qualified. Within a short time, a large number of river vessels were completely manned by Vietnamese personnel and operated under VNN command. For the time being, American advisors remained aboard the boats, but they too would soon pull up stakes and depart. The U.S. Navy's TF 117 would cease to exist on August 25, 1969, and by the end of 1970 all surface combat river forces, including the PBRs of TF 116, would be under the command and control of the VNN.

16

Seawolves Down

Aₛ ɪɴ ᴛʜᴇ Gᴀᴍᴇ Wᴀʀᴅᴇɴ ᴏᴘᴇʀᴀᴛɪᴏɴs, ʀᴀᴘɪᴅ ʀᴇsᴘᴏɴsᴇ ʙʏ ᴛʜᴇ Seawolves to PBR calls for assistance was essential to the success of the Sea Lords program. Consequently, several HA(L)-3 detachments were repositioned as necessary to provide this support.

Det. 3 moved from Vinh Long to the YRBM-20 on the upper Bassac in mid-February 1969. By March 12 it had moved again, this time to Ha Tien on the Gulf of Thailand, at the extreme northwest corner of the Mekong Delta, next to the Cambodian border. Det. 6 worked the Vinh Long area, flying from the LST *Garrett County*, but they increasingly supported Sea Lords operations farther north. Det. 5 moved north from Rach Gia to the YRBM-16, moored near the town of Chau Doc, close to the highly volatile Cambodian border. Det. 4, which had been working out of Dong Tam on the My Tho River in support of Operation Giant Slingshot, moved up to Duc Hoa on the Vam Co Dong River to be closer to the action. Det. 7, based at Binh Thuy, and Det. 1, aboard the LST *Hunterdon County*, continued to cover the lower Bassac River and its environs. The detachments were extremely mobile; they could pick up and change location to meet new situations at a moment's notice, often taking up residence under some very Spartan conditions.

Dick Barr, then a lieutenant (junior grade) with Det. 3, remembers operating from Ha Tien in March 1969. The so-called base was simply a wide spot on the ground near the town. The crews fueled the helos from fifty-five-gallon drums, pumping the fuel into the aircraft by hand. They lived in what was charitably called a villa, rough quarters that lacked such basic conveniences as running water. The Seawolves took showers when it rained and avoided serious intestinal problems by drinking Coca Cola, which was, curiously enough, readily available.

Part of their assigned mission was support of SEAL operations along the Vinh Te Canal. The Seawolves conducted SEAL insertions and extractions and provided gunfire support whenever and wherever it was needed. The SEALs made surprise attacks on NVA/VC bases, kidnapped enemy personnel, and ambushed infiltrators.

The topography along the canal was largely flat plain, and the vegetation mostly saw grass. This enabled the enemy to see from great distances where helicopters were landing. While this made insertions somewhat difficult to conceal, it also offered some opportunities to confuse Charlie. The Seawolves simply applied the old shell-game principle. They flew quickly from one location to another, landing in full view of the enemy, making false insertions into the saw grass. The enemy could never tell with any degree of certainty just where the SEALs were actually being dropped or, for that matter, if any were being inserted at all.

There are many stories about Seawolves pulling SEALs and others out of tight spots in the Delta, but there is at least one about a very talented SEAL marksman who saved the day for some Seawolves, as well as himself.

SEAL R. J. "Bob" Thomas was a favorite of the HA(L)-3 crews at Ha Tien. He was also a terrific shot with just about any kind of firearm, and the helicopter crews liked to get him to demonstrate his considerable skill as a form of entertainment, something that was in short supply at their remote location. According to Barr, Thomas could pick off seagulls with a sniper rifle at incredible distances. No one knew it at the time, but his extraordinary marksmanship would come in handy in the very near future.

In addition to insertions and extractions, the Seawolves of Det. 3 flew regular patrols and made "duty strikes" on Viet Cong and North Vietnamese troops dug in on an approximately two-thousand-foot high mountain peak just inside Vietnam, only a few hundred yards from the Cambodian border. There was enemy activity at several locations on the mountain, but Thomas was particularly interested in a suspected mortar position near the summit as a possible candidate for a nocturnal visit from the SEAL team. To check it out, he hitched a ride with Dick Barr on a Det. 3 patrol on March 23.

Lt. (jg) Randall H. "Randy" Miller was the fire team leader and led the two helicopters on a strike in the area in question. Miller's aircraft took a hit that obliged the two helos to return to base for some quick repair. Then they were in the air again, having switched leads so that Barr's aircraft, Seawolf 305, was in the forward position.

Barr and Miller rolled in from the northeast to the southwest, firing rockets and guns as they approached the Viet Cong position. Barr vividly remembered: "The whole mountain opened up on us. We took a .51-caliber hit in the engine, and the next thing I knew, the gauges started unwinding. I began an autorotation at three hundred feet and managed to get out a very terse transmission to Randy Miller. 'Lost engine, going in,' I said. 'I'll cover you,' Miller responded."[1]

The enemy sensed a kill; ground fire was intense as the helo fell toward earth. One round killed copilot Lt. (jg) Edward W. Pawlowski, and another hit Barr in the foot as he fought the plunging aircraft. Despite his best efforts, Seawolf 305 hit the ground hard in an open area and rolled over, fatally crushing the right door gunner, ADJ3 Howard M. Meute. The other door gunner, AN R. W. "Rick" Abbott, broke both femurs in the crash, but he was still alive. Barr was knocked unconscious by the impact.

To make matters worse, the aircraft began to burn. SEAL Thomas, who suffered a painful back injury, somehow managed to drag Barr clear of the aircraft.

By this time, Miller, ignoring the fusillade of enemy fire, had landed close by, and door gunner Davy Riordan jumped out. As Miller took off again, Riordan dragged Abbott out of the burning aircraft, and all four of the now-stranded Americans put the burning Huey wreckage between themselves and the advancing Viet Cong. It was not a very safe spot, and as the helo burned, the ammunition aboard started to cook off. They stayed where they were because it was the only protection they had. In any case, Thomas could only crawl; Abbott could barely move; and Barr, suffering from a serious foot wound, also had an eyeball dislodged from its socket. It now dangled precariously down his right cheek.

Miller called in Outlaw 21, an Army UH-1D slick from the 175th Assault Helicopter Company flown by 1st Lieutenant Willsey, to help. It attempted a landing to pick up the four men, but was driven off by a deadly barrage of enemy fire. Not, however, before Willsey and one of his crewmen had been hit. Enemy marksmanship was very good that day.

Now several Viet Cong moved cautiously toward the Americans. Barr, who could barely see with his one good eye, gave Thomas his .45-caliber pistol and his two clips of ammunition. It was the only weapon they had among them.

A .45 round has a considerable wallop. It will stop an oncoming man in his tracks, maybe even throw him backwards a few feet. The problem with the .45 automatic is that it is next to impossible to hit anything with it at any distance. Thomas, the consummate marksman, waited until the VC were close enough, took careful aim, and began squeezing off rounds. He brought down a surprised enemy soldier with every shot.

Meanwhile, despite the fact that he and one of his crewmen had been hit, Willsey ordered his copilot to return to the scene and attempt another rescue. As they landed close to the burning Navy helo, the wounded Army pilot managed to bring down two enemy soldiers with shots from an M-16 rifle. Distracted from his headlong assault on the downed navy party, one VC turned to direct his fire at the army helo. Thomas dropped him with a shot from the .45.

Having advanced to within yards of the Americans, the remaining VC now turned and fled to a tree line for cover. Barr and company were loaded into the slick and flown to the army's Third Surgical Hospital at Binh Thuy. If Bob Thomas did not already have a marksman's medal, he certainly earned one that day. A Det 3 fire team returned to the scene and destroyed what was left of Seawolf 305.

March 26 was another difficult day for HA(L)-3. It began shortly after midnight, when Viet Cong forces began a heavy mortar attack on Dong Tam, from which Dets. 4 and 6 were then staging. As crews attempted to get airborne, mortar rounds hit an ammunition dump nearby, which went up in a tremendous explosion. The ear-splitting blast of twenty-two tons of munitions engulfed two helicopters as they were taking off.

Door gunner ADJ2 Vincent G. "Vince" Paone was part of the Det. 6 duty crew that night and was outside when the attack began. He watched transfixed as several mortar rounds landed in the ammunition dump next to the parked helicopters and said to fire team leader Lt. (jg) Robert J. Romanelli, "that thing's going to go." Romanelli replied, "Let's get the birds out of here before it does."[2]

The two duty crews ran to the aircraft and started cranking. Romanelli's helicopter was first off, but just as the chopper lifted into the air, the dump exploded. Paone remembers:

> The shock wave flipped us on our back as if the aircraft was a toy, and we came down hard. We were all shaken badly and had minor injuries, but our copilot, Lt. (jg) Dave Heater, was pinned under the aircraft. To make things worse, the fuel tank had ruptured, and there was jet fuel everywhere. Ammunition in the dump was still cooking off, and fire was falling from overhead. We were afraid it would touch off the fuel, and Heater would be burned alive. Mike O'Brien, the other door gunner, and I grabbed fire hoses and tried to wash down the area around the aircraft until we could get Heater out of there.[3]

The wing helicopter never got off the ground and was demolished by the explosion. The copilot, Lt. (jg) Alfred A. Suhr, was killed. He had reported to the detachment only about three weeks before.

Lt. (jg) William M. "Woo" Ferrell was an off-duty Det. 4 pilot. The detachment's two aircraft and duty crews had been dispatched to Moc Hoa the day before for anti-infiltration operations near the Cambodian border and had not yet returned.

Ferrell was standing by the door in the Det. 4 bunker when the attack began. Someone shouted for him to get away from the door, and he did. An instant later the dump exploded, and the door was blown across the room. Ferrell recalled, "It was a huge boom."[4] Fortunately, the door did not hit anyone, but people who had been standing found themselves on the floor, surprised but unhurt.

Once on his feet, Ferrell ran outside along with everyone else to be met with the sight of one helicopter upside down and another that seemed to be crushed. The pilot and crew members were dragged out of the latter aircraft, but the copilot was already dead. He had been hit by a piece of shrapnel, which had also torn off the main rotor. He had died instantly.

The other helicopter was on its side, and Heater was still pinned under the wreckage by one leg. Ferrell dug furiously under Heater while others tried to lift the aircraft so he could be pulled free, but to no avail.

> The whole area was flooded with fuel, and burning debris from the dump was falling all around. It was literally raining fire. A couple of people were trying to wash the fuel away with fire hoses.

Someone came running up with a fire ax, which was not much good for anything, but Heater saw it and thought someone was about to chop off his leg. Of course, he voiced some strong objections."[5]

Meanwhile, Romanelli went around to the tail of the aircraft and called for people to help him push down on the tail stinger.[6] When they did so, the nose came up and Ferrell pulled Heater free.

In spite of the shower of shrapnel and exploding ammunition, Seawolves ignored their personal safety to help their injured comrades. Door Gunner ADJ2 Dale Odom, who had been in one of the bunkers, was also knocked flat by the explosion, but picked himself up and ran outside to help. He was one of the men who helped to rescue Heater.[7]

A fire truck arrived on the scene and hosed down a large metal ready-box nearby that was full of rockets. That kept it from exploding from the heat and falling debris. Later, it cooked off anyhow and left a deep crater not too far from the bunkers. The next day, there were all kinds of ordnance strewn about. It was a sobering scene of devastation. In addition to the two Det. 6 birds, a non-flyable Seawolf helicopter that was waiting to be heavy-lifted out was also destroyed.

Vince Paone and Mike O'Brien each received a Silver Star for their courage that night, as did three others. Several more, including Ferrell and Odom, received Bronze Stars with combat "V."

Sometimes it seems that tragedy comes in threes. Another loss occurred on April 23, when a low-flying Det. 4 gunship crashed and burned after striking a power line at Cu Chi. The pilots and one crewman made it out of the burning aircraft, but crew chief AO1 Ollie J. Gross died in the inferno. Exploding ordnance aboard the burning helo prevented his rescue.

ART MUNSON'S YEAR OF SQUADRON COMMAND WAS NOW UP, AND Reynolds Beckwith relieved him at Vung Tau as commanding officer of HA(L)-3 on April 25, 1969. Beckwith still held the rank of commander when he arrived, although he had been selected for captain and was just waiting for his number to come up. Munson urged Rear Adm. William R. Flanagan, Commander of Sea Lords Task Force 194 (who also held the tongue-in-cheek title of First Sea Lord), to frock Beckwith so that he would not be at a grade-level disadvantage with the army colonels he would have to deal with to get things done.

Newly frocked Captain Beckwith would not see very much of Vung Tau. Flanagan had been trying to get Beckwith's predecessor to move HA(L)-3 headquarters from Vung Tau to Binh Thuy for some time, but he had met resistance on the grounds that the facilities at Binh Thuy were not complete and could not adequately support the HA(L)-3 "head shed" until improvements were made. But construction had moved ahead rapidly at Binh Thuy, and the admiral thought the time was ripe to get things moving in the right direction. As Beckwith tells it, the first order he received from his new boss was, "get your ass to Binh Thuy."[8]

Thus, after only one night at Vung Tau, Beckwith found himself temporarily divorced from his new command and alone at Binh Thuy, checking out the site to see what he had to work with. As always, some things could have been better, but on the whole, Beckwith was satisfied that the new facilities would suffice.

Consequently, on May 2 an LST began moving the HA(L)-3 headquarters and maintenance unit lock, stock, and barrel to Binh Thuy. The move took place over a period of three weeks, with the usual problems that such an event can create. While all this was going on, however, combat operations out in the detachments continued without letup.

In many respects, Binh Thuy was a better location for HA(L)-3 headquarters than Vung Tau. For one thing, it was a more central place from which to direct the activities of the scattered detachments. Then too, Binh Thuy had twenty-two hundred feet of PSP, and there was more room for administrative and maintenance activities. Unlike the physical limitations at Vung Tau, the additional space and facilities enabled both officers and enlisted men to be quartered on site. Binh Thuy was also the control center for all Game Warden operations, and that afforded more direct communications with commander, Task Force 116, and his staff.

Even as he began setting up shop in the new location, Beckwith found himself dealing with a difficult combat loss. On April 28, a fire team from Det. 3, consisting of Seawolf helos 305 and 320, was assigned a target of several enemy sampans located just a few miles from the Cambodian border. It should be noted that 305 had been the number of the Huey lost on March 23 and had been reassigned. Perhaps it would have been better if that number had been retired.

Capt. Reynolds Beckwith in his new office in Binh Thuy. *Reynolds Beckwith*

During the attack on the sampans, the helos inadvertently drifted over the border, where they were taken under fire by .51-caliber machine guns. Seawolf 320 crashed in Cambodian territory, killing the pilot, Lt. (jg) Richard C. Reardon, the copilot, Lt. (jg) Hal C. Castle Jr., and the gunner, AO3 Michael E. Schafernocker. The other gunner, AN James B. Page Jr., was seriously injured.

The lead ship, Seawolf 305, was also hit, and it made a hard landing near the wreckage of 320. The copilot of 305, Lt. Cdr. James L. Keyes, was able to make contact with Outlaw 29, an army UH-1D slick from the 175th Assault Helicopter Company, and informed the pilot of their predicament. Keyes was also the senior officer and, as such, took charge of establishing a defensive position.

Meanwhile, crew chief and door gunner ADJ1 Lloyd T. Williams thought he saw movement in the wreckage of Seawolf 320. Under heavy

Lloyd Williams received the Navy Cross for his selfless efforts to save his squadron mates and his exemplary courage under fire. *Lloyd Williams*

enemy fire, he made his way to the demolished aircraft in hopes of saving anyone who might have survived. He found Page still alive but badly injured. Through continuing enemy fire, Williams carried the badly injured gunner across an open field to the rest of the group.

Then, ignoring VC bullets, Williams returned to Seawolf 320 to pick through the mangled aircraft for other signs of life, but to no avail. As the enemy began to zero in with mortars, he made a final successful dash for the Seawolf defensive position, where he and the others concentrated on holding off the enemy, hoping that they could do so long enough for help to arrive.

It was not long in coming, but, predictably, the rescue aircraft, Outlaw 29, became the preferred target of the VC as it attempted to land. It was Charlie's chance to make it three for three, and he threw everything he had at the helo. Both the army slick and the escaping Americans were pelted with bullets. After only seconds on the ground, which seemed like an eternity to everyone involved, the Seawolves scrambled aboard, dragging Page with them.

Unfortunately, as the slick lifted off, Lt. (jg) Joseph F. Hart, the pilot of Seawolf 305, was fatally wounded and died on board despite first aid efforts to save him. Gunner Charles Larsen was also hit and seriously wounded, but he survived.[9]

Lloyd Williams received the Navy Cross for his heroic rescue of Jim Page, his efforts to save other crew members of Seawolf 320, and his courage under fire. Jim Keyes and Joe Hart each received the Silver Star, the latter posthumously.

17

The Ca Mau Peninsula

CAPTAIN BECKWITH MUST HAVE WONDERED WHAT HE HAD GOTTEN himself into. Within three days of becoming commanding officer, he had gotten a hard reality jolt when the squadron lost three pilots, a gunner, and two aircraft in combat. That sobering experience had been followed by the relocation of headquarters, which transferred three hundred men and ninety tons of equipment. Then, on May 14, 1969, a Det. 6 helo suffered mechanical failure at My Tho and crashed on takeoff. The aircraft was a strike, but luckily no one was hurt. There wasn't much time to meditate over it all because things were happening fast and furiously.

In June, Det. 4, which had been operating out of Duc Hoa, moved south about fifteen miles to Ben Luc; like Duc Hoa, Ben Luc was also on the Vam Co Dong River. From there the detachment continued to support Operation Giant Slingshot in the vicinity of the Parrot's Beak. The big news of that month, however, was HA(L)-3's acquisition of eleven recycled UH-1Bs, bringing the squadron's total number of aircraft to thirty-three. Two of these were used to expand Det. 2 at Nha Be. As a result that detachment— the only one that was permanently located—also became the squadron's sole double detachment, comprised of four aircraft and a corresponding increase in personnel.

A couple of the new UH-1Bs remained in the maintenance pool at Binh Thuy so they could be shuttled out to the detachments as they were needed to replace battle-damaged aircraft or those undergoing periodic checks. As detachments fanned out around the Mekong Delta, a headquarters fire team was also established to respond to calls in the Binh Thuy area or to temporarily beef up a hot spot in an emergency.

Four of the new aircraft were used to create new detachments to cover the expanding demands of Operation Sea Lords. Det. 8 came into being in early July, and on the ninth of that month, it was dispatched to Tay Ninh for a short time to assist Det. 7 in providing support for surface units on the upper Vam Co Dong River. In September, Det. 9 was created at Binh Thuy and moved to the YRBM-21 near An Long, about twelve miles south of the Cambodian border. Like the LSTs, the YRBMs could accommodate just two helos, with no room to spare. There was a small bunkroom on an overhang just off the flight deck, and the duty crews could be out and turning up aircraft within seconds of a call for help.

Aircraft downed for mechanical malfunctions could cause special problems aboard the YRBMs and the LSTs. If a bird was not flyable, and the detachment flight crews could not repair it quickly on the flight deck, coverage in that detachment's area of responsibility was degraded, and another detachment had to temporarily take up the slack. When that happened, the problem had to be resolved quickly if the rapid-response capability was to remain intact.

It was not just a simple matter of sending out a replacement helicopter, because an LST or YRBM could only hold two Hueys at one time. The offending aircraft had to be repaired on the spot or removed from the flight deck to accommodate the replacement helo. Depending on the nature of the problem and the estimated time necessary to fix it, there were two possibilities. A specialized maintenance team from headquarters might be dispatched, along with the necessary parts, to put the bird back in service. If that approach was likely to take an unacceptable amount of time, the army was called upon to provide a heavy lift helo to bring the inoperative machine back to headquarters in a sling. Meanwhile, the second bird of the detachment was dispatched with a crew to pick up a replacement aircraft.

By July 1969 a mini-gun, mounted on the left-hand side, had replaced most of the flex guns on squadron aircraft. The increase in firepower was significant. Unlike the M-60, the mini-gun had six barrels and could put out some four thousand rounds per minute. Instead of the rat-a-tat-tat of the

Seawolf gunships patrol the Parrot's Beak area during Operation Giant Slingshot.
Navy League

M-60s, a mini-gun burst made a noise like a cow that desperately needed milking. One Seawolf pilot says it sounded more like "a colossal elephant fart."[1]

Several detachments had one aircraft fitted with a .50-caliber machine gun on the starboard side. This provided a fire team with the heavier impact of .50-caliber rounds as well as a standoff capability of nearly twenty-two hundred yards. Some said this heavy machine gun could even clear away foliage to get to an enemy hidden underneath the heavy jungle canopy. In fact, the .50-caliber was so powerful that it actually caused the aircraft to yaw to the left when fired. The drawback to this weapon was that the door gunner had to frequently stop firing to reload. Some of the door gunners, especially those that operated from bases ashore where weight was not so critical, continued to carry M-60s in addition to the mounted mini- and .50-caliber guns. An M-60 could be handheld and might come in handy in an emergency situation on the ground.

Light Attack Squadron Four (VAL-4) arrived in country in March and was fully operational by April 19.[2] Known as the Black Ponies, this squadron was also headquartered at Binh Thuy, with a detachment at Vung Tau. Like the Seawolves, VAL-4 was designed specifically to support the river forces, and, like HA(L)-3, it was frequently called upon to assist other friendlies in the Delta. This was the only navy squadron to fly the fixed-wing North American Rockwell OV-10A Bronco. The aircraft could carry a variety of weapons, including combinations of 20-mm cannon or mini-guns and five-inch Zuni and 2.75 rockets. Its heavier firepower was a welcome addition to the good guys' arsenal. Although the Ponies were based only at Binh Thuy and Vung Tau, their speed allowed them to cover distance quickly and therefore arrive at hot spots in timely fashion.

By MID-1969 THE SUCCESS OF THE BROWN-WATER NAVY AND ITS supporting elements was readily apparent along the major rivers in the middle and lower Delta. Farmers were once more bringing their produce to market, and boatmen were operating on the rivers and canals free from interference by the Viet Cong. In other areas, however, it was a different story, and Admiral Zumwalt had already begun concentrating assets in these places to further the objectives of Operation Sea Lords. His intention was to sever NVA/VC supply lines; to challenge and harass the enemy in his long-established strongholds; and to eliminate or greatly reduce enemy control over the civilian population. It was essential to make as much headway as possible in this regard before the completion of "Vietnamization," that is, when the South Vietnamese would be on their own. ACTOV was already well under way. Indeed, some riverine responsibilities, along with armored gunboats and equipment, had been turned over to the VNN as early as February 1, 1969. There was, however, a way to go before the goals of the program could be completely realized. Meanwhile, for the Seawolves and the Black Ponies, the war now became even more intense than before.

The Ca Mau Peninsula, which spreads over the large southwest portion of the Delta and includes the U Minh Forest, had long been a Viet Cong sanctuary. Indeed, the relatively underpopulated toe of the peninsula, had once been a favorite place for steel-hulled trawlers to off-load war materials and supplies for distribution to VC units throughout the Delta. Market Time coastal patrol forces had put an end to that, and Charlie now had to get his military supplies and reinforcements overland from Cambodia. This required him to use or cross the myriad waterways running from the Cambodian border to forces in the south. Down in the southernmost part of the Ca Mau Peninsula, PCF swift boats of TF 115 had begun in the fall of 1968 to penetrate inland along the rivers. This development not only threatened Charlie's supply lines but also called into question his control over the area. That was something he could not tolerate.

The Nam Can district of the peninsula was home to woodcutters, charcoal makers, fishermen, and farmers, all of whom sold much of their goods and services to the Viet Cong because they were the only market available to them. At the same time, the VC continued to squeeze them for taxes and recruits. Many civilians had left the area because of the ravages of war and the abuses of the guerrillas, but a number remained to eke out a living under very harsh circumstances.

Admiral Zumwalt believed that the establishment of a strong allied presence in the area could have major benefits. Viet Cong forces could be directly confronted and their supply lines severed. Equally important, the area might be made safe for commerce and village life and rehabilitated so that the South Vietnamese government could realistically claim control of the area. This was the kind of thing that Sea Lords forces had been brought together to accomplish.

In mid-December 1968, heavily armed and armored riverine craft of TF 117 in Operation Silver Mace had hit fortified Viet Cong positions and torn down barricades along the rivers of the Nam Can district. In April 1969, search and destroy missions code-named Silver Mace II took place in the same area. Ships anchored offshore in the Gulf of Thailand supported the operation logistically and tactically. Seawolf Det. 1, flying from the *Westchester County* (LST-1167), provided helicopter gunship support as part of this operation and remained offshore after Silver Mace II had been completed to continue strikes against the enemy and to disrupt his efforts to regroup.

As had already been discovered, rough water in the gulf was hard on the PBRs, as well as on helicopter operations. Moreover, the distances from the offshore LSTs to the operating areas in the rivers and canals caused delays in response time that, while only a matter of minutes, could be critical to a PBR or swift boat in trouble. What was needed was a more permanent, close-in staging base, protected from wind and wave and set boldly in the enemy's front yard to challenge his deathlike grip on the area.

The innovative solution was a large floating base, positioned smack-dab in the middle of the Qua Lon River, a few miles upstream from the river mouth near the ruined and largely abandoned town of old Nam Can. Nine (later thirteen) Ammi pontoon barges were connected and held in place against the unusually strong tidal currents by 4-1/2-ton anchors and massive concrete blocks.

This floating aggregation contained barracks, a mess area, a basic medical unit, workshops, and storage facilities. It also served as a staging hub for PBRs of TF 116, PCF swift boats of TF 115, mobile strike forces of TF 117, SEALs, South Vietnamese troops, and a variety of other personnel and equipment. Its defensive armament included mortars, grenade launchers, and heavy automatic weapons. Last but not least, the barges were complete with a flight deck from which Seawolf and army gunships could rearm and refuel. The boats and helicopters provided both strike and defensive capabilities for this self-contained floating fortress in the heart of enemy territory. It was appropriately named Sea Float.

Meanwhile, as part of operations to penetrate inland along the west coast of the Delta, Seawolf assets were repositioned accordingly. Det. 1, based aboard the *Westchester County* and using Sea Float as a staging base, anchored the southwestern extremity of the Ca Mau Peninsula.

In early August, Det. 8 moved from Tay Ninh to the *Harnett County* in the Gulf of Thailand, on the coast at Rach Gia. Det. 3 moved to an LST off Ha Tien in September. That same month, Det. 6 moved for a short time to a small strip near Rach Gia and then to the *Garrett County*, positioned in the gulf off Song Ong Doc. Thus, a four-detachment chain of Seawolf coverage was completed along the west coast from the southern tip of the Delta north to the Cambodian border.

Flying from the ships in the Gulf of Thailand turned out to be no picnic for the embarked Seawolf detachments. Unlike operations in the protected rivers, high winds and rough seas caused the LSTs to roll and pitch, making night takeoffs and landings even more hazardous than usual. Vertigo and razor-thin operating tolerances took their toll.

On August 13, a Det. 8 gunship crashed on a night takeoff from the *Harnett County*, killing AMH3 Richard L. Brown. On the twenty-ninth, that detachment also lost a helicopter in combat. ADJ3 Daniel E. Kelly, one of the door gunners, sustained serious wounds that resulted in the amputation of his leg. Det. 8 lost still another helicopter, along with two door gunners—ATN1 Robert J. Arnold and AT3 Stephen A. Johnson—in a night takeoff from the LST on September 15.

Seawolves aboard the LST *Garrett County*. *Navy League*

As an experiment, the ships tried firing star shells during night takeoffs and landings to illuminate the area, but the idea did not work out well because the intense, unnatural light and the moving shadows produced by the star shells tended to cause rather than eliminate vertigo.

The gunships rearmed and refueled ashore as much as possible between strikes for several reasons. For one thing, it was safer. For another, they didn't have to worry so much about weight and could take on more fuel and ammunition. Most importantly, refueling and rearming ashore was also quicker and usually closer to the action. When a firefight was raging, time was a critical factor; flying from shore, fire teams could get in and out again with full loads in twelve or thirteen minutes.

One thing that Seawolves learned very quickly in the Delta was to always expect the unexpected. Even so, some things could still come as a surprise. One dark night, Det. 6 Hueys struck several motorized junks near the Three Sisters Mountains in the northwest corner of the Delta. As the fire team made its runs in from the gulf, they encountered .51-caliber fire from the enemy holed up in caves in the side of a mountain that overlooked the canals. On this flight, Lt. (jg) Cliff Perrin was in the right (pilot's) seat, while Lt. Cdr. William P. Franklin, the fire-team leader and officer in charge of the detachment, rode in the left (copilot's) place.

In the back of the aircraft, several flares lay in a pile on the floor between the two door gunners. Also in the back was Lt. (jg) Tom Weckworth, a pilot from the off-duty crew. Hoping for a little excitement, he had come along for the ride. On one of the runs in to the target, he got his wish.

Fire from the mountainside was only moderately heavy, but, as luck would have it, a random shot hit the aircraft and ignited one of the flares. The resulting fire was searing and the light intense. Franklin immediately took the controls and turned up the instrument lights, but to no avail. Outside there was only blackness, while inside, the instruments were no more than a blur in the dazzling white glare. He was flying the aircraft more on instinct than anything else. The three men in the back hopped around, trying to keep from being burned while kicking at the pile on the floor.

Franklin knew that if they did not get rid of the flare quickly, it would burn a hole through the floorboards and drop into the fuel tank below. He didn't even want to think about that as he turned the aircraft back toward the gulf and began a rapid descent. His plan was to ditch in the water, hopefully before they were all consumed in a fireball. It was a race against time.

Bill Franklin (kneeling, at right) and crew. When this photo was taken, Admiral Zumwalt had just awarded the men medals for action on the Ong Doc River. *William P. Franklin*

Meanwhile, door gunner McBride was trying hard to kick anything he could out the door. Just before they were about to ditch, he succeeded in jettisoning an M-60 gun. In a phenomenal piece of luck, the gun became entangled in the parachute shrouds and pulled the flare out with it.

Franklin called Rach Gia for an ambulance and headed for the strip. Upon landing, it was determined that, except for some shaken nerves and some minor burns, nobody was seriously hurt. They rearmed and refueled and were soon back in the air, working over the enemy junks with a vengeance. Weckworth remained on the ground, having decided he had had enough excitement for one night.

Unbeknownst to Franklin at the time, his eyes had been permanently damaged by the flare. Over time, his sight would deteriorate, and today he is legally blind.

Along with the new focus of attention on the west coast came plenty of action as the NVA/VC fought to maintain their hold on the area. Swift boats, PBRs, SEALs, and Seawolves were constantly in action.

On the night of November 23, Det. 6 Hueys took on several motorized junks delivering supplies to the enemy ashore. It was a hard-fought firefight, and the trail aircraft, flown by Cliff Perrin, took several hits. One round struck nineteen-year-old gunner John Harpole in both legs. He was bleeding profusely and needed immediate medical attention. With his fuel supply low, Perrin made an emergency night landing on a Coast Guard cutter steaming in the gulf, where Harpole got some quick first aid. Then, having refueled, Perrin made a dash for the army medical facility at Can Tho. Harpole survived but, unfortunately, lost one of his legs.

Because the Seawolf detachments were now scattered all over the Delta, it was even more important than before for the squadron CO to visit each one periodically. Captain Beckwith liked to make at least one operational flight with each of his nine detachments as often as he could. He wanted to get a feel for the combat situation in each area and to see firsthand what his crews were up against. He got a good taste of it on the west coast one dark night, flying as pilot in command of one of Det. 6's Hueys. Bill Franklin flew the other bird, and the two planes worked over the area where John Harpole had been wounded.

Franklin was high, dropping flares, while Beckwith was low, looking for targets. From his perspective above, Franklin suddenly saw green tracers arcing skyward from two positions on the ground and converging on Beckwith's low-flying helo. Charlie had Beckwith dead to rights when Franklin shouted into the mike, "Break left skipper, break left."[3] Beckwith reacted with a violent turn to port, avoiding the concentrated fire by a very thin margin. Then the jungle went dark again.

Franklin thought he had a pretty good fix on the enemy positions and called the Coast Guard cutter patrolling just offshore to request gunfire. The cutter skipper, happy to oblige, lobbed in round after round while Franklin spotted the shots. No one could say for sure what damage had been done to the enemy when it was all over, but Franklin says, "We never got fire from that area again."[4] Beckwith credits Franklin with saving his bacon that night.[5]

THROUGHOUT THE REST OF 1969, HA(L)-3 DETACHMENTS CONTINUED to provide the fastest reaction time for close air support in Vietnam, averaging 11.4 minutes from the time of a call for help to the time a fire team was actually over the unit needing assistance.[6] By this time the location of the detachments had also stabilized, although they continued to move just a bit within their areas as needs dictated. This was a good thing because the crews became familiar with the peculiarities of the terrain and waterways as well as favored VC infiltration routes in each area.

Meanwhile, ACTOV continued, with some eighty PBRs transferred to the VNN on October 10. Vietnamization was becoming a reality, and there was a sense of urgency in the air. Despite what some journalists were saying on television and in the newspapers back home, the good guys were slowly but surely winning the brown-water war in the Delta. It was an inch-by-inch slugfest, but just one year after Operation Sea Lords began, the enemy's logistics and troop replacement problem had increased significantly. Allied forces had seized or destroyed more than five hundred tons of military material and supplies, killed some three thousand NVA/VC, and captured three hundred more.[7]

In December 1969, HA(L)-3 took delivery of four new UH-1L Hueys. These were the first of several unarmed utility helicopters the squadron would receive, along with pilots and crewmen to operate them. They were known as Sealords aircraft, and with them the squadron began to take over the duties of AIRCOFAT, a small navy unit that had been based at Tan Son Nhut air base to provide transportation, mail delivery, and other utility functions to navy activities in the Delta.

The UH-1L was a variant of the UH-1E. Only eight were built, all of them for the U.S. Navy. They mounted the T-53-13 engine and were more powerful than the UH-1B gunships. Similar aircraft were built for the army and designated UH-1M. The navy acquired some of these as well.

The Sealords aircraft were based at Binh Thuy and performed a variety of functions, including some that were considerably more exciting than those previously assigned to AIRCOFAT. While these aircraft continued to deliver supplies, equipment, and personnel to far-flung navy units, they also conducted emergency medical evacuations, made rescues under fire, and engaged in SEAL insertions and extractions. The term *unarmed,* as applied to the UH-1Ls, is somewhat misleading. While no fixed rocket pods or guns were fired from the cockpit, these aircraft routinely carried crewmen with M-60s that could be fired from the door positions when necessary.

Captain Beckwith recalls that, "several of the Sealords pilots came to us right out of the training command."[8] As the new personnel were integrated into the squadron, they were also trained in gunship operations, and most eventually wound up in a detachment.

Beckwith remembers

The UH-1Ls were nice birds. They could fly at max. gross weight despite the hot, humid climate. What's more, they had full instrument panels on both sides and brand-new single-side band radios. (Only the pilot's side of the UH-1B had a full instrument panel.) They came equipped with rotor brakes, so that they didn't have to be backfitted. The bad part was their Teflon rotor heads. They could be easily damaged by debris and had to be checked every thirty hours. We were replacing parts on the UH-1Ls at a great rate.[9]

Maintenance officer Lt. Roger Ek put one of these more powerful helicopters to work early on in one of the imaginative supply capers that Seawolves frequently engaged in. This particular one was to help solve a problem with gunship tail boom shortages. He took one of the new UH-1Ls to Saigon and purchased two fifths of Jack Daniels, which he then flew up to an outpost not far from Moc Hoa where they had refrigeration and good things to eat as a kind of consolation prize for their isolation. But alas, they had no booze. He traded the Jack Daniels for two cases of frozen steaks, which he then flew to the army airfield at Vinh Long, where he traded the steaks for a tail boom and an "overhauled transmission, still in the can."

We loaded the tail boom into the cabin of the L-Model and strapped it in with nylon cargo nets. It stuck out about ten feet on each side. Then we rigged a strap to the transmission, picked it up with the L-Model cargo hook, and flew it to Binh Thuy. The transmission can was stabilized in flight by a small drogue chute from an OV-10 ejection seat. As we approached from the northeast around sunset, the tower said, "We don't have you in sight, but be advised we have some weird experimental aircraft near your location."[10]

Ek and company landed shortly thereafter and unloaded their loot. In such unorthodox ways were the Seawolves kept flying and fighting without interruption.

On December 14, 1969, a Huey gunship from Det. 2 crashed during a low-level reconnaissance mission, killing door gunner AMS1 Larry R. Johnson. That brought the total number of Seawolves who had been killed in action against the enemy in 1969 to seven, while another later died of his wounds. Thirty others were wounded. It was a dangerous business. There is no question, however, that the enemy got the worst of it. For the year, there were 447 enemy casualties by actual body count, with credible estimates of many more.[11]

Admiral Zumwalt's Operation Sea Lords had been a great success, having established an effective 250-mile blockade along the Cambodian border while making significant penetrations inland all along the west coast and in the southernmost tip of the Mekong Delta. Allied forces had succeeded in reducing the flow of supplies to the NVA/VC from Cambodia and had expanded their presence in areas of the Delta previously the exclusive domain of the enemy. For the Seawolves it had been a year of growth. There were more pilots, door gunners, and maintenance and other ground personnel, and there were more gunships, equipped with more lethal weapons. There were now nine fire teams plus an occasional make-up team at headquarters. Neither the brown-water navy nor any other friendly forces in the Delta were very far from rapid-reaction air support provided with alacrity and enthusiasm by the Seawolves of HA(L)-3.

18

Cambodia, Sea Float, and Solid Anchor

As 1970 BEGAN, THE BARRIER ACROSS THE CAMBODIAN BORDER WAS in full operation. Charlie's savage response to Admiral Zumwalt's Sea Lords initiative testified to the debilitating effect the strategy was having on his activities. Even so, it was impossible to completely seal the 250-mile-long stretch, and plenty of military supplies, munitions, and reinforcements were still making it through.

Meanwhile, allied forces continued to strike at the enemy along the rivers and canals all the way down to the tip of the Ca Mau Peninsula. PCF Swift Boats, PBRs, heavily armed and armored assault boats, SEALs, and South Vietnamese ground forces penetrated inland from the Gulf of Thailand to hit Charlie where he lived. The newly arrived Black Ponies now weighed in with some well-placed, heavy supporting fire from their Zuni rocket launchers, 20-mm cannon, and mini-guns, while the ubiquitous Seawolf gunships, flying from bases afloat and ashore, continued to appear out of nowhere to provide their own special brand of fire from the sky wherever and whenever it was needed. While no one could deny that Charlie still operated in the Mekong Delta with strength and ferocity, it was clear his ability to move about with impunity had been seriously impeded.

Black Pony OV-10A Broncos with their Zuni rockets and 20-mm cannon provided the "heavy artillery" for close air support in the Delta. *U.S. Navy/PHC A. R. Hill*

On January 23, 1970, HA(L)-3 received four more UH-1L Sealords aircraft, bringing the total to eight. Ostensibly, they were assigned for the logistic support of Operation Sea Lords, but increasingly they were used for combat-support missions, such as SEAL insertions and extractions, and hot medevacs. They also supported SEAL forays into enemy-held territory to capture key NVA/VC personnel in missions known as "body snatches." In all such endeavors the SEALs were covered by at least two accompanying gunships because the only armament on the Sealords aircraft was an M-60 at each door position. As one Seawolf pilot later wrote, "Two M-60 door guns doth not a gunship make."[1]

On February 20, the Cambodian government delivered three boxes, which it claimed contained the remains of the Seawolf crewmen killed when their aircraft were shot down over Cambodia the previous April. In fact, they contained only the partial remains of Lieutenant Castle and AO3 Schafernocker. An official request was made to the Cambodians for a further effort to recover and return the remains of Lieutenant Reardon, but no one was optimistic.

Accelerated turnover of brown-water navy assets and combat responsibilities to the Vietnamese was now in full swing. In March 1970, the VNN took over Operation Foul Deck along the Cambodian border, renaming it Tran Hung Dao I after a legendary thirteenth-century Vietnamese military commander who twice defeated Mongol invasions from China. North and South Vietnamese alike revered this ancient hero; ironically, both sides invoked his spirit to motivate their respective combatants.

As the South Vietnamese assumed greater responsibility for the fighting, they assigned to each of the combat operations the designation Tran Hung Dao, followed by a distinguishing number. Operation Giant Slingshot, near the Parrot's Beak, thus became Tran Hung Dao II, and so on.

Even as the South Vietnamese took over more of the fighting on the rivers, the Americans continued to provide necessary air support. For the Seawolves and Black Ponies, the job was much the same as before, and certainly just as hazardous. In the early hours of March 29, Det. 3, then staging from Vinh Gia on the Rach Giang Thanh Canal, and Det. 5, aboard YRBM-16 at Chau Doc, received an urgent call for help from a Vietnamese unit that was under heavy attack. Each detachment put in several welcome air strikes with rockets and mini-gun fire that probably prevented the camp from being overrun. Return fire was heavy, but none of the helicopters was hit.

While this action was under way, the Det. 3 birds were diverted by an exigent call from friendlies in another area that was also under attack. The two aircraft broke away and were on top of the site within minutes, delivering the requested air support with customary accuracy and aggressiveness. Finally, out of ammunition and low on fuel, the fire team was relieved at 4:30 AM by army gunships and returned to base. Det. 5 had already been relieved and had returned to the ship.

On April 14, Capt. Martin J. Twite Jr. relieved Captain Beckwith as commanding officer of HA(L)-3. Twite, former executive officer of Helicopter Antisubmarine Squadron Seven (HS-7), had just finished a shore-duty tour at the Naval War College in Newport, Rhode Island, and was due for rotation to an operational command. He was extremely pleased with his good fortune. Because HA(L)-3 was the navy's only combat helicopter squadron, it had become the plum assignment for navy helicopter pilots.

For Beckwith, it seemed like he had just arrived, and suddenly it was already time to leave. Indeed, all of the Seawolf skippers felt that way. During his year as CO, Beckwith had overseen the continuing expansion of HA(L)-3 personnel, aircraft, detachments, and mission assignments. Admiral Zumwalt's Operation Sea Lords had added new complexities and placed greater demands on the Seawolves. Even so, the unique mobility and flexibility of the

Capt. Martin J. Twite relieved Capt. Reynolds Beckwith on April 14, 1970. Note the experimental 19 tube, M-59 rocket pod. *Charles O. Borgstrom*

detachments, combined with an aggressive can-do spirit, enabled the squadron to meet the challenge head on.

Together, the Seawolf gunships and Sea Lord slicks were now flying an average of thirty-one hundred flight hours a month.[2] Captain Beckwith recalls, "I cannot emphasize enough how impressed I was with that generation of young people. The pilots were out flying and shooting every night, and their performance was superb. The same was true for the enlisted men. If they were not flying, they were hard at work trying to keep those old Hueys in the air."[3]

Back in the United States, other young Americans were using their energy to stage antiwar protests with youthful enthusiasm. Mounting casualties and the hostility of the press fanned the flames. Demonstrations by people of all ages had become larger, more virulent, and politically more difficult to contain. To many, the country seemed to be coming apart at the seams. To the Nixon administration fell the difficult task of extricating American forces from Vietnam, while leaving the South Vietnamese with some hope of surviving afterward. Some courageous decisions in Washington and some heavy lifting by American military forces that would remain in country were necessary to transfer the burden of war to the South Vietnamese.

The situation was complicated by the fact that the NVA/VC had virtual free use of territory just across the border in Cambodia. Here were the termini of the infamous Ho Chi Minh and Sihanouk Trails, and here were huge caches of arms, ammunition, and military supplies, waiting for transshipment into the Delta. Here also were enemy staging areas for incursions into South Vietnam. By March 1970, U.S. intelligence estimated that as many as forty-five thousand NVA/VC were in Cambodia. Enemy sanctuaries had existed in Cambodia for some time with the reluctant approval of the Sihanouk government, which was powerless to do anything about them. The Johnson administration had not allowed U.S. forces to enter Cambodia for fear of widening the war, but the new commander in chief was about to change that.

In mid-March 1970, the Sihanouk government was replaced in a coup by anticommunist president Lon Nol, who closed the port at Sihanoukville (renamed Kompong Som) to Communist ships and made known his support for U.S. and South Vietnamese efforts.[4]

Despite the instability of the political environment at home, President Nixon took a deep breath, stepped up to the plate, and approved an allied invasion across the Cambodian border. The invasion involved some fifty thousand Vietnamese troops and thirty thousand U.S. personnel, supported by B-52 strikes and tactical air assets, in the largest allied operation of the war.[5]

The object was to engage enemy forces in their Cambodian sanctuary, destroy arms caches, and disrupt supply routes into the south. American forces and South Vietnamese units with American advisors crossed into Cambodia on April 30, 1970, and Seawolf Det. 4 and Det. 7 supported these operations in the Parrot's Beak area. A few days later, even larger invasions of U.S. and South Vietnamese forces followed.

During this time, personnel from the Seawolf detachments conducted a search of the area where Seawolf 320 had been shot down, in hopes of retrieving more of the remains of their fallen comrades. Success was highly improbable, but the Seawolves used this window of opportunity to make the attempt. With the assistance of a Cambodian officer, they were able to locate some human remains. Fragments were later identified as those of Lieutenant Reardon and AO3 Schafernocker.[6] Ironically, the Cambodian officer enlisted to help in the search had commanded the artillery unit that had shot down the aircraft in the first place.

On the morning of May 9, a joint U.S./Vietnamese naval task force of LSTs, PCFs, PBRs, and a variety of assault and other vessels sailed up the Mekong River to attack enemy staging sites and to supply concentrations in Cambodia. The operation was called Tran Hung Dao XI, and its objective was to root out enemy units along the river and to secure the Highway One ferry crossing at Neak Luong, which was about twenty-two miles north of the border. The Seawolves provided gunship support for the operation.

The *Hunterdon County* moved north from Long Xuyen to a position on the upper Mekong River, one mile south of the Cambodian border. There she became the base for Det. 8, the detachment that was assigned as the primary tactical air support unit for the task force. In order to avoid leaving Det. 8's area of operations in the Rach Gia/Long Xuyen vicinity exposed, one of the fire teams from Det. 2 was dispatched to cover that location.

Dets. 9 and 5 served as secondary units for the Cambodian operation, while Sealords aircraft from Binh Thuy provided command and control, utility, and emergency medical evacuation services. Det. 3, flying out of Ha Tien, also managed to get in on some of the action.

Detachments 8, 9, and 5 were involved in air strikes against bunkers and other structures along the Mekong River. They strafed enemy personnel, rocketed mortar positions, and sank a number of enemy small craft.

Det. 9 door gunner ADJ-2 Anthony J. "Tony" Guptaitis Jr. remembers making fourteen hot turnarounds in one day. On another day, a Det. 5 bird went down with engine problems in enemy territory two miles north of the Cambodian border. Jet mechanic Guptaitis was sent in on a Det. 9 Huey and dropped off to see if he could somehow come up with a quick fix so the aircraft could be flown out. Seawolf mechanics were wizards with engines, and Guptaitis soon had this one running well enough to make it back to base.

Concerned about weight with the touchy engine, the pilot decided to leave Guptaitis behind, but he called the Det. 9 bird that had dropped the mechanic off to come and pick him up. Alone in Indian country during a major operation was not a preferred place to be, and it made Guptaitis very uncomfortable. He was not on the ground long, however. Det. 9 pilot Lt. (jg) Thomas L. "Tom" Phillips later joked: "We took a vote and decided to go back and get him."[7]

Det. 8 door gunner Bill Rutledge recalls flying support for South Vietnamese Marines (VNMC) who were having difficulty moving through a Cambodian town that was heavily defended and fortified by NVA/VC.

> When we arrived over the town, the marines popped smoke to show us their forward area, and we rolled in hot down the streets of the town, all weapons blazing and taking heavy ground fire from everywhere. We put in three strikes within yards of our "friendlies" and had to go back to the ship for a hot turnaround. Our other detachments were doing the same thing, and we had to take turns using the ship's deck. After several hours putting in strikes, the marines began pushing the enemy back. We put in more strikes at the edge of town, picking Charlie off like flies. The fire was intense, and I couldn't believe we hadn't been blown out of the sky. The enemy was entrenched, and jets were called in with napalm. What a sight! Our Det. rearmed and refueled six times that day, as did our other Dets.[8]

Tran Hung Dao XI went pretty much as planned, with the VNMC taking Neak Luong without much trouble. South Vietnamese forces penetrated all the way to Phnom Penh. For political reasons, however, the U.S. contingent of the task force, with the exception of one Seawolf fire team, did not proceed north past Neak Luong. That one fire team beat the South Vietnamese to the Cambodian capital on the ninth to become the first of the allied forces to reach that city.

On that morning, the squadron operations officer, Cdr. Wesley W. Wetzel, flew up with two aircraft from HA(L)-3 headquarters at Binh Thuy to the YRBM-20 at Chau Doc for an armed reconnaissance mission upriver into Cambodia. Because the YRBM could handle just two birds at a time, Lt. Rick French of Det. 5 took off in one of the detachment's Hueys so that Wetzel could land and refuel. Wetzel then left the deck to allow his wingman to do the same. It was all accomplished quickly, but in the process Wetzel's wing aircraft experienced mechanical problems and had to be scrubbed from the mission. French, who was already airborne in the Det. 5 Huey, armed and fueled, replaced the headquarters aircraft.

The armed reconnaissance mission took the two Seawolf helos all the way to Phnom Penh, where they got a bird's-eye view of the city. As it turned out, there was no unusual activity along the river, and the aircraft, having made no strikes, returned to the YRBM-20 without incident.

One result of the Cambodian operation was the boost in antiwar demonstrations in the United States. Consequently, all American components of the incursion were withdrawn completely by June 29. Seawolf and Sealord aircraft logged more than seventeen hundred hours during the operation.

Allied forces captured or destroyed thousands of individual and crew-served weapons and enough ammunition to supply fifty thousand soldiers for a year. Also captured were hundreds of trucks, jeeps, and other vehicles, as well as enough rice to feed six enemy regiments for a year.[9]

While the Cambodian incursion had successfully engaged enemy units and had destroyed large caches of supplies, it had little long-term effect. The South Vietnamese continued their presence on the Cambodian side of the border, but they were not able to completely prevent subsequent operations by the enemy.

MEANWHILE, IN THE SOUTHERNMOST PART OF THE CA MAU PENINsula, Charlie continued to mount determined resistance to Operation Sea Lords initiatives. Det. 1, which had been flying from an LST offshore, was now staging from Sea Float. It was not an ideal basing situation, but here the gunships were now closer to the action and could respond to a call for help much faster. Night takeoffs and landings aboard the rolling LST out in the Gulf of Thailand were also eliminated, making nocturnal flight operations a bit safer in one respect.

The downside of the arrangement was that during takeoffs and landings, pilots and crews were frequently shot at from the nearby shore, and helicopters, while aboard Sea Float, were now vulnerable to a few well-placed mortar rounds from shore. What's more, the fact that the pad on which they were parked was perched directly over fuel tanks created other concerns. Space limitations aboard the floating barge complex did not allow the entire detachment to be permanently based aboard. That meant that the two fire team crews had to rotate between the ship and Sea Float on a twenty-four-hour on, twenty-four-hour off, basis.

It was just as well, because living conditions aboard Sea Float were considerably less than perfect. Pilots and door gunners crowded together in one small compartment that was overrun with cockroaches and rats. Fitful sleep was punctuated by continuous explosions from concussion grenades thrown over the side to discourage the activities of Viet Cong swimmer/sappers. AMS-1 Thurman L. Hicks remembers that officers and enlisted men slept in the same compartment in beds stacked several tiers high. It required the agility of a monkey to get to the top bunk. "Our room was made up of sheets of four-by-eight plywood around the bottom with screen around the top half, and we were able to scrounge up one floor fan that we pointed straight up. The mosquitoes were the size of birds, and no mosquito nets were available. They sounded like buzz bombers all night, along with the concussion grenades every fifteen minutes."[10]

To the enemy, Sea Float was a hated, high-visibility symbol of the American and South Vietnamese government presence. Their apparent inability to do anything about it was not lost on the civilian population. Charlie was willing to go to great lengths, and to expend as many lives as necessary, to destroy it. Door gunner David K. "Dave" Smale remembers at least three separate swimmer attacks on Sea Float while he was there.[11] More than one sapper ended his midnight swim as a victim of concussion grenades or the strong tidal currents. Enemy floaters washing in and out with the tide provided grim evidence of unsuccessful attempts to sink or seriously damage the mid-river fortress. Lt. (jg) Michael L. "Mike" Lagow vividly remembers an event he and the rest of the Det. 1 ready crew witnessed from Sea Float, an event that brought home the seriousness of the swimmer threat and perhaps made the nightly concussion grenade explosions less objectionable. "A Vietnamese patrol boat moored nearby was blown out of the water in front of our eyes. It was a tremendous blast."[12]

There was a lot of enemy activity in this area and plenty of work for the Seawolves. So much so that Captain Twite assigned another helicopter and additional personnel to this detachment. The third gunship was withdrawn a short time later, but the additional personnel remained with Det. 1.

As before, Det. 6 continued to operate from Song Ong Doc. That detachment had lost one of its helicopters to enemy fire on May 22, when it

Sea Float rides at anchor in the Cua Lon River. Remains of the old town of Nam Can that was destroyed during Tet-68 can be seen in the foreground. *U.S. Navy/PHC Arthur Hill*

made a hard landing in enemy territory after taking a number of hits from heavy machine guns, probably .51-caliber. The crew was unhurt and quickly rescued, but the downed helicopter had to be destroyed by fixed-wing attack aircraft to prevent it from falling into enemy hands. Det. 8, back from its Cambodian adventure, returned to its old hunting grounds at Rach Gia, relieving the Det. 2 birds to return to Nha Be and their accustomed area of operations.

Concentration of Operation Sea Lords forces on the Ca Mau Peninsula continued, and soon included three Seawolf detachments. On August 5, Det. 3 left its home aboard an LST off Ha Tien and flew south to take up residence ashore near Ca Mau City, in the center of the peninsula about forty miles north of Nam Can. The two airstrips there—one short and one long—could accommodate fixed-wing aircraft like the Black Pony OV-10As as well as helicopters.

Seawolf crews endured primitive living conditions at first, sleeping in the open and living on C-rations. Nevertheless, it was a good location from which to make life miserable for Charlie, and that was something at which the Seawolves excelled. The detachment's area of responsibility included the southern part of the U Minh Forest, a nasty bit of real estate sprinkled with NVA and VC personnel.

In the meantime, barges full of sand had been floated up the Qua Lon River to reclaim a large swampy area near the old town of Nam Can, turning it into an important operating base. It was called Solid Anchor, partly to contrast it with Sea Float and partly to signify the allied commitment to bringing the area under solid South Vietnamese government control. It would become the major allied base in the area, ultimately replacing Sea Float.

Like the floating fortress, Solid Anchor was strategically located on the Cua Lon River, and, like Sea Float, it was an in-your-face gesture to the enemy because it expanded government authority deeper into an area that, until recently, had been undisputed VC territory. Complete with a U.S. Navy Operations Center, it was home to a number of PCFs and other vessels, as well as SEAL teams and U.S. and ARVN units. In all, about a thousand men were based there.

Solid Anchor boasted a thirty-three-hundred-foot PSP runway. Det. 1 moved ashore there on September 5. Conditions were certainly not deluxe, but they were much better than those on Sea Float. The crews lived in hootches—officers in one and enlisted men in another. Rats and cockroaches were a continual problem; some of the former were reported to be as big as a foot long. Dave Smale remembers, "We owned the days, but the rats and cockroaches owned the nights. We slept under mosquito netting and were careful not to let arms or legs hang out, for fear of being bitten in our sleep."[13]

The HA(L)-3 investment in the southern portion of the Ca Mau Peninsula now included Det. 6 at Song Ong Doc, Det. 3 at Cau Mau, and Det. 1 at Solid Anchor. All three of these detachments worked closely together to cover this area, which was still heatedly contested by a tough, experienced, and dedicated enemy. Soon there were indications that the concentration of efforts on the Ca Mau Peninsula was working to allied advantage. On the waterways—as well as in the forests and rice paddies—farmers, fishermen, boatmen, woodcutters, charcoal makers, and other South Vietnamese civilians began to reappear, cautiously at first, but in increasing numbers.

The locals had begun trading with Sea Float shortly after its establishment, and this practice was now extended to the base ashore. All this was happening despite Viet Cong threats of dire consequences to anyone dealing with the Americans and South Vietnamese. The arrangements negotiated by the

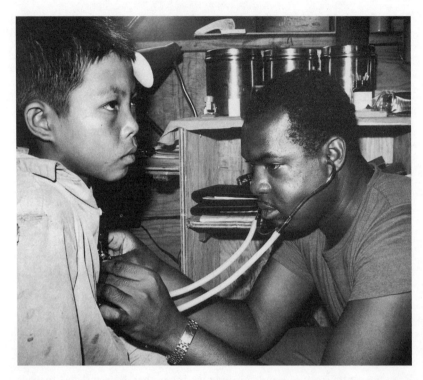

A U.S. Navy corpsman examines a local Vietnamese boy aboard Sea Float. *Naval Historical Center*

locals for their products were far better than those that had been imposed by the Viet Cong, and no goods were confiscated nor were demands for taxes made. What's more, the Americans had begun providing the locals with such small services as basic medical attention, something few of them had ever had access to in the past.

There was cause for some guarded optimism, but everyone involved on the Ca Mau Peninsula knew that much remained to be done before total turnover to the South Vietnamese could be achieved.

19

Bad Day at VC Lake

THERE IS A THEORY—OFTEN ATTRIBUTED TO THE CHINESE, BUT which repeatedly turns up in other cultures as well—that holds that optimism is called for when things look the bleakest because they can only get better. Unfortunately, that theory also holds that the reverse is true. So it was for the Seawolves on the Ca Mau Peninsula in September 1970.

On the fifteenth of that month, ARVN forces ran into considerable enemy resistance on the ground. The site was on the edge of a large, shallow body of water that had been dubbed VC Lake because Viet Cong forces of varying size were frequently encountered there. This day was different, however, because a regular North Vietnamese Army unit supplemented a sizeable number of Viet Cong guerrillas. Together, they proved to be a highly capable force.

Fighting was heavy, and the ARVN troops took a number of casualties. They requested medical evacuation of the most seriously wounded, and Dust-off 86, a U.S. Army slick flown by 1st Lt. Kenneth Ledford Jr. and Warrant Officer Miller responded. Enemy fire was so severe, however, that the helo could not make the pickup without the covering fire of gunships. Because army gunships were not immediately available, the Seawolves were called upon to help.

The Det. 6 fire team at Song Ong Doc was scrambled, and within two minutes they were turning up and ready to go. But just as they were about to lift off, they were told to stand down. Low on fuel, Lieutenant Ledford had decided to retire to Solid Anchor to top off before trying again. That done, the army pilot again contacted the U.S. Navy Operations Center at Nam Can to request gunship support. This time, two fire teams were assigned.

Detachments 1 and 3 each had a gunship down for maintenance, so the remaining birds—Seawolf 313 and Seawolf 306, respectively—had combined to make a two-plane fire team, flying from Solid Anchor. The Det. 6 fire team at Song Ong Doc was scrambled again. Together, the four Seawolves were to escort Dust-off 86 to the combat area and cover the medevac extraction.

Lt. (jg) William A. Pederson flew Seawolf 312 of Det. 6; the copilot was Lt. (jg) William L. Ford. Crew chief AMS3 James P. "Jim" Plona (also known as "Frog"), along with ADJ3 Jose P. "Joe" Ramos, were the door gunners. Except for Ford, who had arrived just a few weeks earlier, this crew had flown together for some time.

Plona recalls that Pederson was an exceptionally skilled pilot who knew the aircraft and its idiosyncrasies well. "When it came to flying, he was one step ahead of everybody else."[1] Indeed, Pederson was well respected and was a particular favorite of the enlisted men in the detachment. "Mr. Pete," as his crew called him, had been with the detachment the longest. In fact, he was about to finish his tour with the Seawolves and rotate home to the States.

It was squadron policy to bring such experienced pilots back to head-quarters at Binh Thuy for about a month before they checked out, so they could train newly arrived pilots. Pederson, however, had done some fast-talking and had persuaded Captain Twite to let him stay with the detachment for his remaining time in country. Even that time was now up, and this was to be his last day on the job, so to speak.

Door gunner Plona had come to the squadron from the USS *Tripoli* (LPH-10), where he had been a crew chief on a Sikorsky H-34 Seahorse, flying utility and medevac flights. After serving two Vietnam tours in that capacity, he volunteered for a stint with the Seawolves, and the squadron scooped him up.

Door gunner Joe Ramos had been around for a while too and had recently volunteered to extend his service in the squadron. He had just returned to the detachment following some well-deserved leave. Morale was high; Pederson's crew knew its business and liked to call itself "The A Team."

When the initial call to scramble came, the Det. 6 fire team was playing horseshoes at Song Ong Doc. In the amount of time it took to sprint to the aircraft, the rotors were turning, and the gunships were about to lift off, when they were called back. As mentioned, Dust-off 86, now low on fuel, had taken time out to refuel at Solid Anchor. It was not long, however, before they were scrambled again, this time rendezvousing in the air with Dust-off 86 and the makeup fire team from Dets. 1 and 3.

This appeared to be a routine medevac extraction. Even though that usually meant they would encounter enemy fire, being shot at was an everyday occurrence. This day, however, the exchange of fire would be something quite a bit more than routine. As the five aircraft approached VC Lake, they could see while they were still some distance out a smoky haze hanging over the area in question. There was a serious battle under way, and the extraction was not going to be easy.

The plan was simple and direct. The four Seawolf gunships formed a kind of protective box with the unarmed Dust-off aircraft in the middle. The two Det. 6 gunships were slightly ahead to provide initial suppressing fire. The Det. 1 and 3 birds took positions on each side of, and slightly behind, the army chopper to protect it as it landed to take on the wounded. The Det. 6 helos would overfly the landing zone and circle quickly to come in behind the Det. 1 and 3 birds to provide follow-up supporting fire. The idea was that the two fire teams would repeat this relay maneuver until the medevac aircraft had made the pickup and was in the clear. As always, mobility was the best defense, and it was essential that the gunships keep moving. So much for best-laid plans.

As the gunships descended rapidly toward the landing zone, enemy response became intense. AO2 Dave Smale, a Det. 1 door gunner who was no stranger to air/ground combat, later described the fire from the ground being "as heavy as I have ever seen."[2] Tracers seemed to be coming from everywhere, and all four Seawolves took hits. Some of the Seawolves say that it was like the enemy had been waiting for them, and indeed they had.

The Viet Cong and the North Vietnamese were only too familiar with allied operations. They knew they had killed and wounded some of the ARVN troops, and from long experience, they fully expected that the Americans would try to airlift the wounded out. They apparently believed they had control of the situation on the ground, and they were now looking at an ideal setup to nail one or more American choppers. It was a bona fide helicopter trap!

Lt. David Speidel was the pilot of one of the two Det. 6 aircraft. Records are incomplete and memories have dimmed somewhat over the years, but it was probably Seawolf 315. The key facts of the shootout at VC Lake, however, are burned into the minds and souls of the participants.

"I was flying the trail bird," says Speidel, "and Bill Pederson had the lead. We arrived on scene along with aircraft from Dets. 1 and 3, escorting Dust-off 86. My bird had a .50-cal. mount manned by first class petty officer George A. "Pappy" Valdespino."[3] The port side door gunner, Henry "Hank" Seeman, had an M-60.

> We were hit early on. I could hear .50-cal. gunfire and said, "Pappy, we're not cleared to fire yet." He said, "I'm not shooting." The next thing I knew, I had lost control of one rudder pedal. We had taken a hit in the control tube that runs under the aircraft and contains the linkage between the rudder pedals and the tail rotor. There was also smoke in the cockpit from a tracer hit. I saw the lead bird go down, but at that point there was nothing we could do to help.[4]

In fact, Speidel was barely able to maintain directional control and was obliged to depart the area. He was able to nurse the aircraft to Ca Mau, where he made a "run-on landing" on the long PSP strip. No one was hurt, but the aircraft was no longer flyable and had to be "hooked out" by a heavy lift army helicopter the next day.

Seawolf 312 had not been so fortunate. As the gunship encountered the gunfire barrage, it was holed several times. Jim Plona believes the fatal hit penetrated the transmission, but to this day no one is certain. In any case, the aircraft suddenly lost all power, and Pederson immediately began autorotation. Because they were almost directly over the LZ when they were hit, they were now descending into the midst of an enemy hornet's nest. There was no help for it, and things began to happen very quickly.

Plona recalls: "Joe was wrapping M-60 ammo around himself, because it was clear we were going down, and we were going to need it on the ground. I tried to get the fifty [.50-caliber machine gun] off its mount, but the ground was coming up fast."[5] Despite Bill Pederson's best efforts, the Huey hit a dike, rolled over, and became a mass of twisted aluminum.

Seawolf 313 of Det. 1 also took several fatal hits, and the engine quit. The pilot, Lt. Richard W. Lambert, also began autorotation. Like Seawolf 312, Seawolf 313 was going down in enemy territory, and it was up to him to keep a bad situation from turning into a tragedy. The pilots and gunners braced for the impact. Crew chief Dave Smale describes his personal dilemma. "I didn't have my belt on and hung on to the pilot's seat for dear life."[6]

Lambert now used what little altitude he had left to jockey the stricken aircraft into the lake. Landing a Huey on water is not a happy thought, since that aircraft tends to roll over to the right and trap its occupants underwater. The pilot had no idea how deep the water was, but he knew the lake option would put a bit more distance between them and the enemy. Lambert's quick decision turned out to be a wise as well as a lucky one.

Lambert, copilot Lieutenant Lagow, and the two door gunners braced for the impact. Lagow remembers that "Dick Lambert did a masterful job of autorotation to put us safely into the lake."[7] The helicopter hit the water with an enormous splash and settled to the bottom, right side up. To everyone's surprise, the water was only about four feet deep, and the top of the helicopter remained high and dry. All four crew members scrambled out without difficulty. No one was injured. Lagow dove back down to retrieve the secure communications gear. Crew chief Smale says, "I climbed out with my .50-caliber gun and scrambled up on top of the helicopter. I remember thinking I had to keep the gun from falling into enemy hands."[8]

Seawolf 306, the Det. 3 Huey flown by Lt. Robert E. Baratko, had also been damaged by enemy gunfire, but his problem was different. They were still flying, but the aircraft had taken a hit in the fuel sump drain valve underneath the Huey, and jet fuel was draining out fast and spewing into the atmosphere. Baratko did not know where they had been hit, but he knew they were losing fuel from somewhere and at a considerable rate. What's more, the main rotor was sucking the fumes up into the aircraft interior, conjuring up an unpleasant vision of fire or an explosion. The situation was quickly going to call for some very tough decisions.

In a recent interview, copilot Lt. (jg) Thomas G. Padon put his finger squarely on the problem: "We were the only gunship still flying."[9] Baratko had no idea how long he could remain airborne, or whether he would have enough fuel to make it back to base, even if he left right away.

Looking down on the scene in the lake, he saw that the crew of Seawolf 313, the other half of his fire team, was okay for the time being. Indeed, Dust-off 86 was at that very moment making an approach to pick up the four very wet but uninjured men.

Baratko now turned his attention to the spot where Seawolf 312 had gone down, looking for signs of life. He saw none, but knew there could be Seawolves down there still alive. If there were, someone was going to have to get them out fast. The enemy seemed to be all around the crash site, but they did not try to close in on the wreckage. They were probably wary of the remaining gunship still overhead but just out of range.

Out over the lake, Lieutenant Ledford in Dust-off 86 had taken the crew of Seawolf 313 aboard and now informed Baratko of his intention to go after anyone who might have survived the crash of Seawolf 312.

Baratko kept a wary eye on the fuel gage as he pondered his next move. It was telling him he had better depart soon, or he too would wind up on the ground as a result of fuel starvation. Still, he knew that if Dust-off 86 was going to have any chance of completing the rescue and getting out in one piece, he had to hang on to provide cover.

Ledford now headed for the downed Seawolf 312 and began a descent escorted by the damaged Seawolf 313. Aboard the Dust-off aircraft, Smale watched in disbelief. "I thought the army pilot was crazy, but he didn't think twice about it. He must have had ice in his veins."[10] Ledford brought the slick in smartly, landing as close as he could get to the wreckage.

Meanwhile, Baratko had positioned himself to provide support and now made a run down the paddy dike at treetop level to draw fire away from the medevac aircraft. He could not use his rockets because the open flame would have ignited the atomized fuel that was still pouring from his aircraft, but he took the chance of having his door gunners fire continuously throughout the run. Another quick glance at his fuel gage told him that time was running out, but Dust-off 86 was still on the ground. He circled again and made another low pass along the dike line, his gunners working hard to keep enemy heads down.

On the ground, Seawolf Mike Lagow and army crew chief Mike Mitchell jumped out of Dust-off 86 even as it flared for a landing and made their way over to the crumpled Huey gunship. It was soggy and very rough going. Mitchell found Jim Plona semiconscious, lying outside the wreckage. He helped him up, and together the two stumbled toward the waiting medevac helo. That was a small miracle in itself, considering Plona's extensive injuries.

"There was mortar and small arms fire all around us," recalls Plona, "and at one point we fell. The people in the helicopter thought we had been hit, but we got up again and made it all the way. We were pulled aboard and I passed out."[11]

Lagow reached the wreck at about the same time that Mitchell found Plona.

A Seawolf gunship begins a low pass. *Conrad Jaburg*

The pilot [Pederson] was dead and the copilot [Ford] was badly injured but still alive. Both were pinned in the wreckage. I tore at the metal with my hands. I don't know how I did it, but I was finally able to free him [Ford]. He was very badly broken up, and I had to carry him to the Dust-off helicopter. There was mortar, machine gun and small arms fire, and the stuff was hitting all over the place. It was the kind of situation where you know you are going to get it any minute but somehow it doesn't happen.[12]

Smale had initially provided covering fire from the medevac helicopter with an M-16, but after a few rounds he too jumped out to help. He found Ramos in the water, outside the bird. He was dead. Smale turned to help Lagow with Ford and then jumped onto the helicopter as it began to lift off.

Eleven men were now on board Dust-off 86, and the army slick was very heavy. "We were overloaded, and he [Ledford] overtorqued the helo to get us out. The two wounded men needed immediate medical attention, and we flew directly to the hospital at Binh Thuy."[13]

Now that the Dust-off was clear of the LZ, Baratko, his fuel gauge registering near empty, hightailed it in Seawolf 306 for Song Ong Doc, where he made a hasty landing and shut down. Copilot Tom Padon jumped out to inspect the underside of the aircraft where the sump valve had been shot away. As he crouched there, "A final trickle of fuel drained out and stopped, leaving a spot about eighteen inches wide on the pad. That was it. That was all the fuel we had left."[14]

The drama was not over yet. A Sealord UH-1L was in the area conducting psychological warfare operations: dropping leaflets and playing tapes urging Viet Cong guerrillas to defect. "It was very boring work," recalled Lt. (jg) William R. Beltz, pilot of Sealord 3. "We had gone into Ca Mau to refuel and were ready to go out again when we were told that the base had received a Mayday from a Seawolf gunship that had gone down at VC Lake."[15] Beltz and his crew took off for the area to see if they could help.

"When we arrived, Dust-off 86 informed us that they had just picked up two wounded and that there were 'two probable dead' still on the ground. They were low on fuel and were leaving the area."[16] Beltz descended for a close look to gauge the extent of enemy firepower. One pass through a hail of bullets answered that question, and he quickly put some distance between himself and the enemy gunners. Just then, another UH-1L arrived with Captain Twite aboard.

Beltz remembers that "the word probable bothered me. I was very concerned that there might be two Seawolves alive down there and that, if something wasn't done, they were going to fall into the hands of the enemy. I decided to go in and see if we could get them out."[17]

It was a very gutsy thing to do. Sealord 3 was unarmed; that is to say, they had no rocket or flex gun capability. AE1 William R. Rutledge was a highly qualified door gunner, but one M-60 and a couple of M-16 rifles were about the extent of their armament.

As Beltz began a fast approach, two army AH-1G Cobra gunships arrived and proceeded to provide cover, but enemy fire remained heavy throughout. Beltz went in close to the dike, but he did not set down because the area he had chosen as a landing zone looked too soggy. As it turned out, it was more than that. Door gunner crew chief Rutledge jumped out of the Huey and landed chest deep in water. As he made his way to higher ground and toward the mangled Seawolf aircraft, copilot Lt. (jg) John E. Farr and crewman AO1 Robert A. Harvey began laying down what supporting fire they could with M-16s. Rutledge also had an M-16, and he fired into the tree line as he approached the downed Huey. When the gun was empty, he threw it away.

"When I reached the wreck, I saw Lieutenant Pederson and checked him and found he was dead. He was too entangled in the wreckage, and I couldn't get him out. Ramos was in the water. I thought he was alive, but when I checked he was gone."[18]

Joe Ramos was still attached to the wreck by his long gunner's belt and, with some difficulty, Rutledge was able to disconnect it from the wreckage and drag him back to the hovering helicopter. The gunship had changed position slightly to get closer to Rutledge, but the ground beneath it was still submerged in water, making it impossible for Beltz to land and for the gunner to heft Ramos' body aboard. Harvey jumped down to help, but even the efforts of both crewmen were futile.

Not about to leave his fellow door gunner behind, Rutledge tied him to the skid with the gunner's belt. By this time, Rutledge was so exhausted he had to be helped aboard the hovering chopper by Harvey. Beltz quickly exited the area, with Joe Ramos dangling beneath the Huey.

The Sealord pilot remembers:

I took off; the two guns [Cobra gunships] followed me out, and one of them (Crusader 32) was shot down right behind me. The fire was extremely intense. I remember it being almost a solid sound . . . one solid roar. Fifty-caliber tracers looked like big basketballs coming up. We took a number of hits but got out of there. The gun that was shot down behind me was immediately rescued by an Army medevac (Dust-off 80) that had arrived while I was on the ground. He followed that gun right down; as he autorotated, the medevac was right beside him, and the crewmen immediately jumped out of the gun and into the medevac. They probably weren't on the ground thirty seconds.[19]

The body of Lieutenant Pederson was recovered the next day without incident, as was the downed Cobra aircraft. The two Seawolf gunships were beyond salvage and were destroyed where they were to keep them from being recovered or used in any way by the enemy.

Bob Baratko was recommended for the Medal of Honor but received the Navy Cross. Tom Padon received a Silver Star. Baratko's two door gunners were recommended for Silver Stars but received Single Action Air Medals. William Beltz was recommended for the Navy Cross but received a Silver Star. His copilot, John Farr, received the Distinguished Flying Cross. Plona later received a Distinguished Flying Cross as well. Other Seawolves received

Bronze Stars, Air Medals, and Purple Hearts. Army 1ˢᵗ Lieutenant Ledford, the pilot of Dust-off 86, received the Navy Cross, while his copilot, WO Miller, and the other Dust-off 86 crewmen received Silver Stars.

Both Bill Ford and Jim Plona survived their injuries and endured long hospital stays. Plona had second-degree burns, a separated right knee, and a crushed left ankle that was so badly pulverized "it was like Rice Crispies." The left leg had to be amputated below the knee. He also suffered two compressed vertebrae, a collapsed lung and a concussion. Ford had at least equally serious injuries, the full extent of which is not known.

Jim Plona remembers his friend and fellow door gunner Joe Ramos with sadness and great affection. "Joe was driven to be the very best," he recalls. "I think of Joe often, and I say a prayer for him each Memorial Day."[20]

20

The War Grinds On

Lt. (jg) Don Thomson reported in to Det. 1 at Solid Anchor on October 14, 1970. Like other Seawolf replacement pilots, he had undergone a relatively short training program in the United States, topped off with a few flights from Binh Thuy. Now he was being introduced to the down and dirty life of combat as a helicopter gunship pilot on the Ca Mau Peninsula.

By the time of Thomson's arrival, Solid Anchor was a going concern, and living conditions for the Seawolves were pretty good by Mekong Delta standards. The crews lived in air-conditioned hootches, with diesel generators providing the electricity.

Initially, all of the American personnel on the base ate in the army messing facility, where the food was described as "uniformly lousy." Taking matters into their own hands, the Seawolves had procured a large charcoal barbecue grill, and with some imaginative trading, they also managed to acquire a walk-in freezer from the army that they installed in their hooch area. The LST in the gulf, part of whose job it was to provide material support for the Seawolves ashore, supplied all of the groceries they needed, including generous quantities of lobster, chicken, steak, and other good things to eat. The Seawolves filled their freezer and ate well. What's more, there was always food left over to trade with the army for other things they needed.

Cooperation between the LSTs and the Seawolf detachments was excellent, and when the helos flew out to the ship for groceries and other necessities, they often brought with them a load of brass cartridge casings that were plentiful ashore. Over time, an LST could accumulate large quantities of brass to trade for Chinese labor in Hong Kong. While they were at sea, the sailors chipped paint and prepared the ship for a cosmetic face-lift. When they went into port for R&R, a brigade of Chinese coolies swarmed aboard and painted the vessel in a couple of days. The bartering arrangement was perfect: the ship's company was spared an onerous job and had more time for liberty ashore, and the Chinese melted down their "wages" and made saleable goods from the brass.

Life at Solid Anchor was about as good as it could get on the Ca Mau Peninsula, but it was hardly luxurious. There was still the strangling heat, the almost continuous drenching rain during the monsoon season, the sour-smelling mud, the insects, the rats, the leeches, the poisonous snakes, and other Delta wildlife, to say nothing of the occasional mortar and rocket attacks. The gunships were parked on a PSP pad between the river on one side and the hootches and a revetment on the other. The aircraft were about as safe as the Seawolves could make them, but there was always concern that Charlie might attack from the river.

The enemy was never far from the perimeter and wanted the Seawolves to know it. Takeoffs and landings were routinely met by hostile ground fire. AO1 Fred T. Stark remembers that, "the majority of the time, either arriving or leaving, you were guaranteed to be fired upon by the VC."[1] Sometimes it was only a lone gunman with an AK-47, sometimes a concerted effort by several NVA/VC, hoping for the ultimate prize of bringing down one of the hated Seawolf gunships. On the plus side, flying out of Solid Anchor got the crews' attention early in each mission and primed them for the action ahead.

The few amenities the Seawolves scrounged together for themselves made life bearable. To newly arrived Don Thomson, things looked like they were going to be relatively pleasant, or in any case not nearly as bad as he had expected. He had to come up to speed quickly, however, and there was no time to relax. The day after his arrival, he was scheduled for an orientation flight to introduce him to the geography and to familiarize him with Det. 1 operating procedures. Navigation was an important part of every copilot's job.

October 15 dawned bright and sunny, a good omen. Only one helo was available that morning, the other having been shot up the day before and temporarily put out of action. Detachment personnel were hard at work mak-

Solid Anchor at Nam Can with a Seawolf gunship parked on the PSP. Seawolf hootches are on the other side of the road (center, at top). *Charles O. Borgstrom*

ing repairs, and headquarters at Binh Thuy had elected not to send a replacement for the short period the bird would be down. The lack of a second aircraft, however, did not interfere with Thomson's familiarization flight, essentially a jog around the operating area. For the most part, everything was proceeding as planned. In the gunship business, that frequently meant that something unforeseen was about to happen.

That morning, a Sealord HH-1K from Binh Thuy flown by Lt. Richard W. "Dick" Barr and Lieutenant (jg) Tom Phillips, landed with parts for the downed bird. The gunship crews set to work immediately to get the aircraft up and operating. Even more welcome was the detachment's mail.

The tempo began to quicken, however, when the U.S. Navy Operations Center received a call from an Armored Troop Carrier (ATC), also known as a Tango boat, that was manned by an all-Vietnamese crew.[2] It had been involved in a firefight and had wounded men aboard who needed medical evacuation. Dick Barr volunteered to fill in for the Det. 1 gunship under repair and make the pickup. The HH-1K was better suited for a medevac mission anyhow, and although it was unarmed like all Sealords aircraft, the two enlisted crewmen each had an M-60 they could fire from the doors if need be. The functioning Det. 1 gunship would provide such cover as might be needed.

This Tango boat, an ATCH, was equipped with a tiny helicopter landing deck, so the pickup would be relatively easy. Off the Hueys went, with Thomson in the left seat of the lead aircraft. The gunship pilot was Lt. (jg) Michael R. "Mike" Suldo, an experienced Det. 1 fire team leader. This was to be his last flight before leaving the detachment. Like most Seawolf pilots and door gunners, he had survived some hair-raising missions and was going home unscathed, or so it seemed. This flight would be a milk run. There is an old adage, however, that you cannot avoid the bullet that has your name on it. Recent sages have added a corollary: bullets addressed "To whom it may concern" are similarly problematic.

Looking back on the flight, "newbie" copilot Thomson recalls: "I had no idea where we were going, didn't have any radio frequencies, didn't know where we were, didn't know anything."[3] Not a problem. Mike Suldo had flown missions like this many times and knew the area like the back of his hand. For the most part, Thomson was a passenger.

Door gunner AE2 Michael W. "Mike" Dobson remembers: "We took off, with the Sealords aircraft flying trail on us, and were soon following a waterway known as the 77 Canal, which was about fifty feet wide. We found the Tango boat nosed up to the bank. It had apparently been hit by a B-40 rocket, which wounded several crewmen."[4]

Old pro Barr landed the HH-1K slick on the little flight deck with ease and took the wounded men aboard. None was seriously injured, and so they climbed on the helicopter without assistance. Meanwhile, Suldo's gunship provided close cover overhead, ever alert for any NVA/VC mischief. No movement was detected in the surrounding area; it was a quick, well-executed, no-sweat pickup.

"When all were safely aboard," Mike Dobson recalls, "the HH-1K took off again and followed us at the seven o'clock position over about two hundred yards of jungle. We broke out into a clearing [a rice paddy] and started to take fire. At this point, we only had about thirty or forty feet of altitude. We didn't see where the fire was coming from, but we opened up into the tree line anyway."[5]

For Thomson it was an unexpected introduction to gunship combat. "All of a sudden I heard both our door gunners open up," he says. "Then we were going into the rice paddy. Mike Suldo had taken a round that had come up through the console between us, and he suddenly slumped over the controls. I grabbed the stick to keep us from crashing into the paddy."[6] The right door gunner, ADJ3 Robert J. Christenson, flipped a catch that let the pilot's seat back fold down; he laid Suldo out flat to check his wound.

Tom Phillips, copilot of the Sealords aircraft that was slightly behind, spotted a man in black pajamas firing up at them with an AK-47. Then the gunship ahead lurched momentarily as Suldo was hit and plunged toward the ground. It recovered as Thomson took over the controls.

The Sealords aircraft also took some hits as Barr jinked to throw off the enemy's aim and to give one of his crewmen a quick shot at him from the open door. Just ahead, Dobson was out on the skid of the gunship, firing behind and under the Sealords aircraft.[7]

Aboard the gunship, Christenson gave Suldo first aid. The pilot had been hit in the thigh, very close to the groin. It was a nasty wound and a close call; an inch or two higher would have had substantially more serious implications and, as he lay on his back, Suldo loudly voiced his concern. Assured that he remained intact in those most important of male matters, he remained quiet for the trip home.

The riverine boats had heard the exchange of gunfire. One of them asked for a report and was told the pilot had been wounded, but he would be okay. Barr set a course for Binh Thuy with the lightly wounded Vietnamese, while Thomson, a bit unsure of his whereabouts, headed back to base. Tracing the canal back to the river, he followed that major waterway to Solid Anchor, where Suldo received immediate medical attention before being flown on to the army's Third Surgical Hospital at Binh Thuy. After being patched up, he was soon on his way back to the States none the worse for wear. Says Thomson: "It really was Mike Suldo's last combat flight in Vietnam and my first. To this day the incident sticks in my memory, as I am sure it does in his."[8]

Despite impressive allied inroads into what had previously been an undisputed Viet Cong sanctuary, the Ca Mau Peninsula continued to be a hot spot. Charlie did not take the allied gains with good grace. What's more, he was well aware of the drawdown of U.S. forces in Vietnam and of the program to turn the war over to the South Vietnamese. Those conditions offered the NVA/VC in the Delta a new reason to be hopeful, and from their point of view, it was essential that they hang on and even improve their situation during the transition. Overrunning and destroying one of the despised allied bases would be a tremendous morale booster, as well as an impressive message to the indigenous population that the VC were still very much in charge.

One of the offending American staging areas was located next to the fishing village of Song Ong Doc on the river of the same name. It was a primitive town with almost nothing in the way of basic amenities and a population of no more than a couple thousand people, many of whom were VC or VC sympathizers. The base was separated from the town only by a concertina wire (coiled barbed wire) fence. Thus, it was not a very secure location. As twenty-four-year-old Lt. (jg) Richard "Dick" Blair put it: "It was like having North Vietnam right next to you."[9]

Det. 6 helicopters flying from Song Ong Doc supported PBRs and other allied watercraft that plied the river and the smaller waterways from the Gulf of Thailand to Ca Mau City. As previously noted, they also covered the area north to the U Minh Forest and south to VC Lake, forming an overlapping network with Dets. 1 and 3.

The PBRs at Song Ong Doc were berthed alongside a couple of barges that contained repair shops for the boats, as well as messing and berthing facilities for the PBR crews. Seawolf personnel lived ashore in two elevated wooden hootches, with tin roofs, plywood floors, and screening to keep out the mosquitoes and the many other varieties of insects and vermin that inhabit the Delta swamps. They took their meals aboard one of the barges with the PBR crews. The food was said to be tolerable, depending upon who you asked.

Each hooch was about twelve feet by twelve feet, with eight bunks, a table, and a couple of chairs. Some overworked generators supplied electricity, but there was no plumbing. Showers were taken from fifty-gallon drums. The hootches were close to the river, and raw sewage from the latrines just ran into the stream. It was enough to give one of today's environmentalists heart palpitations, but it was how the native population had done it for centuries and was thus no big deal. Between the hootches and the water was a bunker made of four-by-six planks covered with sandbags.

The Seawolves flew from an elevated helo pad that was just big enough for the detachment's two helicopters. For the gunship crews that was no big deal either, but, just as it was aboard ship, the two aircraft could not turn their rotors at the same time. The steel revetment walls on two sides of the platform were reinforced with sandbags to protect the gunships from enemy fire. The ends were open so the aircraft could take off and land into the prevailing wind. To get to the aircraft, crewmen used a catwalk about thirty-five feet long that ran from the hootches to the helo pad.

Incredibly, no ground forces of any significance were present to protect the base. There was, however, a Dufflebag unit that placed electronic sensors outside the perimeter and monitored them for enemy movement in the surrounding jungle. Signals came through a rather high antenna that was placed in line with the approach to the helo pad. Whoever erected it clearly had not taken a course in flight safety. One had to fly a bit of a dogleg pattern to get around it just before touchdown. Landings could be hairy at night, but things were no worse there than operating in the dark from a rolling LST in the Gulf of Thailand.

There was no fuel for the Hueys at Song Ong Doc; Det. 6 helicopters usually armed and refueled at Solid Anchor, about a twenty-minute flight away. The gunship crews flew their missions and stayed on station until the last moment, that is to say, when the low-fuel light came on. When that happened, they knew they had just about enough fuel to make it to Solid Anchor before the tank went dry. Because there was a seven-thousand-foot runway there, they could overload the aircraft with both fuel and ammunition and make a running takeoff. Upon arrival back at Song Ong Doc, they had burned off enough fuel to enable them to get airborne for the next flight. It was certainly not an ideal situation, but, as is the case in most wars, operational necessity often trumped prudence and routinely intruded on the peacetime margins of safety.

On the night of October 20, Lieutenant Speidel, fire team leader of the Det. 6 off-duty crew, was making the most of his night off. He was sacked out in the officer's hooch when he was awakened by the sound of incoming fire. "About a month before," he says, "we had been attacked by a U.S. Coast Guard cutter that had mistakenly lobbed several five-inch rounds into the base. I thought this was a repeat at first, but then realized that these were mortar rounds."[10]

Indeed they were, accompanied by rocket and automatic weapons fire as well. Despite the large amount of incoming, the hootches were not hit, and it quickly became apparent that Charlie's primary targets were the barges and the PBRs. The hootches, however, were no more than fifty yards away from those targets and the Seawolves—both the ready and off-duty crews—hunkered down in a makeshift bunker along with a SEAL who had just come up from Sea Float.

Ordnance was exploding all around them. Because of the ferocity of the attack, they expected an imminent attempt by the NVA/VC to overrun the base. That was a matter of some concern, because the only weapons in the bunker were a few .45-cal. pistols. Speidel told the SEAL, "This looks like your kind of thing, so you lead and we'll follow."[11] For the moment, though, the enemy seemed to be concentrating on the barges, and the men of the detachment all stayed where they were. The barrage was so heavy there was not much any of them could do but keep their heads down.

Blair was the fire team leader of the ready crew and remembers it all clearly.

> The twentieth was the day before my birthday. We were asleep in the hooch along with the off-duty pilots when all hell broke loose. The base had come under fire by mortars, rockets, RPGs, and machine guns. The sound was deafening, and once it started there was no let-up.
>
> We were all in our skivvies, but we jumped out of our bunks and piled into the bunker. We could see and hear the stuff coming in. RPG rounds were hitting the steel revetment walls that protected the helos, and there were showers of sparks. My first thought was that we had to get airborne, but it was a thirty-five-yard dash along the catwalk to the helo pad, and it seemed like we didn't have a prayer of making it.[12]

As enemy fire poured into the barge area, the PBRs got under way with minimum damage. The barges themselves were not so fortunate and absorbed the brunt of the attack. The revetments shielding the helicopters, however, performed their job well and, incredibly, the gunships were still intact and flyable, at least as far as anyone could tell.

Just then a round of something hit one of the generators, and there was an enormous explosion. Blair took the opportunity to run back into the hooch for his flight suit and his .45 and then dashed back into the bunker. Now there was another large explosion over on one of the barges. Blair decided that if they just sat there, they would eventually be overrun. Everyone knew what happened to Americans unlucky enough to be captured by the Viet Cong. Blair decided they would make a run for it.

> I took my right door gunner, ADJ-2 Joel F. Trammel, and told the others to follow close behind. Tram and I made it to the helo with stuff going off all around us. He quickly unhooked the rotor blade tie down while I jumped into the aircraft and flicked the battery switch. Damn! The running light switch had been left on and the enemy now knew we were getting ready to take off. I flicked the light switch off and got the rotor turning. By now [Lt. (jg)] Paul Watters, my copilot, and the other door gunner had made it up the catwalk. They jumped in and we were

airborne. As we left the pad, Tram opened up with the .50-caliber gun. The trail ship, flown by [Lt. (jg) Robert E.] Bob Flynn, followed about a minute later.[13]

The first thing Blair did was to call the LST offshore to tell them the base was under heavy attack and to get any and all available close air support assets in the area to respond. Then the two gunships began a series of repeated strikes on the base perimeter, concentrating on spots from which the most fire seemed to be emanating. It was not long before Det. 1 gunships and a couple of OV-10 Black Ponies arrived to add their considerable clout. Blair and his fire team expended their ammunition and repaired to Solid Anchor to rearm and refuel. After repeated air strikes, the shooting on the ground tapered off and finally stopped altogether.

Blair was very concerned about the off-duty crews that had been left on the ground, but no one knew if the enemy had faded into the jungle, as he often did, or was simply waiting for the right moment to launch a second assault. Maybe he was actually in the compound waiting for the helicopters to land. With Charlie, no one ever knew for sure.

> It was still dark, but I decided to go in and see if I could get the other Seawolves out. We dumped our rockets and other ammunition to lighten the aircraft, and with Bob Flynn flying cover, I attempted a landing. We approached from the gulf, flying over the water at ten feet on the radar altimeter. It was a hairy way to do it, but I considered it safer than a normal approach that might expose us to enemy gunners. We landed safely, and I sent one of the gunners to check the bunker and the hootches. Everyone was gone![14]

Unbeknownst to Blair, PBRs had evacuated the remaining crews to the LST *Garrett County*.

The attack was over; the enemy, however many of them had survived, had left the area. When morning came, a large number of enemy dead were found just north of the base, giving mute testimony to the timely effectiveness of the aerial attack. Charlie had been poised to storm the compound, and if that had happened, few if any of the allied personnel on the base would have survived. The bad news was that the enemy had been able to demolish the barges and had made a wreck of the waterfront. When the smoke cleared, the superstructures of the barges had been leveled; what remained were smoking hulks. On the ground, mortar hits had so pockmarked the surrounding area, it looked like a slab of Swiss cheese.

Following the attack, Det. 6 aircraft moved out of Song Ong Doc. The two aircraft staged from the *Garrett County* and other bases ashore to cover their area of responsibility. The enemy had made his point, but the PBRs and the Seawolves had escaped destruction and had given Charlie a bloody nose in the process.

After the Song Ong Doc raid, the end of 1970 seemed to come on fast. It had been a hard year, one that had seen the aggressive execution of Admiral Zumwalt's Sea Lords program, the reshuffling of detachments, and the incursion into Cambodia. There had been no letup of calls for rapid-reaction support of river and land forces.

On the night of November 12, a Det. 8 fire team from Rach Gia responded to a call for help from the Kien An VNN base. Arriving overhead, the Seawolves found that a severe mortar and rocket attack had ceased only minutes before, although small arms fire from sappers continued. Several Vietnamese sailors had been seriously wounded in the attack and required immediate medical evacuation. For the Seawolves, that meant a night landing in an unfamiliar location that had no helipad, a tricky situation at best. The weather in the area was unusually bad and worsening, but the lead aircraft was able to make its pickup from a small wooden pier before heading back to Rach Gia.

The second aircraft, flown by Lt. (jg) Kevin Delaney, was left to evacuate three remaining critically wounded men. Now, however, the base had become completely engulfed in fog and heavy rain, with visibility near zero. Relying on continuous instructions from a PBR skipper, Delaney made his approach to the pier, passing over the PBR at an estimated eight to ten feet without ever seeing it! He felt, rather than saw, his way for the final few feet before the welcome bump of the skids on the wooden pier. The wounded were quickly loaded on board. With fuel low and no letup in the weather, Delaney immediately took off on instruments into the muck and headed for home. Following a quick refueling stop at Rach Soi, the injured men were flown on to Rach Gia where medical help was waiting.[15]

Meanwhile, the interdiction program along the Cambodian border had produced some positive results. Despite this, unacceptable numbers of North Vietnamese and significant amounts of contraband continued to make it across the border and into the Delta. What's more, the Song Ong Doc attack demonstrated that the enemy still had some very sharp teeth.

On the plus side were the significant inroads that had been made in the southwestern part of the Delta. Despite Charlie's persistent attempts to terrorize and intimidate the local population, people were beginning to return to the area. Sea Float had started things rolling by buying local produce and providing modest benefits. Some civilians took advantage of basic medical services. AMS1 Hicks remembers witnessing a corpsman assist a Vietnamese woman in giving birth to a healthy baby.[16] Commerce was slowly being restored to the area, and the South Vietnamese government was beginning to function there.

For the Seawolves, the pace had been hectic, the pressure constant, and the human cost high. Ten men had been killed during the year and a number of others wounded or injured. Combat damage was heavy, and accidents caused by hard use of equipment and personnel combined to take a further toll. A new concern was the rash of crashes that resulted from engine failures in noncombat situations. Eight aircraft were lost during the year from all causes. Others suffered various damages. Patching bullet and shrapnel holes in airframes was, of course, a necessity, but it was an often-deferred job. Operational necessity sometimes caused minor maintenance issues that would normally ground an aircraft to be temporarily put aside until the tempo of operations subsided.

By December 31, the squadron had a total of thirty-five helicopters. The gunship stable consisted of twenty-seven of the venerable old UH-1Bs and two new UH-1Cs. The latter type made it into the Seawolf inventory because the army had begun replacing their UH-1C Hueys with new, more powerful and hard-hitting AH-1 Cobras.

During 1970, the Seawolf gunships flew more than seventy-eight hundred hours, destroying well over a thousand enemy structures, including bunkers. They sank some sixteen hundred vessels, mostly sampans and junks. Some 755 enemy troops, both North Vietnamese and Viet Cong, were confirmed killed by Seawolf fire from the sky, and many more "probables" and "possibles" were recorded.

By the end of that year, innovative gun configurations had proven themselves and were now in routine use. An M-21 mini-gun installed on the left-hand side of the aircraft and fired by the copilot had replaced the M-60 flex gun. Door gunners had experimented with pintle-mounted .30-caliber machine guns for a time, but these were abandoned in favor of a single-mounted .50-caliber machine gun, installed in the right door of one aircraft in each detachment. This weapon gave the door gunner some heavy muscle on that side of the bird.

A mini-gun was mounted in the right door of the second aircraft in some detachments, replacing the .50-caliber gun. Combined, the copilot's mini-gun, the right door gunner's mini-gun, and the other door gunner's M-60 could put out well over eight thousand rounds per minute. Despite the ability to spew out bullets like a garden hose, however, mini-guns had an unfortunate tendency to jam, and right door gunners increasingly took to carrying M-60s as spares just in case.

Some detachments retained the .50-caliber door gun on one aircraft. M-60s continued to be used exclusively in the left-door positions of all squadron aircraft and remained the preferred weapon of many gunners. Seawolf gunships were now well known to the enemy in the Mekong Delta war, and whatever the combination of firepower on any given aircraft, the arrival of a Seawolf fire team on the scene of any action was bad news for Charlie.

Sealord slicks were increasingly used in 1970 to insert and extract SEAL units, covered, of course, by Seawolf gunships. Sealord crews often fired handheld M-60s from the slick's doors, but they had no mini-guns or rockets. The Sealord crews took many of the same risks as Seawolf personnel, without, however, having the same capability to strike back.

Four UH-1Ls were lost during the year. One that crashed at Binh Thuy on June 1 took the lives of Lt. John M. Mulcahy, AO1 Lloyd L. Bowles, and AMS1 Wilbur D. Frahm.

To offset the loss of the UH-1Ls, the squadron had acquired three HH-1K models, which were immediately thrown into the fray, flying combat support and logistic missions. On November 26, one of the new HH-1Ks lost power and had to ditch in the Gulf of Thailand off Song Ong Doc. The aircraft was lost, but the crew was rescued after a short time in the water.

At one point, the squadron tried arming UH-1L and HH-1K aircraft by installing hard points to carry two five-hundred-pound bombs or fuel air explosives (napalm) to clear landing zones. The bombing system employed sighting mechanisms in the chin bubble so that the bombs could be sighted from either the pilot's or the copilot's seat. The hard mounts could also be used to accommodate M-59 rocket pods with nineteen rockets. For reasons that are unclear, these innovations were never used in combat, and the problem may have been related to interservice turf wrangling.

Sealords aircraft continued to serve in an unarmed capacity throughout the war. During 1970, they carried more than seven thousand passengers during more than six thousand missions.[17] As year-end rolled around, merely six Sealords aircraft were left to do an increasingly demanding job.

American troop strength in Vietnam at this point numbered about 280,000, just a bit more than half of what it had been just two years before. Vietnamization was fast becoming a reality, with ground operations in the

Pintle mounted twin-mount .30-caliber guns did not prove satisfactory and were quickly replaced with .50 caliber single mounts on the starboard side of one gunship in each detachment. *Peter Mersky*

Delta now largely in ARVN control. ACTOV was moving ahead with all deliberate speed, and South Vietnamese crews now manned most of the brown-water navy. Air support remained in American hands, but there was now concern over who would provide this critical function in the Delta when the Seawolves and the Black Ponies left.

In mid-December, a Seawolf gunship en route from Ca Mau to Binh Thuy crashed along the way, killing Lt. (jg) Richard R. Buzzell, Lt. (jg) Antonio O. Ortiz, AEC Johnny Ratliff, and ADJ-2 Robert E. Worth. To date, thirty-eight Seawolves had lost their lives in the Delta war.

Seawolves at Binh Thuy and with the detachments celebrated Christmas day in 1970 much like the other U.S. personnel who remained in Vietnam. For the ready crews, of course, there were routine patrols and responses to calls for help. Some Seawolves put up modest decorations. Others thought about home and wondered what the family was doing. Whether long or short timers, most looked forward to going home when their tours were up.

A Seawolf gunship keeps vigil over two swift boats as they patrol a Mekong Delta canal. *U.S. Naval Institute Photo Archive*

On December 25, one of the Hueys brought last-minute Christmas mail to the detachments. It also made deliveries to some of the isolated South Vietnamese outposts around the Delta that still had one or two U.S. Army advisors. They must have been the loneliest people in the world on that special day.

At each little compound, the Hueys landed and shut down. They usually just tossed the mail out and went on to the next mud-walled fort, but this day was different. This was Christmas, and they had something that had to be hand delivered. While the two gunners stood guard over the aircraft, the pilots went inside for some brief, friendly conversation with the American advisors and to present them with some high-octane Christmas cheer. The Seawolves had just about bought out the Binh Thuy PX's supply of Jack Daniels and Pinch and the like for this project. Compliments of the Seawolves, guys, and Merry Christmas![18]

21

Door Gunners

A SEAWOLF DOOR GUNNER HANGS FROM A HUEY GUNSHIP THAT IS careening wildly through the sky at treetop level. The noise of a laboring jet engine and whirling blades provides background music for the staccato sound of a handheld M-60 machine gun. Swinging precariously over the sweltering jungle, one foot on a skid while firing beneath his aircraft, he provides cover for the gunship in front of him. It has just made its run and is now especially vulnerable to enemy ground fire. His target concentration is intense, and he seems oblivious to the red-hot metal filling the air around him.

What would any reasonable man think of such a bizarre scene? His first reaction would almost certainly be: This is insanity! But for those familiar with the ways of war in the Mekong Delta, other words would quickly come to mind: words like "skill," "daring," and "incredible courage." Everyone would agree on one point, however: it was not a job for the faint of heart.

Tales of Seawolf derring-do tend to emphasize the role of the pilots. They unflinchingly flew their beat-up old Hueys into the heart of a firefight, with guns and rockets blazing, or plucked an American from under the nose of an enemy primed for the kill. Their story is well documented in the many citations and awards that they received for audacity and valor. Most Seawolf pilots, however, will quickly point to their gunners as the indispensable players in any gunship saga. To qualify and serve as a Seawolf door gunner was to become a member of a warrior elite. Door gunners were special, and they knew it.

To begin with, no one was ever shanghaied or even coaxed into becoming a Seawolf door gunner. All were volunteers who could opt out at any time. Almost none of them ever did. Indeed, it was not uncommon for a door gunner to finish his one-year tour and sign up for another one. Bill Rutledge probably holds the record in this category with a total of three-plus consecutive tours.

For the most part, gunners were young, many barely out of high school. The majority were in their early twenties, some still in their late teens, all bursting with the hormones of youth, full of piss and vinegar. Any door gunner older than twenty-five was getting along in years, and someone over thirty was considered a senior citizen.

To some observers, door gunners seemed indifferent to death; in fact, combat did begin to seem old hat after a while. One gunner remembers: "After flying so many combat missions and hanging outside the helo on a nine-foot gunner's belt, shooting, you don't think about death and become either stupid, fearless, or both."[1] Some gunners remember that combat from a maneuvering gunship provided a rush of adrenaline and an indescribable high. When each mission was over, they experienced the satisfaction of a man-size job well done and a sense of having beaten the odds one more time.

A kind of warrior stoicism permeated the Delta atmosphere and helped to sustain those who routinely engaged the jungle enemy. Door gunners may also have entertained a youthful conviction of immortality, especially in the early stages of a tour. They quickly tempered that perception, however, when a fellow gunner, sometimes a close friend manning the gun at their side, was killed or severely wounded. Always sobering, such experiences rarely caused a gunner to throw in the towel. He just gritted his teeth and returned to his guns with a vengeance, years older and a bit savvier about life and death.

Seawolf gunners and pilots alike had a visceral sense of responsibility to their fellow Americans and other friendly forces under fire, particularly those in imminent danger of being killed or captured by a ruthless enemy. "The best way to put it," says door gunner John P. Lynn, "[was that] nobody was ever left in trouble."[2] Right from the squadron's very beginning that theme had quickly developed, until it had become each Seawolf's first and last commandment. It is a theme voiced over and over again in the recollections of

A door gunner scours the riverbank for bad guys who ambushed a PBR (center). *U.S. Naval Institute Photo Archive*

pilots and gunners alike. Although that rule was unofficial and unwritten, no Seawolf could ignore it and retain the respect of this exclusive fraternity.

Door gunners were inspired by the fact that they were part of a close-knit team that operated largely on faith: faith in the skill and daring of the pilots they flew with, and well-earned pride in their pilots' faith in them. Door gunner Sam Taylor remembers that relationship vividly. "My pilot and copilot," he said, "I would have walked through hell for. You fly with the same crew and have the same combat experiences and you build a mutual trust. You depend on each other."[3]

Indeed, every crew was a family of sorts. Each man knew he was an essential part of that family, with a critical job to do, and each had a sharp understanding that others counted on him to do it well. The respect and confidence of one's fellows was a compelling inducement to excel, to consistently turn in a flawless, 110-percent effort. Each crew member, pilot and door gunner alike, was acutely aware that, in the helicopter gunship business, the cost of a shoddy performance might well be a trip home for someone in a body bag. Was there fear? Of course. But it was not so much fear of death as it was fear of not being up to the job, of letting your crew down. That was the ultimate disaster.

Most men were chosen to be door gunners before reporting to the squadron and were given some stateside training in the relatively new, and still developing, art of helicopter gunship warfare. The U.S. Army, which had pioneered the concept, provided the training, usually at places like Fort Benning, Georgia, Fort Rucker, Alabama, or Fort Eustis, Virginia. It was a good introduction to the UH-1B as a weapons system, but, as might be expected, it did not completely prepare gunners for the enormous challenge they would suddenly come face to face with in country. There they would learn from the school of hard knocks, and in the process, they would find that they frequently had to modify and adapt the procedures and doctrine they learned back home to fit the Delta environment and the navy's rapid reaction concept. In the end there were only two basic goals: get the job done, and survive.

Some enlisted men came to the squadron strictly as support personnel, with no intention of joining a flight crew, but they were swept up in the challenge of combat and decided they wanted to become part of a gunship team. Even though they had no stateside crew training, those evaluated as having "the right stuff" were given a chance to qualify. Several highly motivated people were picked up in this manner. Regardless of where they came from and what their skills might be, they had to show they could cut it as a gunship crewman before being sent off to a detachment. Combat-tested gunners, often those on their second tours, checked out the newbies carefully and were not inclined to coddle them. Even after reaching their detachments, new gunners were usually paired with seasoned veterans of six or eight months and got some hard combat under their belts before they were accepted as authentic warriors.

As might be expected, some door gunners were ordnancemen with considerable technical knowledge of guns and other weapons. Others, who had no ordnance experience whatsoever, were engine mechanics, electricians, structural mechanics, electronic technicians, and other aviation ratings. Virtually none of them, however, not even the ordnancemen, had ever actually fired a machine gun in deadly combat. In all other U.S. Navy squadrons, only pilots or naval flight officers got to fire guns or launch weapons of any type. This was a unique opportunity for enlisted men, and they took it very seriously. Each door gunner quickly became more familiar with his guns than he was with his toothbrush, and more adept at the grim business of combat than Joe civilian back home in suburbia was with mowing his lawn or driving the family car.

Besides their prowess with their weapons, Seawolf door gunners had to be jacks-of-all-trades and masters of a variety of technical skills because they operated in detachments that were geographically removed from normal support

A door gunner readies his gunship's M-60 flex guns aboard the LST *Harnett County*. *Peter Mersky*

facilities. Returning from grueling, often back-to-back combat missions, door gunners maintained and repaired their aircraft and kept them fueled, armed, and flying on a round-the-clock basis. When a detachment was shorthanded, as was often the case, the gunners substituted adrenaline for sleep. Seawolf door gunners were tough, relentless, and very, very good at what they did.

Door gunners perform maintenance on one of their gunships aboard the LST *Harnett County. U.S. Navy/PH3 Steve Howk*

There are many stories of door gunners' courage and tenacity, too many to tell in one chapter or one book, for that matter. One of the most memorable, however, took place on March 26, 1971. On that day, twenty-year-old AN Norman B. "Norm" Stayton was the left door gunner, manning an M-60 machine gun on the lead gunship of a light fire team that was flying from the short strip at Rach Gia.

The fire team leader was Lt. O. C. Fowler, and the copilot was Lt. (jg) Joseph E. Love Jr. The crew chief and first gunner, AE1 Russell Underwood, flew the right door, manning a .50-caliber machine gun. The trail aircraft commander was Lt. (jg) Terry R. Ogle.

The two Seawolf gunships were escorting a small convoy of Mike boats (LCMs) along the Can Gao Canal. Their mission was to deliver ammunition, fuel, and supplies to one of the outposts in the area. Stayton remembers somewhat wryly that he had little regard for that kind of an assignment and considered this one especially boring. That feeling would soon change in a rather dramatic way, but for the moment, all was quiet. Stayton knew, however, that in the Delta anything could happen, so he fought to stay alert.

The aircraft was getting low on fuel, and Fowler elected to refuel at the nearby Rach Soi PBR base, leaving Ogle's crew to cover the convoy. When

Terry Ogle poses with his gunship. *Terry Ogle*

he returned, it was Ogle's turn to do the same. The whole refueling evolution took only minutes for each aircraft, but that was enough time for things to happen. Ogle remembers that, as he hurried back to join the convoy, he saw smoke rising from the scene when he was still about ten miles away.

"It rose from the Mike boat and built to over two thousand feet. We were flying at one thousand feet and had to look up to see the tops. No one said a word. We didn't have to. We knew what had happened."[4]

An NVA/VC unit ashore had attacked the convoy. One of the Mike boats, laden with jet fuel, had been hit by a rocket and had exploded in a ball of fire. Burning fuel was spewed over a wide area in the water. Three of the boat's four crewmen were killed almost instantly, but one American in the water seemed to still be alive.

Stayton recalls: "We spotted him through the smoke and fire in the water. He was struggling to crawl out onto the bank but was not having much success. He was clearly hurt, although we could not tell the extent of his injuries at that point. O. C. Fowler said simply, 'We need to help him.'"[5]

The VC barrage from the village was intense. Stayton remembers, "There was machine gun and B-40 rocket fire coming from everywhere. We made a run at the village to suppress it and then returned over the man in the canal."[6]

It seemed there was not a lot the gunships could do other than to keep the VC away from him. It was very frustrating for the Seawolf crews, and Stayton recalls, "We weren't doing him much good sitting up there on our butts."[7] The young door gunner volunteered to do something about it.

> Lieutenant Fowler brought us in low and slowed down enough for me to jump out with a Mae West [inflatable life jacket]. The surface of the water was aflame, but I knew how to splash and keep a path clear ahead of me. I got to the wounded man quickly. Fire from shore was still heavy, but the gunships were doing their best to hold it down to a dull roar. The man in the water was blistered from his feet to his head. There is only one way to describe it: the poor guy was fried. He was awfully gutsy though, and he was not giving up.
>
> "We've got to get out of here," I told him. I grabbed a small sampan that was pulled up along the bank and tried to lift him in. I wrapped my arms around him, and his skin peeled off. "My arm," he said. I saw it was loose and hanging by a shred of flesh. He had no control over it, but it was his, and he was not about to let it go. I stuffed the arm into his shorts and was able to get him into the sampan. Then I paddled out into the canal, so one of the helicopters could pick us up.
>
> Lieutenant Fowler came around and tried to hover over us, but the rotor wash kept blowing the little sampan away. On one try I was able to grab a skid and hold on.
>
> Russ Underwood [AE1 Russell L.] hung out of the helicopter on his long gunner's strap and tried to get hold of the man, who was lying in the bottom of the boat, but he couldn't quite manage it. I shouted at the man, "You've got to sit up." Somehow he did, and Russ grabbed him by his good arm. The skin just peeled off, and he fell back into the canal.[8]

It was decision time again, and it was one that would have taxed the courage of the bravest of the brave. Stayton knew that, if he went back into the water, he would probably not be able to save the injured man. He had seen just how badly burned the man was and knew he would almost certainly not make it, even if by some miracle Stayton could get him to safety. By this time, there was even a growing question in Stayton's mind as to whether he could save himself. Meanwhile, they were still being shot at from shore, and the hovering helicopter was a big fat target in a shooting gallery.

The gunner still had a firm grip on the skid and could easily have pulled himself back aboard the helicopter. Who could have blamed him? For Stayton, however, that was not an option. "I let go of the skid and went back into the canal."[9]

The gunships continued to provide cover to hold down the enemy fire. "I managed to get us back to the bank again and found a larger sampan that had a motor. Somehow I lifted the man in and tried to get the motor going, but it wouldn't start. Just then several PBRs arrived on the scene. My God, I thought, they'll think we're VC. I stood up and started to wave my arms. "We're Americans," I shouted. Of course they couldn't hear me, but I guess they got the idea."[10]

One of the boats now got in close enough to pick up Stayton and the injured man. By this time, Fowler was flying on fumes and left the area briefly to refuel. Ogle now decided to try to pick up Stayton and his charge from the boat. "We dumped all our remaining ammunition overboard so I could hover and maintain control of the helicopter."[11]

Ogle made his approach to the stern of the boat and turned sideways to set his skid on the aft end. The boat was small, and the maneuver was tricky. As he maneuvered into position, he could no longer see the boat beneath him and descended using instructions from his gunners. The problem with the burned man's skin prevented a successful transfer. Anywhere he was touched, it would simply peel away. It is hard to imagine how painful it must have been. Nothing was working, and Ogle was ultimately obliged to break off and try something else. "I felt bad about the situation," says Ogle, "because I knew that time was of the essence."[12]

The boat now put Stayton and the burned man ashore on a dike that ran along the canal so that Ogle would have a better chance at picking them up. "This wasn't that easy either," says Ogle. "As I remember it, I had to straddle the dike, never completely weight down, but in a slight hover."[13] This time, they were able to load the burned man and Stayton aboard. By now Ogle was also critically short of fuel and set down at the Rach Soi PBR base, where the burned man was picked up by a waiting Dust-off helicopter and hurried to the hospital in Saigon. He was barely alive.

Norm Stayton put his feet on the ground at Rach Soi and was surprised to find that he couldn't stand on his right leg. For the first time, he realized he had been hit and was bleeding. Moments later, Fowler picked him up and whisked him off to Rach Gia, where he received first aid from a corpsman attached to the Seabee detachment there. He was later medevaced to the hospital in Saigon, where he was treated for multiple injuries suffered during the incident.

The army sergeant Stayton rescued is believed to have died shortly afterward. Considering the fact that the man's burns covered most of his body, his death was not unexpected. Still, there was always hope. He was, after all, an American in trouble, and that is why Stayton would not leave him. It was what Seawolves did. Stayton's wounds were treated, and he was later returned to his detachment. He was awarded the Navy Cross for his bravery. On August 15, 2003, at a ceremony attended by many of Stayton's fellow Seawolves, a new enlisted berthing facility at the navy base in Norfolk, Virginia, was named Stayton Hall in his honor.

Despite traumatic combat experiences, door gunners were often back in the saddle, so to speak, as soon as possible. Even serious, life-threatening wounds did not seem to deter them or persuade them to relinquish their warrior role easily. The case of AO3 James A. "Jim" Wall is a classic example.

Wall was a Texan, complete with a drawl. A friend described him as "one of those kind of guys that you like at first sight" and having, "a grin that could have set the Devil himself at ease."[14] He checked into the squadron in June 1970 and quickly got into some heavy combat while assigned to Det. 2 at Nha Be. Four months later, his gunship was supporting South Vietnamese ground troops on a mission north of the base, when he received a chest wound that almost ended his life. Fellow door gunner Fred "Terry" Meeks administered some timely and efficient first aid that probably saved Wall's life, while pilot Lt. Clint Davie nursed the damaged gunship back to Nha Be. Visiting Wall in the hospital at Saigon, Davie gave the gunner what he thought would be the good news that he would be ordered home. His days as a door gunner had come to an end.

Wall was visibly upset. "No way," he said. "I'm staying to finish my tour."[15] After two months in the hospital, he was permitted to return to the squadron and served in a non-flying status extending well into the following year.

In April 1971, some of the detachments were experiencing a critical shortage of door gunners. The available gunners were flying missions on an almost daily basis. The situation was especially bad at Rach Gia, where they were flying around the clock. Wall, who was now fully recovered from his wounds, saw his chance to get back on a crew and volunteered to help fill the gap. On the nineteenth, he and Bill Rutledge were flown down to Det. 8 at Rach Gia to relieve their exhausted comrades. It was a temporary assignment for Rutledge, but Wall was to be a permanent member of the detachment.[16]

Norm Stayton sporting his TF 116 black beret at the dedication of Stayton Hall more than thirty years after his incredible act of courage. *Norman B. Stayton*

Door gunner ATN3 Michael J. "Mike" Madrid, who was to be Wall's roommate, took the new man to their billet, and the two went off to dinner at the army mess hall. It was good to have a new gunner in the detachment, especially an experienced one. Madrid and the other Det. 8 gunners were worn out from too many back-to-back missions.

It's strange what people remember about times of emotional trauma. Madrid recalls the meal at the army mess hall that day because, in all probability, of the events that followed. It was "very poor army spaghetti," he says, "with acceptable garlic bread and lime Kool-Aid with brown sugar sweetener."[17]

Madrid was well aware of Wall's previous brush with death, and as he sat there, he wondered why Wall would want to lock horns with fate again. "I wanted to ask him, 'What are you doing here? Haven't you done enough?'"[18] He didn't ask the question, though. Maybe he knew the answer; he was, after all, a Seawolf door gunner himself.

After dinner, Madrid went back to his room for some well-earned rest and immediately fell into a sound sleep. Jim Wall went down to the short strip to prepare for the flight. There, Russ Underwood, the petty officer in charge of the detachment, briefed him on the area of operations. Otherwise, Wall, as an experienced gunner, knew the ropes well.

Wall was part of the ready crew that night. He hadn't even had a chance to unpack his seabag. That was okay; he could do that later. This was where he wanted to be. He would fly the left door on the trail bird manning an M-60, while Bill Rutledge would man a mini-gun on the right side of the same aircraft.

They flew a routine combat patrol south of Rach Gia while it was still light. There were signs of enemy activity, but they made no contact. The enemy preferred darkness, and it was a well-worn cliché that, in the Delta, the VC owned the night. (Understandably, many Seawolves took issue with that claim.)

Returning to the long strip to refuel, the two gunship crews settled down to wait for the call to scramble that they knew would come. The call came around 9:00 PM, and the two gunships headed south again for a spot not too far from the Gulf of Thailand. Sure enough, Charlie was on the move.

They struck fast, in hopes of surprising him. The lead bird rolled in on a rocket run. But Charlie had heard them coming, and his response was immediate. The door gunners on the lead bird worked the area over as they flashed by. The trail bird rolled in to cover the lead and to put in its own strike. Rutledge and Wall were concentrating on muzzle flashes on the ground.

Both gunships put in several strikes. The sky was filled with red tracers from the air and green tracers from the ground. Charlie was feeling his oats (or rice) and was not giving an inch. All too soon the gunships were out of ammunition and had to return to base. There they quickly rearmed and refueled. Rutledge recalls that Wall was all thumbs-up and smiles. It was good to be back in harness. Soon they were in the air again and headed back to the same spot. Charlie was waiting for them.

The lead bird made its run, the trail gunship with Rutledge and Wall right behind. As they rolled in, Wall shouted, "taking heavy fire."[19] He was hanging way out of the aircraft on his strap, trying to protect the lead bird as it finished its run. Rutledge remembers vividly what happened next.

"I started taking fire on my side, and it was heavy. We were taking hits in our bird. Then I felt a dull thud of an explosion on Jim's side. I was still firing as I looked over to see if he was okay. He fell over toward me and I called out 'gunner hit.'"[20]

The aircraft was in a dive and headed for the ground, still taking heavy fire. Rutledge continued shooting while the pilot, Lt. (jg) Thomas S. Parrett, struggled to regain control. He recovered just before hitting a dike line. The lead bird came in behind to cover them, and the two gunships made their escape.

Rutledge now turned his attention to his fellow door gunner. It was one of those moments that one remembers forever. It took only a moment to realize that Wall had a fatal head wound. It had killed him instantly.

The gunship limped back to the short strip, made a run-in landing, and shut down. Underwood jumped from the lead aircraft and ran back to help, but there was nothing he or anyone else could do.[21]

One of the U.S. Navy's largest enlisted berthing facilities at the U.S. Naval Station, Norfolk, Virginia, was named in Wall's honor. The James D. Wall Manor was dedicated on April 28, 2000. The ceremony was attended by more than thirty of his squadron mates, his sister, and his daughter, who had been just eighteen months old at the time of her father's death.

The loss of a squadron mate was always hard, but it was something that crews learned to deal with. Sometimes the grim reaper visited in other unexpected ways that brought an emotional response from the most experienced and combat hardened of door gunners.

On a dark night in early 1970, the Det. 8 ready fire team was called out to provide air support for a South Vietnamese compound that was under heavy attack. It was one of those mud-walled outposts—gratuitously referred to as forts—that dotted the Delta in strategic locations. It was manned by members of the regional and popular forces, known to the Americans as Ruff Puffs.[22] Without immediate help, there was little chance the defenders of this friendly outpost would survive.

Bill Rutledge (along with many other veterans) attended memorial services for fallen Seawolves at Patriots Point, South Carolina, in November 2004. *Richard Knott*

As the Seawolf fire team neared the scene, they could tell it was bad by the sound of the American advisor's voice. They could see the flashes from the enemy mortar tubes and, charging into the fray, concentrated their fire accordingly. Suddenly, they were told to put all of their efforts into the east end of the compound because the enemy was overrunning it. All of the friendlies had moved to the west end to make their stand. The Seawolves directed their fire as instructed and took several hits in the process. After three strikes, the South Vietnamese troops were able to retake the east end of the compound, but the situation remained precarious.

Several of the South Vietnamese defenders had their families with them, a common occurrence in these Ruff Puff forts. Indeed, they had probably lived in the nearby area before the war. Some of these civilians had been seriously wounded and thus had to be evacuated. Since the aircraft had expended all of their rockets and most of their machine-gun ammunition by this time, they were now light enough to take on a few passengers. The fire team leader elected to do so, and the two gunships landed at the west end, where the critically wounded were loaded aboard. There were three adult women and one little girl in one aircraft. The other bird also took as many wounded civilians aboard as they could.

The NVA/VC were still firing, and bullets were flying everywhere. Some of the South Vietnamese soldiers were terrified and tried to climb onto the helicopter where Bill Rutledge was one of the door gunners. He and the other gunner were obliged to use their M-16s as clubs to knock them off. It was one of the hazards of this kind of rescue attempt. Rutledge hit two that were hanging on the skids with his rifle butt, and they fell a few feet to the ground.

As we moved away, we turned our attention to the wounded. The left door gunner was attending to two of the women. The little girl had a heavy, bloody bandage on her chest. Her mother had a head wound and had lost her right hand. The stub was wrapped in a cloth. She was trying to give the child to me to hold. I took the little girl and held her on my lap while her mother wailed and rocked back and forth.

The little girl's eyes were open. She was looking up at me and blood was foaming at her mouth. I knew she was not going to make it. A few minutes later she closed her eyes, stopped breathing, and was gone without a sound. I pulled her to me with tears running down my face.

When we landed at the surgical unit, the wounded were off-loaded and the little girl was taken away. We rearmed, refueled, and flew back to Rach Gia to wait for the next scramble.[23]

22

Of SEALs and Seawolves

WHEN THERE WAS AN ESPECIALLY TOUGH AND DIRTY JOB TO DO IN the jungles and rice paddies of the Mekong Delta, it was a good bet that the SEALs would be involved. The SEALs' modus operandi was much like that of the VC themselves, and they habitually gave Charlie a very nasty taste of his own medicine. Having accomplished their mission with precision and alacrity, they quietly faded away into the jungle. They were aggressive, highly disciplined, and ruthless, and, like the VC, they did some of their best work under the cover of darkness.

The Seawolves were always on hand to insert and extract them, and to provide air support. Indeed, the Seawolves and SEALs frequently operated together throughout the war, and over time they developed a solid bond of friendship and mutual respect.

Retired Rear Adm. Tom Richards, affectionately known to SEALs, Seawolves, and others as "The Hulk," was guest speaker at the Seawolf reunion in November 2004. Well known as an aggressive SEAL team officer in the Mekong Delta, Richards had, on more than one occasion, called on the services of the Seawolves and Sealords and was never disappointed. He began his speech by saying, "If it were not for you guys, I would not be here tonight."

SEALs practice rappelling from a Seawolf gunship at Nha Be. *U.S. Naval Institute Photo Archive*

He then went on to describe an event in which he was wounded and the Seawolves pulled him and other SEALs out of an extremely tight situation under heavy enemy fire. His high regard for the Seawolves was clearly heartfelt. Other SEALs have similar recollections.[1]

In his book, *Combat Swimmer: Memoirs of a Navy SEAL,* retired Capt. Robert A. Gormley says of the Seawolves, "When we called, they came fast and they were effective." He also remarks, "I don't know a single SEAL who operated in Vietnam and wasn't saved by those guys at least once. They were the best helo crews I had ever seen. The Seawolf crews were real heroes."[2]

Door gunner AE2 Mike Dobson vividly remembers an incident early in 1971, when a lone Seawolf crew and a platoon of beleaguered SEALs put it all on the line to stand together, no matter what. Despite official policy, and without regard for reasonable prudence, warriors facing extreme circumstances sometimes band together to do what they have to do.[3]

On this very dark night, a small SEAL team had unexpectedly made contact with a much larger enemy unit, and the SEALs were pinned down. The enemy was clearly aware that SEAL units typically carried a limited supply of ammunition that could be quickly consumed in a firefight of any intensity or extended period. Indeed, a six- to eight-man SEAL team might carry no more than four thousand rounds of ammunition, a pretty small amount for a serious firefight. The SEALs had to make every bullet count and hope for some help to arrive before they ran out of wherewithal and were left completely at the mercy of the enemy.

In this instance, the good guys' prospects did not look encouraging, but took a turn for the better when a fire team from Det. 1 at Solid Anchor arrived. The Seawolves could discourage an immediate, all-out attack, but Charlie was tenacious and could afford to wait.

The Seawolves could see sporadic enemy muzzle flashes, and the SEALs were able to mark the enemy's location with tracer rounds. The gunships rolled in on a rocket run to get Charlie's attention and to do as much damage as they could to the larger and more heavily armed enemy force. A rocket run at night close to friendlies on the ground was always a hazardous undertaking, but everyone understood that situations of this kind demanded such a response.

Mike Dobson recalls: "Normally, gunners would retreat back into the aircraft as the rockets started firing, because of the intense field of sparks, rocket caps, and molten slag in the air. This time, the SEALs were in big trouble, and we stayed outside and continued to concentrate fire on the VC position all through the rocket run."[4]

The Seawolf fire team then set up a wagon-wheel pattern overhead that allowed the two aircraft to cover each other when turning away from the enemy, always a vulnerable moment at low altitude. The highly accurate fire from the door gunners kept enemy heads down, but it did not prevent them from firing into the SEALs' position. With the Seawolves overhead, however, the SEAL team was relatively safe for the moment.

Morning was not far off, and when there was enough light, Sealords aircraft, covered by the gunships, would be able to land and make the extraction. Indeed, when dawn came, it would be Charlie who was in the exposed position if he elected to hang around that long. The prospects of capturing or killing a few hated SEALs, however, might be too enticing to pass up. Charlie would probably hang on until the last possible minute and then make his move, one way or another. Therefore, it was up to the two Det. 1 aircraft to keep the enemy engaged during the final hours of darkness and prevent them from overrunning the SEALs.

As always in circumstances like this, time flew by quickly, and with no immediate help on the horizon, the decision was soon made to initiate a refuel shuttle, so that at least one aircraft would remain on station. Dobson's aircraft was the first to return to Solid Anchor, where it was hot refueled and rearmed in what surely must have been record time.

Back on station, they found the SEALs still hunkered down and Charlie still probing and trying to make them expend their ammo. The trail bird was making threatening passes while carefully conserving its ammunition for an anticipated enemy assault. The pilot had saved a few rockets, and the two aircraft made a coordinated rocket attack before the trail bird broke off and headed for Solid Anchor and a drink of jet fuel.

While Dobson's aircraft maneuvered overhead, Det. 3 was alerted to prepare to join Det. 1 and execute an extraction of the SEALs at first light. Meanwhile, the lone Det. 1 gunship set up in alternating left and right circles overhead, so that the door gunners could share the ammunition expenditure until the other Det. 1 aircraft returned. With a little luck, the shuttle would keep Charlie at bay until daylight. Then came the unexpected.

Dobson's gunship received a disconcerting call from Solid Anchor. The fuel pumps had broken down, and it was impossible to refuel the trail bird in time for it to relieve the lead aircraft. For the moment at least, the crew of the lone Det. 1 aircraft was on its own.

What to do? Maybe another detachment would relieve them before they ran out of fuel. Maybe not! Other detachments were conceivably engaged elsewhere. The pilot reviewed his options.

There was a hint of gray in the eastern sky, but it was still dark on the ground below and would remain so for a while yet. They could stay until they had just enough fuel to make it to the nearest outpost at Hai Yen, leaving the SEALs to their fate, or they could stay on station until all they had left was fumes. It would be light enough then to risk a landing next to the SEALs. They had their handheld M-60s, an M-79 grenade launcher, a couple of M-14s, and a few personal side arms, along with whatever the SEALs had left in the way of ammunition, to hold off the VC until help arrived—or until they all ran out of ammunition and were overrun.

It was decision time, and the pilot put it to the crew. If they were to make it home unscathed, they would soon have to depart in order to make it safely to Hai Yen. Such a choice would certainly be in line with squadron doctrine, and no one—except perhaps they themselves—could have blamed them for making it. To a man, the answer was the same. "No way! We stay!"[5]

The pilot informed the SEALs of their intentions. When the time came, the gunship would make one last rocket run, and, using its remaining few drops of fuel, land alongside the SEALs.

On the ground, Charlie must have noted that the second aircraft had failed to return. He could not have known what that meant, but he certainly knew that the helicopter circling above had been there for some time and would soon have to leave. The enemy would still have time for the kill, with enough left over to make a safe departure. If there was one thing Charlie had proven over and over again, he excelled in the practice of patience.

In the gunship cockpit, the low-fuel light came on. It seemed much larger than usual, more like a big red eye warning that time was fleeting. It got everyone's attention. There were now less than twenty minutes before flame-out. It was relatively quiet below, but occasional flashes told them that Charlie was still there, waiting. The crew was silent as the gunship continued its lonely orbit, each man occupied with his own thoughts.

Precious fuel was burned as the minutes went by. It was almost light enough to attempt a landing when the radio came alive. Det. 3 was inbound, about five minutes out. Det. 6 was also inbound.

"Det. 3 arrived first, and after one quick orbit to orient the gunships, we headed to the nearest landing site available, which was about six miles at [the village of] Hai Yen."[6] There was no jet fuel available there, but it was a relatively safe spot to set down. "The low-fuel light had been on for what seemed like an eternity, but somehow the old girl got us down safely yet another time."[7]

The extraction went well, and some grateful SEALs were lifted out without further incident. "A couple of hours later, the refueling pump was back in action at Solid Anchor. Our sister ship soon arrived, and we siphoned fuel from them and returned to base for another day of flying."[8]

ON APRIL 14, CAPT. CHARLES O. "CHARLIE" BORGSTROM RELIEVED Capt. Marty Twite as commanding officer of HA(L)-3. Charlie Borgstrom was a gregarious guy and a hard charger who had just come from serving on the faculty at the Naval War College in Newport, Rhode Island. His varied career included two tours as an airship pilot and one on the ice in Antarctica as operations officer during Deep Freeze 65 and 66. He had been designated a helicopter pilot in the late 1950s; in the late 1960s, he organized, commissioned, and served as commanding officer of Helicopter Combat Support Squadron Five (HC-5). Now he had the chance that every red-blooded helicopter pilot dreamed of, an opportunity to show his stuff as CO of the navy's first and only helicopter gunship squadron of the Vietnam War.

As with former COs, there was no time for a leisurely introduction to the job. Jim Wall had been killed in action a few days after Captain Borgstrom's arrival. Indeed, things were hot all over the Delta. Borgstrom set his jaw and went to work. As the drawdown of Americans in Vietnam continued, there was plenty to do.

ON THE NIGHT OF APRIL 29, THE SEALs AGAIN GOT CAUGHT ON the ground, but not before doing what they came to do. Their mission this time was to assault a known NVA/VC camp hidden in the jungle and to rescue American prisoners reportedly held there. There was no confirmation that Americans were actually there, but even the report was enough to cause a rescue attempt. It was the kind of job for which SEALs could work up a lot of enthusiasm.

The team was inserted into an area not far from the camp by two Sealord slicks covered by two Det. 6 gunships. The insertion went as planned and without incident. Making their way to the enemy camp, the SEALs found no

Capt. Charles O. Borgstrom relieved Capt. Martin Twite on April 14, 1971. *Charles O. Borgstrom*

Americans there, but shot the place up pretty badly. They also took four prisoners of their own in the process. Hopefully, with a little coaxing, the prisoners could be persuaded to reveal information about enemy operations in the area and whether there had ever actually been American prisoners at the camp.

Charlie now mounted a counterattack, determined to stop the SEALs and their reluctant traveling companions from escaping. One of the SEALs had suffered a stomach wound and required immediate medical attention.

The extraction was difficult. During the first attempt, the pilot of one of the Sealords aircraft and a door gunner on one of the gunships were hit, and the two aircraft were obliged to return to base. Det. 3 at Ca Mau was scrambled to get the SEALs out. AMSC Kenneth E. Wheeler was crew chief and a door gunner on one of the Det. 3 birds.

Approaching the extraction area, both gunships and the remaining Sealord aircraft came under intense fire. The gunships produced a barrage that kept Charlie's head down while the Sealords aircraft slipped in and picked up several SEALs and their prisoners. Now, with the remaining Det. 3 gunship laying down suppressive fire, Chief Wheeler's aircraft descended into the middle of it all to rescue the rest of the SEALs, including the wounded man.

As the aircraft flared for a landing, Wheeler maintained a steady fire and, upon landing, jumped down with his M-60 and kept the pursuing enemy at bay while the SEALs lifted their wounded comrade into the aircraft before piling aboard themselves. Outside, the chief's gun jammed, and the SEALs standing in the door covered him while he too scrambled aboard the departing gunship. Enemy fire again became intense, and the aircraft took several hits in the tail boom but kept on going.

The SEALs had accomplished their mission, having determined that no friendlies were held captive. They also netted four prisoners for interrogation. What's more, the SEALs and the gunships clearly scored a number of enemy kills during the engagement. The cost, unfortunately, was one pilot, one gunner, and one SEAL wounded and three aircraft damaged.[9]

All of the wounded Americans recovered.

There are many stories of Seawolves responding to SEALs in trouble. Veteran Seawolf pilot and fire team leader Tom Phillips recalls one instance when the reverse was true. The incident occurred in the Army Engineers Officers' Club at Binh Thuy, a popular establishment largely because army nurses from the Third Surgical Hospital frequented it.

On the night in question, a jeepload of Seawolves and SEALs visited the club to curb their thirst and relax a bit. SEALs and Seawolves made club

managers apprehensive, but according to Phillips, this little group was "actually being quiet and reasonably well-behaved."[10] One of the Seawolf pilots, an
officer of somewhat diminutive size, had struck up a conversation with one of
the nurses, when a burly army officer who had had too much to drink stepped
in and accosted him, making abusive comments and pushing and shoving
him. One of the SEALs tried to intervene, but the army guy just pushed him
aside. Bad move! The SEAL, says Phillips, "laid the army officer out with one
punch. The guy was out cold before he hit the deck. Just like in the movies."[11]

There was dead silence in the bar as the small navy group got ready to
defend itself. The SEAL looked around the room and said in what Phillips
described as "a slow, loud, menacing voice: 'Nobody messes with Seawolves
while SEALs are in the bar.'"[12] Silence again, while the navy guys waited for
the place to erupt. Nothing!

Suddenly, as if on cue, people took up their drinks and went back to their
conversations. Nobody even bothered to check the man on the floor to see if
he was okay. He got up a few seconds later and made a discreet exit.

23

Winding Down? Who Says?

MAY 23, 1971, WAS A MODERATELY BUSY DAY FOR DET. 5 AND HALF of Det. 9. The latter detachment, which worked from the YRBM-21, moored just south of the Cambodian border, had one of its aircraft down for combat damage and repair at Binh Thuy. No replacement was available, and since it was against squadron policy for one Seawolf aircraft to operate alone except in extreme circumstances, the remaining flyable Det. 9 aircraft was working with Det. 5 in a heavy, three-helo fire team. The combined team now covered both the Det. 5 and Det. 9 areas of operation.

On this day, the three aircraft had made a morning patrol along the Vietnam/Cambodian border and had provided some air support for a friendly ground unit in the Det. 5 operating area. So far, it had been a so-so day.

Lt. Lew Madden, the Det. 5 fire team leader, was senior. He decided it would be a good time to use the team's temporarily heavier firepower to advantage in a daylight attack on an NVA/VC position situated in the three sisters' mountains. This area had several mountainside caves that were protected from air attack by .51-cal machine guns.

Charlie knew from experience Seawolf gunships almost always operated in pairs. His gunners had but a few moments to fire, with minimum exposure to themselves, as each Huey turned away.

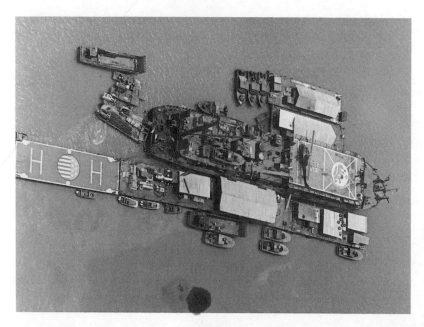

The YRBM-21, together with associated barges, PBRs, and other river craft just south of the Cambodian border. Note the Seawolf insignia painted on the flight deck. *Barry Solomon*

On this day, the Seawolf attack was prompted by the theory that Charlie would not expect a third aircraft. Sure enough, he opened fire with everything he had, laying it on especially heavily as the second Det. 5 gunship turned away. At that point the third Huey, from Det. 9 and flown by Tom Phillips and Stephen A. "Steve" Hanvey, both lieutenants (junior grade), came down out of a haze layer and unloaded into the mouth of the cave. All fire from the enemy position ceased, causing the Seawolves to speculate that at least a few of the enemy gunners had gone to meet their ancestors. Having successfully sprung their trap, Lew Madden elected not to press their luck, and the three aircraft returned safely to the Det. 5 base at Chau Doc.

The crews turned in early to get as much rest as possible; they would need to rise bright-eyed and bushy-tailed, or something of the sort, to respond to the inevitable nocturnal call to scramble.

The call came sometime after midnight on the morning of the twenty-fourth from the army's refueling outpost at Moc Hoa, about fifty nautical miles almost due east of Chau Doc and only a few miles south of the Cambodian border. It had become a somewhat nightly routine at Moc Hoa for the enemy to probe the outpost sporadically and lightly with mortars. There was no real danger that the facility would be overrun during these probes, but the personnel stationed there always felt better in such situations when they knew the Seawolves were in the air somewhere close by. Perhaps they just wanted Charlie to be reminded that an all-out assault would bring an almost immediate response from the ubiquitous helicopter gunships.

In any case, the two Det. 5 and the single Det. 9 aircraft launched from Chau Doc and headed east toward Moc Hoa. The province senior advisor informed them en route that the brand-new outpost at Hoa Binh was under fire and in need of immediate assistance. (South Vietnamese Ruff Puffs and two U.S. Army Advisors manned Hoa Binh, as they did at most other of these crude fortresses.) Hoa Binh was located in the Plain of Reeds at the strategic intersection of two canals. It was also smack on a main enemy infiltration and supply route into the Mekong Delta from Cambodia. A typical small Delta outpost, Hoa Binh consisted of a couple of bunkers and several basic wooden buildings that housed the South Vietnamese and their families, along with a few domestic animals.

Like other similar outposts, Hoa Binh's claim to fortress status came from the fact that twelve-foot-high mud walls topped with barbed wire surrounded it. The approaches to the compound were reportedly seeded in random fashion with land mines. Hoa Binh was on an almost direct line between Chau Doc and Moc Hoa.

As before, Madden was the fire team leader, but because the team was now in the Det. 9 operating area, Phillips was in the lead, handling the communications. They saw a flash in the distance where the fort should be. It was the ammunition bunker going up. Phillips switched to the Hoa Binh frequency, and an American advisor came up on the radio instantly. "He knew who we were. Everybody knew who the Seawolves were, especially the diminishing number of Americans left in the boonies as the Vietnamization of the war took effect in the Delta."[1]

The word from inside the compound was bad. The first rounds had killed the senior Vietnamese officer and his XO and wounded one of the Americans. The voice on the radio was that of the injured American in the compound, an army sergeant with a broken leg. According to Madden, this was one of the coolest guys he had ever encountered. "Everything was falling apart around him, the enemy was on top of him and still he spoke calmly and without emotion. I guess he knew that panic wouldn't help. Every word had to count."[2]

Two companies of North Vietnamese regulars from just across the Cambodian border had somehow navigated the minefield and had already taken two of the walls. A number of enemy troops were in the compound. Phillips told the American sergeant to hang on, that they were about five minutes out. The American replied calmly that five minutes would probably be too late.

The fire team was already at maximum power but now began a shallow descent to squeeze out a few extra knots. The needles of the airspeed indicators in all three aircraft were now banging against the red lines.

As they bored in, the fort was in flames and the light played havoc with the pilots' night vision. Even though it was a dark night, burning buildings lit up the whole area. Steve Hanvey remembers that he could even see several sampans in the canals.[3] They were apparently the enemy troop transports and supply boats supporting the assault. The friendlies, meanwhile, had pulled back and were huddled in a bunker on a corner of the northern wall.

Tom Phillips recalls: "We rolled in for a rocket attack without even a single pass for orientation. I didn't even get a chance to put on my chicken plate. A quick call [was made] to ask the voice where he wanted it. 'Right on the southern wall,' was the immediate reply."[4]

Rockets had a significant impact if they ran true, but they were the least accurate of the Hueys' weapons even under the best of conditions. In this case, the two gunships were moving too fast for a good run. The pilots knew it, but they hoped the shock of the attack would slow the enemy down. Phillips made his run parallel to the south wall, targeting the enemy just outside the compound. Both rockets missed the intended mark, but now there was an incredible piece of luck! The second rocket, which had sailed over the compound entirely, found a sampan in the canal on its own. The little boat just happened to be Charlie's ammunition barge, and the result of the hit was like a volcanic eruption.

The explosive impact met Phillips's aircraft head on as it made a low turn over the canal. The pilot's involuntary reaction was to jerk the controls. At fifty feet, flying at an excessive rate of speed, and in a 40-degree bank, the old Huey had a reaction of its own. Its overstressed hydraulics system locked up.

The controls would not move. Phillips shouted to Hanvey to cycle the hydraulics to release the lock. Hanvey was busy at his copilot's job, namely, firing the mini-gun. Between its distinctive, low-throated roar and the noise from the chattering door guns, he could not hear the pilot's frantic call for help. The other two gunships followed behind, increasing the noise level by their added firepower.

Phillips now forced himself to let go of the collective control lever. With his hand momentarily free, he reached over and flipped the switch that cycled the hydraulic system. It kicked back in immediately, and Phillips regained control of the aircraft. That was a squeaker. The crew had no idea there had been a problem until he told them much later.

The air assault had come not a second too soon for the friendlies on the ground. A number of the North Vietnamese were now retreating over the south wall, but plenty of them were still inside the walls. The voice on the radio told the Seawolves that anyone they saw in the compound was fair game, and the three aircraft poured it on. In the light from the fires, the gunship crews could see bodies lying all over the compound.

Incredibly, the whole engagement had taken barely ten minutes, but to the Seawolf crews it had seemed like an hour. Both gunships were almost completely out of ammunition, although each had a few rockets left. Madden now informed the American sergeant that they were going to Moc Hoa to rearm.

As the gunships headed away from the compound, they received another call from the American. The enemy had seen the two aircraft depart and was coming back again over the demolished south wall. The fire team turned around and attacked them with its last rockets. The North Vietnamese pulled back again, but not very far.

Once more, as the three aircraft attempted to depart, the enemy attacked. The assault had already been very costly, and Charlie must have wanted this outpost in the worst way. He probably suspected that the defenders had suffered significant losses and that he was within a hair's breadth of capturing the compound. The gunships still had enough fuel to remain on station, but no ammunition. Somehow, they had to make Charlie believe they could still deal him a substantial blow.

The three aircraft turned around again and swept low over the attackers. The door gunners now resorted to rifles, pistols, and grenade launchers. Even the .45 Phillips carried and Madden's 9-mm side arms were brought to bear in an attempt to convince the enemy that the gunships still had teeth.

"It was a pitiful display of firepower," remembers Tom Phillips. "My left gunner contented himself with dropping smoke grenades as fast as he could pull the pins. To our amazement, the voice [on the ground] reported that the attack had stopped and they were falling back across the wire."[5] The bluff worked!

Phillips later speculated that Charlie might have thought the smoke grenades were marking targets for another incoming fire team and didn't want to be caught in the compound when the fully armed gunships arrived. In any case, Madden, Phillips, and company now departed the area with a low fuel state and virtually nothing left in the way of ordnance with which to fight.

At Moc Hoa the aircraft were quickly refueled and rearmed as the crews quaffed Cokes and wolfed down sandwiches that had been prepared for them. The crew of Madden's bird passed up the sandwiches to deal with a new, and potentially hazardous, problem. The Huey had experienced serious vibrations upon landing, and the fire team leader now commandeered a jeep, climbed on top, and inspected the rotor. He found a hole in one blade about two feet from the tip. It was, remembers Phillips, "about the size of a large softball."[6] What's more, the stainless steel trailing edge of the rotor blade had also been damaged, so that the metal was torn and ragged. Not good! Madden was now dealing with rotor imbalance, a very serious problem in a helicopter. That kind of damage required mandatory downing of the aircraft.

Up on the jeep, Madden used a pair of tin snips to trim the rough trailing edge. Then he pounded it with the butt of his 9-mm automatic to flatten it and wrapped it with some ordnance tape that covered the hole as well. Jumping back in the cockpit, he started the engine, lifted off, and put the helicopter into a hover. He landed a minute or so later. Still vibrating! He repeated his fix on the rotor blade, this time more carefully. "That's better, not so bad."[7]

Everyone knew that the temporary fix might get the helicopter back in the air, but further violent maneuvering could cause the rotor to shatter or break off a couple of feet from the tip. If that happened, it would be all over for the crew.

Any helicopter pilot will tell you that damage like that to a rotor blade is never acceptable. Well, almost never! Phillips thought Madden should sit out the impending return to Hoa Binh. He and his crew would return with the other Det. 5 gunship. Madden replied that, as near as he could tell, the spar had not been damaged, and he was convinced his fix would hold. Phillips was not so sure.

Madden's concern now was the Americans and other friendlies in the compound with no air cover. Maybe it was already too late. Charlie had made it clear by his suicidal attacks that he was determined to take the compound whatever the cost. Madden was the senior officer present, and he had made his decision. He declared the aircraft up and ready. To his crew he said, "This is a volunteer flight. If anyone doesn't want to go, no one will hold it against him."[8]

Without further discussion, the copilot and two door gunners climbed on board, followed by the flight team leader. Madden elected to leave his Vietnamese interpreter behind, partly because of weight considerations, but partly because he felt it unnecessary to risk any more lives than he had to. All three birds started their engines and took off. It was time to get back to Hoa Binh.

Meanwhile, the enemy had evidently decided that the gunships were not coming back, but they had waited a bit to make sure. Now, as the Hueys arrived on the scene, they found several of the NVA inside the compound again. The friendlies were somehow holding out up in the northern corner. The buildings were still burning, although not as brightly as before, and the bad guys could be clearly seen. This time, the initial air attack was a gun run. They fired first at the enemy on the walls and then at those left inside the compound. That accomplished, the gunships then made a rocket run against the retreating NVA outside the compound.

Several wounded friendlies inside the walls had to be evacuated. But a landing helicopter silhouetted by the fire would be a perfect target for the enemy still out there in the darkness. Madden elected to make the pickup himself. Before he could do so, however, his Det. 5 wingman challenged his decision. He was concerned that Madden's damaged rotor might shatter from the stress of the takeoff, particularly with the added weight of the additional people. It was a good point, and he insisted that he be allowed to make the pickup. Phillips now injected himself into the discussion, declaring that he was in the best position to do the job. The problem was immediately resolved by the arrival of an army Dust-off helicopter that had been listening to the radio exchange as it approached.

"Seawolf, this is Drama 01. You're not horning in on my turf, are you? Why don't you *all* cover me? I'm the Dust-off; you're the gunships."[9]

Lew Madden broke in, "Sounds like a plan, 01: we do guns; you do medevac . . . Turn on my call . . . break . . . 52, lead him in; 98, follow him; I'll cover high."[10]

It was a good plan, executed as ordered, but even good plans often go awry. Drama 01 landed in the compound in a small open space between two burning hootches. The evacuation went quickly, and the Dust-off aircraft lifted off as soon as the last man was aboard.

At that precise moment, a mortar round landed just forward of the aircraft. There was a huge explosion, so powerful that it seemed to throw the army helicopter into the air. Madden remembers a huge cloud of fire and smoke.[11] He also thinks the pilot must have pulled back sharply on the controls. In any case, Tom Phillips recalls, "Out he popped from the compound like a champagne cork, and came fluttering down outside the walls, and in the minefield."[12] Fortunately, he landed right side up, and no one was hurt. Everyone inside was able to exit the aircraft and make it through the minefield and across the wall without setting off any mines. The Seawolves provided covering fire.

A Vietnamese Air Force AC-47 gunship now arrived on the scene and immediately began hosing down the whole area surrounding the compound. "It was a scary thing," recalls Madden. "Because of the language barrier, we kept getting in each other's way. I was sorry I had off-loaded my Vietnamese interpreter, because the Vietnamese gunship pilot and I were not able to communicate."[13]

The AC-47 pilot now banked sharply to enable his gunners to blanket the target area with fire. From his close-up vantage point, Phillips remembers a scene made vivid by the tracers: "It was like a stream of red that merges into a continuous flow . . . Surreal . . . Nightmarish."[14] Madden describes it as "a river of fire."[15] When the AC-47 was finished, it was pretty certain that nothing was left alive in the area immediately outside the compound.

After a quick trip to Moc Hoa to refuel and rearm, the fire team returned to cover the landing of an ARVN airmobile group that inserted fresh troops into the compound to relieve the surviving defenders. The Seawolves then returned to Moc Hoa one last time to refuel before calling it a night.

Lew Madden and his two birds returned to Chau Doc, while Tom Phillips sat his gunship down safely on the YRB-21. All three aircraft had been repeatedly hit during the operation. Madden's bird with the damaged rotor blade was deemed not safe for flight back to Binh Thuy, and the other Det. 5 aircraft was so badly holed that both were hooked out by heavy lift helicopters.

Hoa Binh was rebuilt and remained a thorn in the enemy's side.

24

Fun at the Beach

"HEY, WOW, MAN, GOT SOME BAD NEWS FOR YA. WE GOD DAMN GOT our ass kicked by Charlie. Mr. Hanvey, Mr. Cleverton [sic] Shin, & Elliott (newbie) are all in 3rd Surge B/T & they medevaced Sol back to the world."[1] So wrote AO2 Nelson "Buzz" Landy to his friend ADJ2 Anthony J. Guptaitis Jr., who had recently left Vietnam after his door-gunner tour with the Seawolves.

In early July 1971, Det. 9 had moved from the YRBM-21 to the *West-chester County* (LST-1167), located just off the mouth of the Bassac River. Later that month, the detachment transferred again and began operating from the *Windham County* (LST 1170), anchored at the same location. The detachment's operating area was the nearby coastal terrain that Lt. Cdr. Charles R. "Charlie" Hall, Det. 9's officer in charge, described as "the boon-docks of Vietnam. In fact," he says, with tongue in cheek, "it was so remote that the people living there thought they were still fighting the Japanese."[2]

Actually, the only people living there were the bad guys, and they knew very well whom they were fighting. Much of the area had been designated a free-fire zone, an area from which noncombatants had been cleared. North Vietnamese regulars and Viet Cong guerrillas, however, operated there on a continuing basis. It was bona fide bad guy land, and except for the LST, there were no active friendly outposts in the immediate vicinity.

On August 28, Det. 9 launched a daylight patrol that was really more of a training flight. The fire team leader, Lt. Gilbert A. Evans, was newly qualified; this was his first flight in that capacity. Lieutenant Hanvey, who had some serious combat under his belt, was AHAC in the trail bird. Charlie Hall recalls that Evans was told to put in a strike at a location near the beach that they knew the enemy used, although it was not certain that anyone was actually there on this day. In any case, it was a good chance to get in some target practice and to break in a couple of new gunners. To this end, each aircraft carried a trainee in addition to the two regular door gunners, for a total of five crew members.

The day was sunny and clear, the kind during which the enemy holed up under some triple canopy to rest and prepare for some nocturnal mischief. Consequently, except for the whap, whap, whap of the rotor blades, the jungle was eerily quiet. There was no movement below. Even the vegetation seemed to be in repose.

The two Hueys put in the required strike and found no sign of the enemy. Then they scoured the surrounding area, with similar results. The gunners contented themselves with creating targets out of inanimate objects and shredding them. It was good training. There was no return fire, and none was expected. If the enemy was down there, he was not stupid and was certainly not about to reveal his presence to a pair Seawolf gunships in broad daylight.

The two aircraft each carried a typical fuel load for shipboard operations that allowed them to remain airborne for precisely eighty minutes. But time flies when you're having fun, and all too soon it was time to return to the ship. As they headed toward their floating home, however, they discovered a large black squall squatting menacingly over the ocean between them and the ship. A prudent helicopter pilot did not fly directly into a squall if he could help it. The official squadron history records that this one was laced with "violent and numerous thunderstorms."[3]

One option was to divert to a base or fueling outpost ashore for a drink. Unfortunately, there was nothing close by, but the Hueys had enough fuel to fly to one of the bases upriver, provided they did not wait too long to commit. It was, perhaps, the most prudent choice, but it would leave the operating area uncovered for a short period. It seemed like a waste of time.

Another option was to try to sneak under the squall to get to the ship. Seawolves did things like that as a matter of routine, and it was no big deal. Evans chose the third option, which was an attempt to circumnavigate the squall to get to the ship. He could see that the weather was fine on either side of the black clouds. The ship was bound to be in the clear on the other side.

As it turned out, however, the squall covered a much more extensive area than it was thought, and it took more time and precious fuel to circle to the outer limit than had been anticipated. Sure enough, it was clear there, but there was no ship. Bad news! Evans now led the two Hueys around the other side. Still nothing. Damn! It must be sitting under the squall. Okay, they would have to slip under the weather and find it. Again, no big deal.

Hanvey, flying in the trail bird, was not so sure. The rain was very heavy, and the ceiling was low. None of the LSTs had anything in the way of sophisticated navigation aids. The last thing Hanvey wanted to do was run out of fuel tooling around under the squall. Of course, the beach was within reach if they had to make an emergency landing, but that would put them down in hostile territory, not an especially pleasant thought. Even though they had found no sign of the enemy during their patrol, everyone knew that Charlie was not far away. Hanvey recommended they head for the nearest friendly outpost while they had just enough fuel to make it. Evans still believed he could find the ship.

The two aircraft descended and headed into the squall, flying underneath it just above the surface of the ocean. Visibility was so lousy that they passed the ship without seeing it. They tried again, with the same result. Evans was talking to the ship, but the people aboard could do very little to help. The helos' fuel state was now critical, and it would take much too long for the LST to weigh anchor and steam out from under the squall.

The Hueys headed for land, but they now lacked sufficient fuel to reach a friendly outpost. Barry Solomon, the right door gunner on Hanvey's aircraft, remembers a very uncomfortable feeling. "By this time," he says, "we were low on fuel, and I mean *really* low."[4]

The two Det. 9 Hueys would have to land ashore, and they would need some cover. Hall alerted the world to the fast developing problem. Det. 7 at Dong Tam was first to take action. Unfortunately, however, that detachment was not all that close; it would take a good twenty minutes or more for personnel to make it to the area. To make matters worse, one of the Det. 7 aircraft had suffered battle damage and was down for repair.

Barry Solomon sits in front of a gunship that was heavily damaged during a night attack on the YRBM-21. *Barry Solomon*

Single Hueys, of course, were not permitted to operate alone except in emergency circumstances. Fellow Seawolves were in trouble, and as far as Det. 7 pilot Lt. (jg) Howard M. "Mike" Reid was concerned, this was clearly one of those times. He, copilot Robert A. "Bob" Young, and their two gunners launched immediately. Because the second Det. 7 gunship was down, Lt. (jg) John M. "Mike" Masica and his crew were left out of the scramble.

Seawolves, however, were very resourceful people. If he couldn't be part of the action, perhaps he could be on hand to witness it. Masica buttonholed the pilot of an army O-1 Bird Dog light observation aircraft that had just arrived from Vinh Long and cajoled him into taking him to the scene. The army pilot didn't need much coaxing. Things at the beach were about to get very interesting.

Meanwhile, Evans, Hanvey, and company broke out of the weather and approached the shoreline. Several miles inland was a tiny air facility at Long Toan, but it was abandoned and, for some reason, listed on the chart as unusable. No fuel there. More to the point, it was also in an ideal location for an enemy ambush and not any place the Seawolves wanted to put down, even if they could make it that far.

The two Hueys were now running on fumes and would have to land within minutes or risk flameouts. Before reaching shore they spotted a sandbar a half-mile or so out that looked inviting. It was plenty large enough for both aircraft, but Evans decided not to land there because the tide was out. If they became stranded before someone could get to them with fuel, the Hueys would be engulfed at high water. Instead, they headed for the beach.

Evans landed on the sand near a little inlet, very close to where they had put in a strike a short time before. Hanvey put his aircraft down close by, with the right door facing inland so that the .50-caliber gun could be brought to bear in case of attack. It was a wise move. Both aircraft were shut down, and Hanvey told right door gunner Solomon to remain on board, with his gun at the ready. Except for Solomon, both crews exited the aircraft and took defensive positions on the sloping sand beach. They were armed with M-60s, M-14s, M-16s, and side arms and were somewhat protected by the slope of the beach.

Opposition was not long in coming. It started with a few shots from the tree line across the inlet that quickly became many, as more of the enemy arrived. Where in hell had they all come from? The gunships had just scoured that area and encountered nary a soul.

The hunters were now the hunted. And what a prize! Two intact Seawolf helicopter gunships and their crews had fallen into the enemy's lap. Charlie must have been elated at his good fortune and was certainly going to make the most of it.

Automatic weapons fire now became heavy, and it was evident that the defensive position they had chosen on the beach was not, in fact, very defensible. Soon fire was coming from both flanks, as well as from the tree line across the inlet. The aircraft themselves were nice fat targets. Solomon recalls: "Bullets were flying all around and hitting the helicopters. I sprayed the bank with the .50."[5] That action seemed to have a momentary effect, but it was just that—momentary. The situation deteriorated further, as mortar fire began from the tree line.

The enemy mortar crews seemed to be having a difficult time zeroing in, probably because they could not see the aircraft from their position because of the slope of the beach. Nevertheless, a lucky shot could disable or destroy one or both of the helicopters. If that happened, there would be no way for the Seawolf crews to escape.

As the fire became intense, the enemy began to advance toward the men hunkered down on the sand. Evans ordered everyone back to the Hueys; they all made a run for it, the enemy close behind. Buzz Landy remembers them screaming and "shooting at us like you wouldn't believe."[6] Incredibly, everyone reached the aircraft, the gunners standing outside and covering them with their M-60s until everyone scrambled aboard. Solomon recalls that Evans got a hot start and had to do it over again, but Hanvey started clean and was first off.[7] No one strapped in or bothered with helmets. There was no time. They made it off the beach by the skin of their teeth but didn't get very far.

Hanvey's bird could not have been much more than a hundred yards off the beach and twenty or thirty feet in the air when it was hit by enemy fire. Whatever it was that scored the hit disabled the controls, and at that altitude the crash was instantaneous. Both pilots were thrown through the windscreen. The three gunners were also thrown clear, probably out the doors. All five men came to the surface in what Steve Hanvey estimates was ten or twelve feet of water.[8]

Evans's aircraft, meanwhile, made it to the sandbar that they had passed on the way to the beach and landed safely with all its crew. They did not have enough fuel to do much other than to watch the drama taking place in the water.

Hanvey was badly cut up, bruised and bleeding from his encounter with the windscreen, but otherwise, he seemed intact. Looking around to make sure the rest of his crew had made it out, he counted three heads near by, swimming toward the sandbar, which was a good distance away. "Where's the fourth one?" he asked himself.

Then he saw him. AMS2 Thomas E. "Tom" Elliott was making his way with great difficulty, but in the opposite direction, toward the beach and the waiting VC. My God, thought Hanvey. What's the matter with him? He must be dazed.

There was just one thing to do. Hanvey, a former lifeguard and a superb swimmer, took off after Elliott, who seemed to be struggling as he made for the beach, his head disappearing below the surface from time to time. He must be hurt, Hanvey thought. The VC were firing at them both now, but it was no easy matter to hit small bobbing heads from a distance that was about the length of a football field.

Hanvey overtook the gunner about seventy-five yards or so from the beach. Elliott was still neck deep in water, but he could now just touch bottom and had begun to wade ashore when Hanvey caught up and grabbed him. "What in hell are you doing?" the pilot shouted at him. Elliott looked back and said, simply, "I can't swim."[9]

Hanvey was dumbfounded. Everyone in the navy knew how to swim. Anyone who didn't was taught, either during officer training or boot camp. It was a hard-and-fast requirement. How did Elliott ever get away with it? Charlie Hall would later speculate: "He must have bought his [qualification] with a bottle of scotch."[10] No matter; there was no time to deliberate over it.

"Okay," said Hanvey, the lifeguard. "I'm going to drag you out to the sandbar, but if you try to pull me under I'm going to let you go, understand?"[11] Elliott nodded that he did. Hanvey grasped him in a traditional chest hold and, keeping his mouth and nose above water as best he could, swam slowly away from the beach, bullets plinking in the water around them. Why the Viet Cong missed the chance to go in after them while they were so close to shore will never be known.

It was slow going, but eventually Hanvey and Elliott caught up with the other swimmers. The sandbar seemed a long way off, and there was some question whether they could all make it. There were, however, no really appealing options. The enemy on the beach continued shooting, but whether the angle of fire was too low, the distance was too great, or the NVA/VC were just lousy shots, no bullets met their intended targets.

Out on the sandbar, Evans and his crew were safe for the moment, but there was not enough fuel left for an attempt to rescue Hanvey and his crew. Such a move would certainly have resulted in everyone taking a swim. Their only option was to sit tight. Back aboard the ship, things were moving with all deliberate speed. Jet fuel had already been pumped into drums and was being loaded into a boat even as the LST approached the coast. Time was of the essence. In a few hours, the incoming tide would decide the fate of the stranded gunship, and two crews would find themselves swimming—with no place to go.

While all of this was happening, Mike Reid, copilot Bob Young, and the crew aboard the Det. 7 gunship had been hightailing it for the site of the action. They now arrived on the scene and circled low to find Steve Hanvey and crew in the water, making their way slowly, and with some difficulty, toward the distant sandbar. Reid's gunship was too heavy at this point to make an immediate rescue attempt. He would have to get rid of some of the weight.

The enemy, meanwhile, was belatedly launching a few small sampan-type boats, presumably to go after the Americans in the water. With the arrival of Reid's gunship, they apparently thought better of it and were now retreating up the beach toward the tree line and cover. Turning sharply and making a steep descent, Reid headed in toward shore, firing both rockets and guns at the hastily retiring enemy. Charlie had waited too long. Reid fired all fourteen rockets on that one pass, relieving the aircraft of a significant amount of weight and stopping some of the runners in the process. His door gunners picked off a few more as the gunship streaked by. Now it was time to rescue the waterlogged crew.

In the meantime, Mike Masica had arrived in the army O-1 aircraft and was now circling overhead with a bird's-eye view of the action. "Reid's gunners were throwing out ammunition and tool boxes, anything that wasn't bolted down. Even so, the weight of nine men in that underpowered UH-1B was going to be cutting it very close."[12]

Arriving over the swimmers, Reid settled into a hover and slowly lowered his skids into the water. He had wisely maneuvered the aircraft so the men were obliged to climb aboard on the right side, where he could see them. On the beach Charlie suddenly realized that there was only one gunship instead of the customary two. It could not rescue the people in the water and take the enemy under fire at the same time. The NVA/VC soldiers regrouped and began firing at the hovering Huey, scoring several hits on the tail boom. The

Captain Borgstrom sits in the cockpit of a Sealords aircraft. *Charles O. Borgstrom*

left door gunner returned the fire, even as the men in the water were pulled aboard.

The weight and balance now began to change drastically, and the right door gunner rudely slammed Lieutenant Hanvey's crew up against the rear bulkhead as they entered the aircraft to prevent the center of gravity from moving too far forward. Reid now struggled to hold the hover until the last man was aboard. He did so with considerable difficulty, and he could not

Mike Reid was awarded a Distinguished Flying Cross, his second in just a little over a month. *Mike Reid*

keep the Huey from slowly settling. Hanvey was the last one to board, and water was now lapping at the belly of the Huey.

With the engine straining, Reid, uttering a bit of prayer, carefully began transitioning to forward flight. He could feel the overloaded Huey protest and threaten to settle further. Slowly, however, it began to come up and move toward the sandbar. It was heavy and sluggish with the weight of the extra five men. Reid also wondered how much water he had scooped up. For some long minutes he held his breath as the gunship strained and clawed for a few feet of altitude.

Finally, the Huey broke free. They were too heavy to go very far, however, and Reid set the overloaded gunship down on the sandbar with a sigh of relief. To those who were there, not the least of whom were those who had been rescued, it was a grand exhibition of helicopter airmanship. Masica had watched it all from the catbird's seat aboard the army Bird Dog. "That was some of the finest flying I've ever seen."[13]

Having been alerted—like everyone else—by the LST, Captain Borgstrom had also launched in a Sealords slick from Binh Thuy. He now arrived and landed on the sandbar to evaluate the situation firsthand. Every one of Hanvey's crew had been injured to some extent in the crash. Barry Solomon had also been shot in the left ankle and was the most seriously injured.

Their big chance having dissolved before their eyes, a frustrated enemy disappeared into the jungle. Having assured himself that a boat from the LST was on its way with fuel for Evans's Huey, Charlie Borgstrom loaded Hanvey and company aboard the slick and took off. With no rocket pods, flex M-60s, or mini-guns, the lighter and more powerful Sealord slick soon had the five injured and exhausted crewmen ensconced at the Third Surgical Hospital in Binh Thuy.

The boat soon arrived at the sandbar, and after taking on fuel, the surviving Det. 9 gunship returned to the ship. Although it had some combat damage, it seemed to be functioning normally. Reid now joined his single Det. 7 gunship with the single Det. 9 aircraft aboard the LST to make up a combined ready fire team. The two aircraft, each sporting a number of brand-new bullet holes, answered calls for assistance that night. It was business as usual. Other detachments shifted to fill in the Det. 7 operating area as necessary.

Steve Hanvey and crew all received Purple Hearts for their various injuries. Hanvey received a Silver Star for his selfless and courageous rescue of door gunner Tom Elliott. Mike Reid was also recommended for a Silver Star, but was awarded a Distinguished Flying Cross instead, his second in just a little over a month.[14]

25

Turning Out the Lights

BY MID-1971, THE MEKONG DELTA WAS GETTING TO BE A LONELY place for Americans. U.S. Navy crews, who had developed the brown-water idea into a highly efficient combat concept, had divested themselves of their riverine craft and equipment and gone home. Even Solid Anchor, which had been reclaimed from marshland along the Cua Lon River and built into an important naval facility on the Ca Mau Peninsula, had been turned over to the VNN in April. The South Vietnamese now had exclusive responsibility for all combat operations in the Delta, with the notable exception of those conducted by the Seawolves and Black Ponies.

The SEALs were still very much in evidence in the Delta, but even some of their operations were now being conducted with Vietnamese SEAL units, who would soon be going it alone. For the two navy squadrons as well, the handwriting was on the wall. Like their surface counterparts, they would soon be leaving, but they would not turn over their aircraft and equipment to the Vietnamese. Both squadrons would remain intact until they were disbanded. Meanwhile, they continued to provide close air and rapid-reaction support to ARVN and VNN forces as needed.

Vietnamization in the Delta had become a reality, but some military observers were less than optimistic about the long-term ability of South Vietnamese forces to hold their own against the north. Many South Vietnamese had their doubts as well. While the VNN was performing the riverine task reasonably well, other signs were less encouraging. HA(L)-3 XO Cdr. William J. Mulcahy remembers visiting Solid Anchor with COMNAVFORV Rear Adm. Robert S. Salzer later in 1971. The two officers were appalled to find that the facility, which only months before had been turned over to the VNN in perfect condition, had been stripped of everything that could be sold, including washbasins and associated copper piping.[1]

They were mainly concerned, however, about close air support for Vietnamese riverine operations and for ARVN/Ruff Puff forces throughout the Delta. The VNN had no air arm of its own, and a belated and undersized effort to bring the VNAF up to speed was, in itself, a cause for pessimism.

South Vietnamese personnel had flown with the Seawolves in the past as observers and translators, but it was not until July 1971 that any degree of serious training of VNAF pilots and gunners began. Ten Vietnamese pilots and ten gunners reported to Seawolf headquarters, Binh Thuy, on the first of that month. The pilots, who had been trained at Fort Rucker, were well qualified to fly the UH-1B, and several won praise from the Seawolves for their airmanship. The purpose of the program, however, was to familiarize them with the rapid-reaction concept and support of brown-water forces. The idea was that, upon completion of their training, they would return to their own service and form the initial cadre of VNAF personnel skilled in support of river operations.

The Vietnamese attended ground school, made a few familiarization flights at Binh Thuy, and by July 19 moved out to the detachments for on-the-job-training. Two pilots and two gunners were assigned to Nha Be, while a team of one pilot and one gunner was sent to each of the other detachments, where they were integrated into the daily operations schedule. By September 13, all but one pilot and one gunner had successfully completed the course, accumulating about seventy-five flight hours in the process.

A second group of pilots and gunners reported on September 20, and after a short familiarization period at Binh Thuy, their names began to appear on the daily flight schedules out in the detachments. Several of these remained on duty with the Seawolves into 1972 and became very proficient in providing rapid-reaction, close air support.

Capt. Charlie Borgstrom and others hoped that the VNAF would take over the functions of the Seawolves and Sealords and carry on in the proud tradition that the U.S. Navy had established. A paper Borgstrom coauthored with Cdr. Donald "Don" Nichols at the end of the year reflected this hope. "Through the Seawolves Vietnamese Indoctrination and Familiarization program," it stated, "a firm foundation has been laid for the outstanding record of HA(L)-3 to be continued by the Vietnamese Air Force and it's most capable personnel." It also included recommendations for a scaled-down VNAF air support program at four key locations in the Delta, manned by the already trained Vietnamese crews.[2]

Neither Borgstrom nor Nichols was naive, however, and their recommendations stated only what should and could be done. They expressed more hope than conviction.

Meanwhile, life went on for the remaining American Seawolves as they continued to support Vietnamese ground and river forces. Det. 1 was still at Solid Anchor, covering the southernmost tip of the Ca Mau Peninsula. Because the squadron facilities there were largely self-contained and independent, day-to-day Seawolf operations continued pretty much as before, even though the base itself was now run by the VNN.

Det. 2, with a three-helo heavy-fire team, still flew out of Nha Be, guarding the Long Tau shipping channel and convoying high value ships through that dangerous strip of water to and from Saigon. That detachment also continued to make life miserable for the NVA and the VC that were still slogging it out in the mangrove swamps of the Rung Sat Special Zone. Indeed, intelligence information gleaned from prisoner interrogations in late July confirmed enemy fear of "the helos that strike at night."[3] The enemy was so fearful that they had taken to moving their campsites every night in a not-altogether successful effort to confound the aggressive searches and attacks by Det. 2 gunships.

Det. 3 was still at Ca Mau, working from the long strip located northeast of town. This detachment continued to cover part of the infamous U Minh Forest and frequently operated in cooperation with Det. 1 throughout the southernmost part of the peninsula.

Det. 4 was now based at Ben Luc, supporting VNN PBRs and other assorted river units. Its efforts were concentrated on Operation Giant Slingshot, now known as Tran Hung Dao II. An important part of Det. 4's mission was to interdict North Vietnamese regulars who were now crossing into South Vietnam via the Parrot's Beak. Dufflebag unit seismic sensors, seeded along known infiltration routes, generated many of the detachment's contacts there.

Det. 5 remained at Chau Doc. Its area had been greatly increased in size when it took on Det. 9's duties in early July as the latter was moved south to

No letup for Charlie. A Det. 2 gunship makes a low pass over a defoliated area of the Rung Sat Special Zone. *U.S. Naval Institute Photo Archive*

work from an LST off the mouth of the Bassac River. Det. 5 was now conducting interdiction operations all along the barrier south of the Cambodian border, from the Gulf of Thailand east into the Plain of Reeds, at which point Det. 4 took over.

Det. 6, which had been operating from an LST in the Gulf of Thailand off the mouth of the Ong Doc River, had moved on May 15 from the *Garrett County* to the Phu Loi army airfield just north of Saigon. From there it operated with Vietnamese naval units along the waterways, targeting enemy logistics efforts, infiltrators, and resurgent Viet Cong tax collectors. Fortunately, this detachment was also well positioned to assist friendly forces when the enemy launched concentrated attacks around Tay Ninh in October.

Det. 7 continued to operate from the Dong Tam army base, spending much of its time responding to calls from Ruff Puff units holding tiny fortress outposts and from ARVN forces making sweeps of areas where the enemy was reported to be stirring. One could not help but wonder what was going to

Captain Borgstrom addresses pilots and gunners of Det. 5 at Chau Doc in September 1971. *Charles O. Borgstrom*

happen in the not-too-distant future when a frantic call for rapid-reaction air support would be met with nothing but silence.

Det. 8, which had moved ashore from one of the LSTs in February, was now operating from Rach Gia in support of Operation Search Turn, which had been turned over to the Vietnamese at the end of 1970 and now had a Vietnamese name of its own.

Since July, Det. 9 had operated first from the *Westchester County* and then from the *Windham County* off the mouth of the Mekong River, covering a remote region along the southeast coast and for some distance inland. This detachment was equipped with UH-1M Hueys, which had larger rotors and more powerful engines that made shipboard operations from a rolling LST somewhat safer. These were a gunship version of the UH-1L. In October, Det. 9 moved to Binh Thuy to become an all-purpose detachment, adding its considerable muscle to this central area and making its presence felt wherever needed.

These were, for all intents and purposes, the final locations of the detachments prior to squadron disestablishment.[4]

Combat operations in the Delta in 1971 involved a variety of missions, some of which have been described in previous chapters. Lt. Cdr. Charlie Hall, the officer in charge of Det. 9, drummed up some of his own. While operating from the LSTs off the southeast coast, he had made it a point to pay visits to ARVN/Ruff Puff outposts throughout his area to establish working relationships. The South Vietnamese were more than glad to have the Seawolves nearby, and communications with these forces turned up some good targets.

On one especially good day, Det. 9 destroyed as many as sixty-five enemy sampans hidden along the river banks.[5] In early August, the detachment, then flying from the *Windham County*, also did battle with a large junk just off the coast in the South China Sea. A PCF swift boat arrived on the scene and took the damaged enemy vessel, along with members of her crew, into custody.

A number of successful SEAL/Seawolf operations were conducted throughout the Delta. Their purpose was to gather intelligence, capture enemy personnel for interrogation, disrupt enemy operations, and destroy enemy camps and equipment in the process. Bill Mulcahy remembers one mission in particular in 1971 that made his pucker factor surge. The objective was an NVA/VC camp, complete with a crude medical facility and an ammunition dump, located on an island in the Mekong River not far from Dong Tam. It involved a daylight SEAL insertion by two Sealords Hueys staging from Dong Tam and covered by Det. 7 gunships. The mission involved a descent into an excruciatingly tiny LZ that had room for just one slick at a time. Mulcahy was flying one of the Sealords aircraft; as he recalls, there was no margin for error.

> We were heavy going into that small clearing surrounded by trees and a huge stone Buddha. The clearance was minimal, and it had my whole-hearted attention. The Huey was really loaded down with people, and it was an almost vertical approach. As we neared the ground, I got a low RPM light and a horn, and I knew it was going to be a hard landing or worse. There was nothing much I could do about it.
>
> The SEAL team commander was very sharp. He realized immediately what was happening and told his men to jump. They all did from about twenty-five feet in the air. That lightened the Huey significantly and gave me back control. Unfortunately, the SEAL team radioman,

who had a heavy PRC-25 radio strapped to his back, broke his leg on landing. The good news was that he was otherwise unhurt and would be okay. Being relieved of all that weight probably kept us from crashing. Anyhow, the SEALs waved us off and disappeared into the jungle to do their thing, while we went back to Dong Tam to wait. Thirty minutes later came the call for extraction from the same tiny LZ.

We had burned off some fuel and were lighter this time, but I was still concerned about getting out of that confined space with all those guys aboard. It was going to be almost straight up, with no transitional lift.

The landing went okay this time, and the SEALs piled in. We were being shot at, of course, but that was to be expected. We made it off and were almost clear when suddenly there were loud sounds like we were taking hits. Actually, it was the rotor blades coming in contact with the treetops. Moments later, we broke clear and made it back to Dong Tam without further ado. You can say what you want about those old worn-out Hueys, but they were tough.[6]

All of the detachments engaged the enemy throughout the year, but during the last five months, the NVA/VC seemed to back off a bit with regard to the number and ferocity of offensive operations. It was almost like they had suddenly lost interest. If the tempo had slackened, it was certainly not because of any lessening of effort or commitment by Seawolf personnel. More likely it was the result of the South Vietnamese forces pacifying and taking control of much of the Delta. Over a six-year period, the enemy had suffered many severe setbacks. Now he had reason to hope that his fortunes were about to change for the better. It was no secret that the last of the Americans, including the hated Seawolves, were about to leave. All Charlie had to do now was wait.

On September 20, during a routine daylight patrol in Hau Nghia Province west of Saigon, a Seawolf gunship "disintegrated in mid-air."[7] Everyone on board was killed: the pilot, Lt. (jg) Arnold W. Barden Jr.; the copilot, Lt. Cdr. Lawrence L. Cover; and door gunners, ADJ-2 Charles H. Goldbin and AMS-1 Harold E. Cowen.[8] A rotor blade had broken off in flight, and the gunship was torn apart as it plummeted to earth. It was every helicopter pilot's worst nightmare, the kind of accident from which there is no reprieve.

That night, Capt. Charlie Borgstrom sat down to write the customary letters to the families of the four men. He took the loss personally. Bill Mulcahy would later say of his boss: "I loved the guy. He was a good human being who cared about his people. I can't praise him enough."[9]

Rotor blades do not break off in flight for no reason. Indeed, they are more sturdy than one would think, remaining intact despite severe combat damage or even encounters with treetops. In this case, "a careful inspection of the wreckage revealed what looked like intentional scoring or etching of the blade, probably with a hack saw, so that it would break after a few hundred hours. The area in question was covered by a cap so it was undetectable except by magnaflux."[10]

It was rumored that several army Hueys involved in fatal accidents had been found to have rotor blades that were similarly scored. All had reportedly come from the same factory in the United States at about the same time. HA(L)-3 personnel speculated that the crash of a Seawolf gunship that had taken place for no apparent cause in December 1970 was the result of the same kind of thing.[11]

Until his death many years later, Captain Borgstrom was convinced, as were others, that the scoring was an act of sabotage committed by an antiwar activist in the States.[12] Sadly, such acts during the duration of the Vietnam War were not unheard of. In this case, the investigation was not able to confirm sabotage, but for some Seawolves, the suspicion of betrayal lingered on.

In mid-November, a Det. 5 gunship flown by Lt. (jg) Gerald E. Campbell took several hits that disabled the aircraft and necessitated an autorotation into a marsh. An army UH-1D rescued all four crew members, and the Seawolf gunship was later hooked out by a heavy lift helicopter.

Seawolf and Sealords aircraft returned the favor later that same month, rescuing army helicopter crews on three different occasions. Lt. Gill Evans lifted out four crewmen from a CH-46 that had been downed by enemy fire on the twenty-fifth and flew them to the Army's Third Surgical Hospital. That same day, Lt. (jg) Timothy Sharp rescued a flight engineer from a downed CH-53 a few miles from Nha Be. Not to be outdone, Captain Borgstrom, flying a Sealords slick, rescued eight army personnel from a downed HH-1H some fifteen to twenty miles north of Dong Tam.[13]

At the end of 1971, the squadron had a total of thirty-five Hueys, twenty-nine of which were gunships spread over the Mekong Delta and six of which were Sealord slicks based at Binh Thuy.[14] Despite a decrease in enemy activity, the gunships had devastated enemy camps, destroyed hundreds of structures, and sunk more than a thousand small craft on the waterways. All told, the Seawolf Hueys flew more than twenty-five thousand hours, while the Sealords racked up well over nine thousand, for a grand total of almost thirty-five thousand flight hours. Except for the loss of five men, 1971 had been a pretty good year.[15] It was time to think about wrapping it all up and going home. From that point on, things moved rather swiftly.

Bill Mulcahy relieved Charlie Borgstrom as commanding officer of HA(L)-3 in a hangar ceremony on February 1, 1972. Combat operations began to cease as the detachments turned in their aircraft one or two at a time. Det. 9's officer in charge, Charlie Hall, had recently been promoted to commander and was now the squadron maintenance officer. He had the unenviable job of preparing the Hueys for shipment back to the United States.

Meanwhile, pilots, gunners, and support personnel left as fast as transportation could be arranged, and Mulcahy saw his new command shrink rapidly before his eyes. By the end of February, personnel numbers were down to fifty men.

Mulcahy and his executive officer, Commander Nichols, made the last flight of the Seawolves at Binh Thuy late that month. Those squadron members who were left, along with a few bystanders, went outside to watch the event and to participate in some small way. Men on each side of the runway released smokes as the Huey gunship approached. Mulcahy made a couple of mock rocket runs through the smoke before landing to the applause of the small audience.

On March 16, Helicopter Attack Squadron (Light) 3 was officially disestablished.[16] It all ended much as it had begun. There was no band, there were no speeches, and there was no ceremony. Most of the Seawolves had already departed, and there was no one to witness the event. In a manner of speaking, Bill Mulcahy simply turned out the lights, and HA(L)-3 passed into history.

Epilogue

Every two years, the Seawolves hold a reunion, a gathering of men who have been tested in combat and have not been found wanting. They come together to talk about an exceptional time in their lives, to renew old friendships, to relive old firefights, and to honor those of their number who gave the last full measure of devotion.

The gatherings are always large, because the Seawolves encompass groups of men who served at different times over more than a five-year period. Most of the gunship crews belonged to the small, isolated detachments scattered throughout the Mekong Delta and did not even know some of the other people who were in the squadron at the same time. But they all shared the same kind of unique experiences. Deadly combat brings with it a penetrating perspective: a sharper take on such things as fear, courage, loyalty, comradeship, and death. They know things that most men do not, and it binds them together in an intimate brotherhood.

Some stayed on in the U.S. Navy after the Vietnam War and served with distinction until retirement. At least two Seawolves attained flag rank. Most returned home, raised families, and had noteworthy civilian careers. Some passed on and are sorely missed at the biannual gatherings. To many, it is hard to believe that it all happened so long ago.

Capt. Robert Spencer (right), first commanding officer of HA(L)-3 poses with Capt. William J. Mulcahy (left), last commanding officer of the squadron, at a Seawolves reunion in Patriots Point, South Carolina, in November 2004. *Richard Knott*

Most Seawolves are still living, still striving, still turning in that 110 percent effort that characterized their contributions in Vietnam. Many are graying or balding, and more than a few have lost some of the spring in their step. Still, there is a hint of swagger in their walk and a lingering trace of panache in their manner that distinguishes them from others of their generation.

Their guns are silent now, but the sights and sounds of war in the Mekong Delta will remain with them always. They are still Seawolves. Those who know the story understand why that is something special!

In Memoriam

Not for fame or reward
Not for place or for rank
Not lured by ambition
Or goaded by necessity
But in simple obedience to duty
As they understood it
These men suffered all, sacrificed all
Dared all—and died.

Confederate Memorial at Arlington
National Cemetery

Seawolves and Sealords Killed in Action

Name	Rank/Rating	Death Date
John Leon Abrams	Lt.	July 13, 1968
Robert Joseph Arnold	AT1	September 15, 1969
Arnold Winfield Barden	Lt. (jg)	September 20, 1971
Lloyd Lane Bowles	AO1	June 1, 1970
Richard Lee Brown	AMH3	August 13, 1969
James Francis Burke Jr.	Ens.	August 1, 1967
Richard Howard Buzzell	Lt. (jg)	December 19, 1970
Gill Lester Carter	ADJAN	August 17, 1967
Hal Cushman Castle Jr.	Lt. (jg)	April 28, 1969
Roger Dale Childers	AOAN	September 13, 1966
Lloyd Alford Cone	AMS3	May 8, 1968
Lawrence Leroy Cover	Lt. Cdr.	September 20, 1971
Harold Edward Cowen	AMS1	September 29, 1971
Donald Fred Fee	ADJ2	July 21, 1967

Name	Rank/Rating	Death Date
Wilber Dale Frahm	AMS1	June 1, 1970
Thomas Edward Gilliam	Lt. (jg)	August 22, 1967
Charles Henry Goldbin	ADJ2	September 20, 1971
John Davis Gollahon	Lt. (jg)	June 30, 1968
Ollie James Gross	AO1	April 23, 1969
Joseph Felder Hart	Lt. (jg)	April 28, 1969
Larry Richard Johnson	AMS1	December 14,1969
Robert Dennison Johnson	Lt. Cdr.	September 1, 1967
Stephen Ayer Johnson	AT3	September 15, 1969
Christopher L. Maher	ATN2	January 16, 1975*
Howard Michael Meute	ADJ3	March 23, 1969
John Martin Mulcahy	Lt.	June 1, 1970
Earl Kenneth Norris	Lt. (jg)	January 31, 1969
Antonio Alivarez Ortiz	Lt. (jg)	December 19, 1970
Edward Louis Ott III	ADJ1	September 1, 1967
George Merritt Page	AN	June 12, 1969
Edward Wesley Pawlowski	Lt. (jg)	March 23, 1969
William A. Pederson	Lt. (jg)	September 15, 1970
Jose Pablo Ramos	ADJ3	September 15, 1970
Johnny Ratliff	AEC	December 19, 1970
John Richard Reardon	Lt. (jg)	April 28, 1969
Raymond Douglas Robinson	AMH3	July 13, 1968
James Henry Romanski	Lt. (jg)	July 13, 1968
George Henry J. Rush Jr.	ADJ2	August 27, 1967
Michael E. Schafernocker	AO3	April 28, 1969
Alfred H. Suhr	Lt. (jg)	March 26, 1969
James Arthur Wall	AO3	April 19, 1971
Walter Ray Winters	ATR2	October 3, 1970
Dennis Michael Wobbe	AMS3	July 13, 1968
Robert Earl Worth	ADJ2	December 19, 1970

*Christopher L. Maher received a serious head wound on March 15, 1968. He died of that wound on January 16, 1975.

Notes

Chapter 1 The Mekong Delta

1. Dick Stanger, interview, April 27, 2000.
2. Saigon is now known as Ho Chi Minh City.
3. William C. Westmoreland, *A Soldier Reports* (New York: Doubleday and Company, 1976), 185.

Chapter 2 An Enemy Called Charlie

1. Viet Minh was the short name for the Vietnamese *Doc Lap Dong Minh Hoi*, which translated means League for the Independence of Vietnam. It was created in 1941 and fought under Communist leadership against both the Japanese and the French.

2. Viet Cong was a derisive name for Vietnamese Communists. It refers to South Vietnamese guerrillas who united after the departure of the French to topple Ngo Dinh Diem and to reunite South Vietnam with the Communist north. The formal name was National Front for the Liberation of South Vietnam, an organization created in Tay Ninh Province on December 20, 1960.

3. Ngo Dinh Diem was prime minister and then the first president of the Republic of Vietnam from 1954–1963, when he was assassinated.

4. The French did have fixed-wing air assets, but they were not usually available to the boats. When they were, they often took too long to respond.

5. It has been estimated that, up until 1965, the Viet Cong received as much as 70 percent of their supplies and equipment by sea.

6. Phil H. Bucklew, "Report of Recommendations Pertaining to Infiltration into South Vietnam of Viet Cong Personnel, Supporting Materials, Weapons, and Ammunition" (Washington, D.C.: Operational Archives, Naval Historical Center, 15 February 1964).

7. The Swift Boat (PCF) was 50 feet in length, with an aluminum hull and two 475-horsepower diesel engines. It had a top speed of twenty-five knots and a draft of 4 feet, 10 inches. The Swift Boat carried twin-mounted .50-caliber machine guns atop the pilothouse and an 81-mm mortar mounted together with a .50-caliber machine gun aft.

8. For a moving account of river combat in the Mekong Delta, see Thomas J. Cutler's *Brown Water, Black Berets: Coastal and Riverine Warfare in Vietnam* (Annapolis: Naval Institute Press, 1988).

Chapter 3 The First Seawolves

1. The patrol boat river (PBR) was designed by the Hatteras Yacht Company of North Carolina, but the first production contract for 120 boats was awarded to United Boatbuilders of Bellingham, Washington.

2. So-called by American forces, this weapon was actually a Soviet 12.7-mm heavy machine gun, which the NVA/VC used as an antiaircraft gun against allied helicopters. It packed a substantial wallop and had an effective range of almost five thousand feet. For specialized missions, the PBRs were known to carry recoilless rifles and 60-mm mortars. Some had 20-mm canon mounted forward.

3. "Indian country" was a term used to describe a particularly hostile area controlled by the Viet Cong. Bill Fawcett, ed., *Hunters and Shooters: An Oral History of the U.S. Navy SEALs in Vietnam* (New York: Avon Books, Inc., 1995), 83.

4. The PBR-2s were 32 feet long, had 11-foot, 8-inch beams, and a twenty-two hundred pound increase in displacement. They were capable of speeds of up to twenty-eight knots.

5. The army unit was called Sea Wolves (two words), as opposed to Seawolves, the navy's one-word version.

6. Vung Tau, located in Phuoc Tuy Province on the South China Sea. During the French colonial period, it was called Cape Saint Jacques. Blessed with beautiful beaches and a pleasant atmosphere, it was used extensively as an "in-country" R & R retreat for American and other allied forces during the Vietnam War years.

7. Larry Gillespie, interview, May 1, 2000.

8. Ship's Deck Log, USS *Tortuga* (LSD-26) (College Park, Md.: Modern Military Records Section, National Archives II). Entries for 00–04, Saturday, July 9, 1966, and 20–24, Tuesday, July 12, 1966.

9. Usually, but not always, army slicks inserted and extracted SEALs by helicopter.

Chapter 4 Gunships for the Navy

1. PBR personnel began to arrive in February 1966; the first boats were delivered on March 21.

2. Recollections of Rear Adm. Norvell G. Ward, U.S. Naval Institute Oral History Collection, # 8-477, 78.

3. Frank Koch, interview, April 17, 1999.

4. Official Seawolf Web site (www.seawolf.org), "Mail Call," e-mail dated June 17, 1999, 13.

5. Frank Foster, interview, April 16, 1999.

6. Larry Gillespie, interview, May 1, 2000.

7. Ibid.

8. Foster interview.

9. Burton B. Witham Jr., interview, March 30, 1999. Captain Witham became Commander Task Force 116, with headquarters at Binh Thuy, on May 18, 1966.

10. LSDs were 457 feet long; the LSTs were only 328 feet in length.

11. See comments of Thurman L. Hicks, Seawolf Web site—www.seawolf.org/stories/hicks_story.asp.

12. Remarks of Rear Adm. Kevin F. Delaney at the Seawolf Reunion, May 28, 1994.

13. Daniel E. Kelly, *Seawolves: First Choice* (New York: Ballentine Publishing Group, 1998), 78.

14. www.seawolf.org, "Mail Call."

15. Michael Peters, interview, March 13, 1999.

16. Allen E. Weselesky, interview, April 4, 2000.

17. Frank Koch, interview, May 20, 1999. Information on this action is also taken from the *Lakeland* (Florida) *Ledger,* February 7, 1967: 1.

18. Burton B. Witham Jr., interview, April 14, 1999.

Chapter 5 In the Thick of It

1. Frank Koch to Dick Knott, correspondence dated June 23, 1999.

2. Frank Foster, interview, April 16, 1999.

3. Ibid.

4. Ibid.

5. The PRUs, or provisional reconnaissance units, were Vietnamese police units trained by the CIA. Their methods included assassination and torture, but they were very effective in dealing with the Viet Cong.

6. Foster interview.

7. Frank Foster, officer in charge, Det. 27, to commanding officer HC-1, correspondence dated August 5, 1999.

8. HC-1 officer in charge, Det. 27, to detachment liaison officer, Lt. Cdr. D. J. McCracken, correspondence dated November 24, 1966.

9. Officer in charge HC-1 Det. 27, Memo to commander Riverine Patrol Force (CTF 116) dated March 5, 1967.

10. Westmoreland, *A Soldier Reports,* 184.

11. Alfred J. Banford Jr., interview, March 12, 1999.

12. Ibid.

13. Michael J. Peters, interview, March 13, 1999.

14. Ibid.

Chapter 6 Navy Again

1. Commander U.S. Naval Forces Vietnam, Navy News Release 19F-68: 4-4-4. *See also* Cutler, *Brown Water, Black Berets,* 178; James D. Sprinkle, "Helatkron Three: The Seawolves," *Journal of the American Aviation Historical Society* (Winter, 1998): 294; and Seawolf Web site—Seawolf.org/history: 4.

2. Mobile Riverine Forces employed a number of other watercraft, such as command and communications boats (CCBs) and assault support patrol boats (ASPBs). SEALs typically used strike assault boats (STABs) or water-jet-propelled light SEAL support craft (LSSCs) for waterborne insertions and extractions.

3. Alfred J. Banford Jr., interview.

4. Michael J. Peters to Dick Knott, correspondence dated May 3, 1999.

5. Peters, correspondence.

Chapter 7 Ready or Not

1. Lee Levensen, interview, April 27, 1999.

2. Conrad J. Jaburg, *As It Was in the Beginning* (an undated, three-page description of how HA(L)-3 came into being), 2.

3. Jack Bolton, interview, March 12, 2000.

4. Indoctrination of navy Seawolf pilots was moved to the army training facility at Fort Rucker, Alabama, in September 1968. Enlisted crewmen underwent UH-1B maintenance and door gunner training there.

5. Jack Bolton, fax dated January 25, 2000.

Chapter 8 All in One Sock

1. Robert Spencer, interview, April 16, 1999.
2. Jaburg, *As It Was in the Beginning*, 3.
3. Spencer, interview.
4. Spencer, follow-up interview, September 9, 1999.
5. Spencer, from a speech at HA(L)-3 Seawolf KIA Memorial Dedication, Patriots Point, Charleston, South Carolina, November 6, 2004.
6. Spencer, interview, September 9, 1999.
7. Joseph N. Laseau, interview, March 8, 2001.
8. Ibid.
9. Ibid.
10. The Douglas AC-47 gunship was a World War II–era propeller-driven, reciprocating-engine aircraft. Originally adapted for military use from the passenger/cargo–carrying DC-3, it became a highly effective gunship during the Vietnam War. The AC-47 carried three side-firing mini-guns, each able to fire more than four thousand rounds per minute.
11. Matt Gache, interview, December 15, 1999.
12. Ibid.
13. Ibid.
14. Ibid.
15. Anthony Reynolds-Huntley to Dick Knott, e-mail dated March 29, 2003.
16. Huntley e-mail.
17. Combat Air Crew Wings awarded to enlisted air crewmen in World War II and the Korean War were not officially awarded during the Vietnam conflict. Some HA(L)-3 commanding officers sanctioned the practice of awarding them unofficially to qualified enlisted air crewmen. In recent years, the navy has corrected its oversight by approving the award retroactively to all qualified Seawolf door gunners and certain other enlisted crewmen of the Vietnam conflict.

Chapter 9 Up Close and Personal

1. Conrad Jaburg and Dick Knott, e-mail exchange, November 12–13, 2000.
2. Ibid.
3. "Pilot with a Magic Hat," *Naval Aviation News* (August, 1968): 18–19; and interviews with squadron personnel.
4. William H. "Charlie" Johnson, interviews, February 25, 2000, and March 29, 2003.
5. CS1 "Charlie" Johnson, "The Flying Cook," www.seawolf.org/stories/cs1.Johnson.html. Edited in accordance with Johnson interview.
6. Ibid.

7. Ibid.

8. Ibid.

9. Michael J. Peters to Dick Knott, correspondence dated May 3, 1999.

10. Spencer, interview, September 9, 1999.

Chapter 10 The Whisperer

1. Jack Bolton, interview, July 5, 1999.

2. Ibid.

3. Dick Stanger, interview, April 27, 2000.

4. An MSB was 57 feet, 2.4 inches long, with a wooden hull. Its two diesel engines could push it along at about twelve knots. MSBs were typically crewed by six men and mounted two .30-caliber machine guns forward and a .50-caliber machine gun aft in a raised gun tub.

5. Bolton, fax dated January 27, 2000. Edited in Bolton, interview, March 12, 2000.

6. Ibid.

7. Ibid.

8. Ibid.

9. Ibid.

10. Ibid.

11. Ibid.

Chapter 12 Tet '68

1. General Giap later became minister of defense of the Socialist Republic of Vietnam.

2. Thomas Anzalone, interview, November 26, 1999.

3. Joseph S. Bouchard, interview, November 21, 1999.

4. Audiotape titled "Sounds of Battle" made available to the author by Joseph S. Bouchard.

5. Bouchard, interview.

6. Undated letter from Mother Superior Dynnpa of the Good Shepherd Convent, Vinh Long.

7. Capt. L. M. Kraft to Commander Bouchard, correspondence dated May 31, 1976, on the occasion of his retirement from the U.S. Navy.

8. Michael S. Louy, interview, December 13, 1999.

9. Wendell Maxwell, interview, November 6, 2004.

Chapter 13 Of Seabirds and Lawnmowers

1. Michael S. Louy, interviews, December 13, 1999, and May 22, 2004; and e-mail to Dick Knott dated June 28, 2000.

2. Ibid.

3. Ibid.

4. Cdr. Joseph S. Bouchard to the Navy Department, correspondence dated September 25, 1998.

5. Glen L. Wilson, correspondence to the secretary of the navy dated October 8, 1998.

6. Allen E. Weselesky, interview, April 4, 2000.

7. Wilson, correspondence.

8. Thomas Crull, correspondence to the chief of naval operations dated September 28, 1998.

9. C. J. Roberson, correspondence to the secretary of the navy dated October 13, 1998.

Chapter 14 Keeping the Faith

1. James R. Walker, interview, November 25, 2000; and undated Distinguished Flying Cross award signed by Adm. John J. Hyland, U.S. Navy.

2. Robert W. Spencer, interview, September 7, 1999.

3. Arthur Munson, interview, November 3, 2000.

4. Otto Gercken, interview, November 26, 2000.

5. Walker, interview; and undated Air Medal award signed by Vice Adm. E. R. Zumwalt, U.S. Navy.

6. Walker, interview; and undated Navy Cross award signed by Secretary of the Navy John H. Chafee.

7. Ibid.

8. Undated citation signed by Adm. John J. Hyland, Commander in Chief, U.S. Pacific Fleet, of the Distinguished Flying Cross award to Lt. (jg) Alan James Billings; and Billings, interview, January 9, 2000.

9. Billings, interview.

10. The U.S. Army's "Dust-off" helicopters were charged with casualty evacuation. Each Dust-off bird typically had a pilot, copilot, and two medical crewmen, one of whom was the crew chief. They routinely landed in hot landing zones to pick up the wounded, often under extremely hazardous circumstances. Dust-off crews were highly respected for their dedication and daring.

11. Billings, interview.

12. Ibid.

13. Ibid.

14. George C. Heady, interview, January 6, 2000.

15. Billings, interview and undated citation.

Chapter 15 Zumwalt, Sealords, and Vietnamization

1. Adm. E. R. Zumwalt became chief of naval operations on July 1, 1970. He was promoted over many more senior admirals, the youngest officer to be appointed to this post.

2. Sea Lords was the acronym for South East Asia Lake, Ocean, River, and Delta Strategy.

3. Otto Gercken, interview, November 4, 2000.

4. Frank Uhlig Jr., ed., *Vietnam: The Naval Story* (Annapolis: U.S. Naval Institute Press, 1986), 303.

5. OV-10a Broncos could carry M-60 7.62 machine guns, a 20-mm canon, SUU-11 mini-guns, 5-inch Zuni rockets, and 2.75-inch rockets in varying configurations.

Chapter 16 Seawolves Down

1. Richard W. "Dick" Barr, interview, June 24, 2000. *See also* Command History of Helatklron Three dated April 16, 1970, Chronological Narrative for Calendar Year 1969, 1–2.

2. Vincent G. Paone, interview, January 10, 2001.

3. Ibid.

4. William M. Ferrell, interview, January 10, 2001.

5. Ibid.

6. The tail stinger was a piece of metal projecting downward from the tail boom that prevented the tail rotor from coming in contact with the ground during takeoffs and landings.

7. Undated citation signed by Vice Adm. E. R. Zumwalt Jr., of the Bronze Star award to Lt. (jg) Dale Glen Odom.

8. Reynolds Beckwith, interview, December 2, 2000.

9. Details of the shooting down of Seawolves 320 and 305 and the subsequent rescue by Outlaw 29 are taken from the Chronological Narrative for 1969, Squadron History, declassified, October 25, 1972.

Chapter 17 The Ca Mau Peninsula

1. William P. Franklin, interview, January 23, 2001.

2. For a good look at the Black Ponies see Kit Lavell, *Flying Black Ponies: The Navy's Air Support Squadron in Vietnam* (Annapolis: Naval Institute Press, 2000).

3. Franklin, interview.

4. Ibid.

5. Reynolds Beckwith, interview.

6. HA(L)-3 memorandum dated February 27, 1970, to administrative assistant, chief of staff, COMNAVFORV, summarizing squadron accomplishments during the previous year (see item 6).

7. Edward J. Marolda, *By Sea, Air, and Land: An Illustrated History of the U.S. Navy and the War in Southeast Asia* (Washington, D.C.: Naval Historical Center, 1994, 278.

8. Beckwith, interview.

9. Ibid.

10. Roger Ek, "Seawolf Swapp," Seawolf Web site—www.seawolf.org/stories/story1.asp

11. Casualty statistics taken from declassified enclosures to Command History of Helatkltron Three for Calendar Year 1969.

Chapter 18 Cambodia, Sea Float, and Solid Anchor

1. Tom Phillips, "Scramble Seawolves!" Part 2:2, Seawolf Web site—www.seawolf.org/scrmbl02.asp.

2. HA(L)-3 memorandum dated February 27, 1970, (see item 10).

3. Reynolds Beckwith, interview.

4. Lon Nol was the defense minister in Prince Sihanouk's government. His action against North Vietnamese sanctuaries and his support of the Cambodian incursion by U.S. and South Vietnamese forces ultimately led to his downfall and the rise of the Khmer Rouge to power in 1975.

5. Phillip Gutzman, *Vietnam: A Visual Encyclopedia* (London: PRC Publishing Ltd., 2002), 87.

6. U.S. Army, Central Identification Laboratory, Hickham AFB, Hawaii, CILHI 2000–059.

7. Anthony J. Guptaitis Jr., and Tom Phillips, combined interview, November 6, 2004.

8. William R. Rutledge, interview, January 9, 2003.

9. Gutzman, 87–88.

10. Thurman L. Hicks, "War Story," Seawolf Web site—www.seawolf.org/stories/hicks_story.asp.

11. David K. Smale, interview, March 25, 2002.

12. Michael L. Lagow, interview, May 7, 2002.

13. Smale, interview.

Chapter 19 Bad Day at VC Lake

1. James P. Plona, interview, April 12, 2002.
2. David K. Smale, interview, March 25, 2002.
3. David Speidel, interview, April 8, 2002.
4. Ibid.
5. Plona, interview.
6. Smale, interview.
7. Michael L. Lagow, interview.
8. Smale, interview.
9. Thomas G. Padon, interview, April 10, 2002.
10. Smale, interview.
11. Plona, interview
12. Lagow, interview.
13. Ibid.
14. Padon, interview.
15. William R. Beltz, interview, April 12, 2002.
16. Ibid.
17. Ibid.
18. William R. Rutledge recollections taken from "VC Lake Battle, 15 September 1970, Another Perspective." See Seawolf Web site—www.seawolf.org. *See also* Rutledge, interview.
19. William R. Beltz, recollections taken from "Incident at VC Lake," *Journal of the American Aviation Historical Society* (Winter, 1988). *See also* Beltz, interview.
20. Jim Plona, recollections taken from "Outpost Hotel, July 1970," the HA(L)-3 Web site. *See also* Plona, interview.

Chapter 20 The War Grinds On

1. Freddie T. Stark, "War Story," Seawolf Web site—www.seawolf.org/stories/stark_story.asp.
2. An armored troop transport (ATC) was a modified LCM-6 that was heavily armored and armed with turret mounted 20-mm canon, 40-mm rapid fire grenade launchers, M-60 machine guns, and rocket pods. It had a seven-man crew and could carry about forty combat-equipped troops. Maximum speed was six to eight knots.
3. Don Thomson, interview, February 26, 2002.
4. Mike W. Dobson, interview, November 23, 2002.
5. Ibid.
6. Thomson, interview.
7. See the Seawolf Web site—www.seawolf.org—for Tom Phillips's description of the incident in "Scramble Seawolves!" Part 2:3–4.

8. Thomson, interview.

9. Richard Blair, interview, December 3, 2002.

10. David Speidel, interview, April 8, 2002.

11. Ibid.

12. Blair, interview.

13. Ibid.

14. Ibid.

15. Message 250830Z Nov 70 from Helatkltron Three to SecNav, Info CINC-PACFLT, COMNAVFORV, DEPCOMNAVFORV, CTF 116. (Message recommending the Navy Cross be awarded to Lt. (jg) Kevin Francis Delaney.)

16. Hicks, "War Story," 5.

17. Philip D. Chinnery, *Vietnam: The Helicopter War* (Annapolis: Naval Institute Press, 1991), 73.

18. "Maudlin Mission," *Wolfgram* (Winter 2002): 6–8. (The *Wolfgram* is the newsletter of the Seawolf Association.)

Chapter 21 Door Gunners

1. William R. Rutledge, interview, January 19, 2003.

2. John P. Lynn. From the documentary *The Seawolves of Vietnam*, Tully Entertainment.

3. Sam A. Taylor. From the documentary *The Seawolves of Vietnam*, Tully Entertainment.

4. Terry Ogle, e-mail dated September 3, 2003.

5. Norman B. Stayton, interview, July 13, 2003; and Stayton e-mail dated July 20, 2003.

6. Stayton, interview.

7. Ibid.

8. Ibid.

9. Ibid.

10. Ibid.

11. Terry Ogle, e-mail dated September 3, 2003.

12. Ibid.

13. Ibid.

14. Bill Schieber, e-mail to Gordon Peterson, January 11, 2000.

15. Gordon L. Peterson, "AO3 James A. Wall: Hero & Patriot," *Wings of Gold* (Summer 2000): 43. Reprinted with permission from *Seapower,* the magazine of the Navy League of the United States.

16. Rutledge, who had volunteered for a second tour, was now one of the squadron's three NATOPS door gunners. NATOPS gunners were some of the most experienced in the squadron and were used to check other gunners to make sure they

were using their guns safely and with maximum effectiveness. This was often accomplished during combat strikes. NATOPS gunners were also used on occasion to fill in when a detachment was shorthanded.

17. Peterson, article, 44.

18. Ibid.

19. Rutledge, interview.

20. Rutledge, undated and unpublished manuscript, "Combat Action of April 19, 1971: When AO3 Jim Wall Gave His Life in the Service of His Country as a Helicopter Door Gunner," 1. *See also* Rutledge, interview.

21. Jim Wall's medals include the Air Medal, the Bronze Star, the Distinguished Flying Cross, and the Purple Heart.

22. Popular Forces were originally organized under the authority of province chiefs to provide security for their own villages. Regional Forces were originally called the Civil Guard and were formed to protect strategic points in the Mekong Delta. These organizations were later combined into Regional and Popular Forces and were eventually absorbed into the South Vietnamese armed forces. The Americans dubbed them Ruff Puffs.

23. Rutledge, interview.

Chapter 22 Of Seals and Seawolves

1. Tom Richards, speech delivered at the Seawolf Reunion banquet, Charleston, South Carolina, November 6, 2004.

2. Robert A. Gormly, *Combat Swimmer: Memoirs of a Navy SEAL* (New York: Penguin Putnam, 1999), 122, 148.

3. Michael W. Dobson, "War Story," Seawolf Web site—www.seawolf.org/stories/dobson_story.asp. *See also* Dobson, interview, November 23, 2002.

4. Ibid.

5. Ibid.

6. Ibid.

7. Ibid.

8. Ibid.

9. Kenneth Wheeler, Seawolf Web site—www.seawolf.org/stories/wheeler.html. *See also* ADJ2 Madison Freeman, Seawolf Web site—www.seawolf.org/stories/adj2_freeman.html.

10. Tom Phillips, "Scramble Seawolves!" Part 3: 3–4.

11. Ibid, 4.

12. Ibid.

Chapter 23 Winding Down? Who Says?

1. Thomas L. Phillips, "Scramble Seawolves!" Part 5: 3, Seawolf Web site—www.seawolf.org/scrmb105.asp. Information in this chapter is also taken from an interview with Tom Phillips on March 22, 2004.

2. Lewis D. Madden, interview, March 28, 2004.

3. Steve Hanvey, interview, March 22, 2004.

4. Phillips, Scramble Seawolves, 3.

5. Ibid., 7.

6. Ibid., 8.

7. Madden, interview.

8. Ibid.

9. Phillips, "Scramble Seawolves!" 10.

10. Ibid.

11. Madden, interview.

12. Phillips, "Scramble Seawolves!"

13. Madden, interview.

14. Phillips, "Scramble Seawolves!" 11.

15. Madden, interview.

Chapter 24 Fun at the Beach

1. Nelson Landy, letter to ADJ2 Anthony J. Guptaitis Jr., August 30, 1971. The personnel to whom Landy refers are Lt. (jg) Stephen A. Hanvey, Lt. (jg) Thomas F. Cleverdon, ADJ2 Norman A.L. Shinkoethe, and AMS2 Thomas E. Elliott.

2. Charles R. Hall, interview, April 24, 2004.

3. Command History of Helatkltron Three for Calendar Year 1971, Chronology entry for August 28, 1971, 8.

4. Barry Solomon, interview, 17 March 2004.

5. Ibid.

6. Landy, letter.

7. Solomon, interview.

8. Stephen A. Hanvey, interview, March 22, 2004.

9. Ibid.

10. Hall, interview.

11. Hanvey, interview.

12. John M. "Mike" Masica, interview, April 8, 2004.

13. Ibid.

14. Reid had already been awarded one Distinguished Flying Cross for action on July 27, 1971, when, flying a single gunship that had been damaged by enemy fire, he provided essential cover to a SEAL team in extremis.

Chapter 25 Turning Out the Lights

1. William J. Mulcahy, interviews, April 17 and April 23, 2004.

2. Cdr. Donald Nichols, and Capt. Charles O. Borgstrom, "The Seawolves: Past . . . Present . . . Future?" December 1, 1971.

3. Command History of Helatkltron Three for Calendar Year 1971, Enclosure 1, Chronology entry for July 28.

4. Locations of detachments and information on their activities were taken largely from Command History of Helatkltron Three for the Calendar Year 1971, Enclosure 2, Narrative, 2-4, as well as an annotated map and information provided by HA(L)-3 commanding officer Captain Borgstrom.

5. Charles R. Hall, interview, April 24, 2004.

6. Mulcahy, interview.

7. Command History, Chronology entry for September 20.

8. Commander Cover was the senior officer, but he was flying as copilot because he was not yet a qualified AHAC. He had arrived at the detachment as officer in charge just six days before.

9. Mulcahy, interview.

10. Charles O. Borgstrom Jr., interview, August 18, 1999.

11. On December 19, 1970, a Seawolf gunship en route from Ca Mau to Binh Thuy crashed near Kien Long. The pilot, Lt. (jg) Richard H. Buzzell, copilot, Lt. (jg) Antonio A. Ortiz, and door gunners AEC Johnny Ratliff and ADJ2 Robert E. Worth were killed in the crash.

12. Borgstrom, interview.

13. These rescues are recorded on page 11 of the Command History Chronology.

14. Nineteen gunships were UH-1Bs, and ten were UH-1Ms; four of the Sealords aircraft were UH-1Ls, and two were UH-1Ks.

15. Seawolves killed in 1971 were Barden, Cover, Cowen, Goldbin, and Wall.

16. CNO message 111716Z dated March 1971.

Glossary of Acronyms and Terms

ACTOV: Accelerated turnover plan, the U.S. Navy's part of the Vietnamization program

AHAC: Attack helicopter aircraft commander

AMMI pontoons: Developed by the Naval Facilities Engineering Command, these pontoons were decked over and used for a variety of platforms, including mobile basing.

ARVN: Army of the Republic of Vietnam

ATC: Armored troop carrier

ATCH: An ATC with a small helicopter landing deck

Black Ponies: A fixed-wing Light Attack Squadron (VAL4) that flew OV10A Bronco aircraft in support of riverine forces and other "friendlies" in the Mekong Delta.

Body snatches: Kidnapping enemy personnel for interrogation.

BUPERS: Bureau of Personnel

Charlie: Nickname for the Viet Cong (VC) based on the words "Victor Charlie" of the phonetic alphabet.

Chicken plate: A kevlar vest worn by pilots and door gunners.

CHNAVADVGRU: Chief Naval Advisory Group Vietnam

CNO: Chief of Naval Operations

CO: Commanding officer

COMUSMACV: Commander U.S. Military Assistance Command Vietnam

COMNAVFORV: Commander Naval Forces Vietnam

Det.: Detachment. A Seawolf detachment was normally made up of two gunships, eight or nine pilots, and eight or nine door gunners.

DFC: Distinguished Flying Cross

Dinassauts: Division Navales d'Assault, an earlier French version of the American Mobile Riverine Force (MRF).

Dust-off: U.S. Army helicopters that performed medical evacuation, often under fire.

FAC: Forward air controller

FFAR: Folding fin aerial rocket

Fleshette: An antipersonnel rocket warhead containing some twenty-four hundred steel projectiles. Also referred to as "nails."

Free-fire zone: An area from which all innocent civilians and water traffic had been cleared. Anyone found there was assumed to be enemy and was dealt with accordingly.

FTL: Fire team leader

Guns: An abbreviated name for helicopter gunships.

HAC: Helicopter aircraft commander

HAL: Helicopter Attack Light Squadron

HC-1: Helicopter Combat Support Squadron One

HE Warhead: High explosive rocket warhead

HHFT: Heavy helicopter fire team consisting of three helicopter gunships

Hootch: A slang term for a living accommodation. In Southeast Asia, it was typically a small berthing structure consisting of a wooden platform, louvered and screened sides, and a wooden, metal, or tent roof. Seawolf detachment hootches could usually accommodate eight to ten people; some were larger.

Hot landing zone: An LZ that is under fire.

HS: Helicopter Antisubmarine Squadron

Huey: The popular name for the Bell UH1 series of helicopters. The name is derived from its earlier HU designation.

JP4/JP5: Jet fuel

LCM: Landing craft mechanized. Also called a Mike boat

LCPL: Landing craft personnel large

LHFT: Light helicopter fire team consisting of two helicopter gunships

Limpet mines: Mines that were attached to ships, barges, and other large watercraft by swimmers and timed to detonate after the swimmer had safely left the area.

LSD: Landing ship dock

LZ: Landing zone

MACV: Military Assistance Command Vietnam

Market Time: Patrols conducted by the Coastal Surveillance Force of Task Force 115 to interdict vessels attempting to supply the Viet Cong by sea.

Medevac: Medical evacuation

MRF: Mobile Riverine Force (Task Force 117)

"Newbie": A new man in the squadron; also known as an FNG, for f—ing new guy.

MSB: Mine sweeping boat

Nails: *See* Fleshette

NASM: National Air and Space Museum

North Vietnam: The Democratic Republic of Vietnam

NVA: North Vietnamese Army; the actual name was the People's Army of Vietnam, or PAVN.

NWIP: Naval warfare information publication

PBR: Patrol boat river. These 31-foot boats were used by the River Patrol Force (Task Force 116) to patrol the waterways of the Delta and to interdict enemy forces.

PCF: Patrol craft fast; also known as Swift Boats, these 50-foot, aluminum-hulled, twenty-five knot boats were used in Operations Market Time and Sea Lords

PRV: Provincial Reconnaissance Unit

PSP: Perforated steel plating used for temporary runways and aircraft parking areas

ROE: Rules of Engagement

RPG: Rocket propelled grenade

Ruff Puffs: American and Australian nickname for Regional and Popular Forces, essentially South Vietnamese Militia used primarily to man outposts and protect villages.

Sampan: A small watercraft used in the rivers and other internal waterways. Most sampans were usually propelled by paddling or sculling, but they might even have a small motor and/or a sail.

SAR: Search and rescue

Scramble: Launch

SeaBees: CBs; construction battalion

SEAL: Sea, air, land; U.S. Navy commando-type forces trained to operate in enemy-held territory for reconnaissance and a variety of other clandestine purposes.

Sea Lords: South East Asia lake, ocean, river, and delta; strategy put into effect by Vice Adm. Elmo R. Zumwalt in 1968.

Sealords aircraft: Unarmed HH1K and UH1L helicopters used for logistics, SEAL insertions and extractions, medical evacuations, and other combat support missions.

SERE: Survival, evasion, resistance and escape

Sissy belt: A slang expression for the belt and strap worn by door gunners to keep them from falling from the helicopter during combat.

Slick: An unarmed helicopter. The army used them primarily for transporting assault troops and for medical evacuation. The navy used them for inserting and extracting SEALS, psychological warfare, medical evacuation, and logistics. *See* Sealords aircraft

Swift Boat: *See* PCF

Tango boat: An armored troop carrier

Tet: Vietnamese New Year

TF: Task Force

TOC: Tactical Operations Center

VAL: Light Attack Squadron

Viet Cong: Derisive term for Vietnamese Communists.

Viet Minh: From *VietNam Doc Lap Dong Minh Hoi*—Communist insurgents who fought against the French.

Vietnamization: The process of phasing out U.S. armed forces in South Vietnam while strengthening and expanding the South Vietnamese military forces.

VNAF: South Vietnamese Air Force

VNMC: South Vietnamese Marine Corps

VNN: South Vietnamese Navy

WP warheads: White phosphorous rocket warheads; also known as Willie Petes.

XO: Executive Officer

YRBM: Yard, repair, berthing, and messing; a non-self-propelled vessel that provided a base for ten PBRs and two Huey gunships and their crews.

Bibliography

Articles

Chapelle, Dickey. "Water War in Vietnam." *National Geographic* (February 1966): 270–96.

Cook, John. "The Attack Helicopter." *U.S. Naval Institute Proceedings* (October 1972): 97–100.

Dodd, Daniel. "Navy Gunship Helicopters in the Mekong." *U.S. Naval Institute Proceedings* (May 1968): 91–104.

Miller, Richard T. "Fighting Boats of the United States." *U.S. Naval Institute Naval Review* (May 1968): 296–329.

Peterson, Gordon I. "The War Without Heroes?" *Sea Power* (May, 1999): 1.

Rose, Dick. "Seawolves of the Mekong Delta." *Vietnam Chronicals: Air War Vietnam*, vol.1 (1991): 28–33.

Rosier, Bill. "Pilot with the Magic Hat." *Naval Aviation News* (August 1968): 18–19.

———. "Seawolves in the Delta." *Naval Aviation News*, (March 1970): 16–17.

———. "Seawolves on the Prowl." *Naval Aviation News* (January 1967): 26–28.

Sprinkle, James D. "HELATKLTRON THREE: The Seawolves." *Journal of the American Aviation Historical Society* (Winter 1988): 290–310.

Tyler, David G. "Seawolves Roll in Across the Mekong Delta." *Naval Institute Proceedings* (January 2002): 42–49.

Wells, W.C. "The Riverine Force in Action." *U.S. Naval Institute Naval Review* (1969): 46 ff.

Weselesky, A.E. "The Seawolf Helo Pilots of Vietnam." *U.S. Naval Institute Proceedings* (May 1968): 128–30.

White, Peter T. "The Mekong: River of Terror and Hope." *National Geographic* (December 1968): 744–87.

Books

Chinnery, Philip D. *Vietnam: The Helicopter War.* Annapolis: Naval Institute Press, 1991.

Croizat, Victor. *The Brown Water Navy: The River and Coastal War in Indo China and Vietnam, 1948–1972.* Poole, UK: Blandford Press, 1984.

Cutler, Thomas J. *Brown Water, Black Berets: Coastal and Riverine Warfare in Vietnam.* Annapolis: Naval Institute Press, 1988.

Forbes, John, and Robert Williams. *The Illustrated History of Riverine Force: The Vietnam War.* New York: Bantam Books, 1987.

Gutzman, Philip. *Vietnam: A Visual Encyclopedia,* London: PRC Publishing Ltd., 2002.

Hooper, Edwin B., Dean C. Allard, and Oscar P. Fitzgerald. *The United States Navy and the Vietnam Conflict.* Vol. I: *The Setting of the Stage to 1959.* Washington, D.C.: Naval History Division/Government Printing Office, 1976.

Kelly, Daniel E. *Seawolves: First Choice.* New York: The Ballantine Publishing Group, 1998.

Marolda, Edward J. *By Air Land and Sea.* Washington, D.C.: Naval Historical Center, 1994.

Marolda, Edward J., and Oscar P. Fitzgerald. *The United States Navy and the Vietnam Conflict.* Vol.2: *From Military Assistance to Combat, 1959–1965.* Washington, D.C.: Naval Historical Center, 1986.

McGuire, John F., ed. *River Patrol Force.* An unofficial, undated publication of Task Force 116.

Mersky, Peter, and Norman Polmar. *The Naval Air War in Vietnam.* Annapolis: Nautical & Aviation Publishing Co. of America, 1981.

Rottman, Gordon L. *The Vietnam Brown Water Navy: Riverine and Coastal Warfare 1965–69.* Hong Kong: Concord Publications Co., 1997.

Schreadley, R.L. *From the Rivers to the Sea: The United States Navy in Vietnam.* Annapolis: Naval Institute Press, 1972.

Uhlig, Frank, Jr., ed. *Vietnam: The Naval Story.* Annapolis: Naval Institute Press, 1986.

Zumwalt, Elmo R., Jr. *On Watch: A Memoir.* New York: Quadrangle Press/The New York Times Book Co., 1976.

Public Documents

U.S. National Archives, *Ship's Deck Log, USS* Belle Grove *(LSD-2)*. (1966).

U.S. National Archives, *Ship's Deck Log, USS* Jennings County *(LST-846)*. (1966).

U.S. National Archives, *Ship's Deck Log, USS* Tortuga *(LSD-26)*. (1966).

U.S. Navy. *Commander U.S. Naval Forces Vietnam, Navy News Release.* Release 19F-68 (1968).

U.S. Navy. *Command History of HELATKLTRON THREE for Calendar Year 1969.* Declassified 10/24/72.

U.S. Navy. *Command History of HELATKLTRON THREE for Calendar Year 1970.* Declassified 10/25/72.

U.S. Navy. *Command History of HELATKLTRON THREE for Calendar Year 1971.* Declassified 10/25/72.

U.S. Navy HELATKLTRON THREE, Standardization Manual (Operating Procedures), 1 April 1968.

U.S. Navy. *THE "SEAWOLVES" PAST . . . PRESENT . . . FUTURE?* (1 December 1971).

Unpublished Works

Jaburg, Conrad. *"As It Was in the Beginning."* A three-page, undated description of the early days of HA(L)-3.

Nichols, Donald, and Charles O. Borgstrom. *"The Seawolves: Past . . . Present . . . Future?"* An eight-page history of HA(L)-3 from 1966–1971.

Phillips, Tom. *"Scramble Seawolves!"* A fifteen-part account of the Seawolf experience, available on the Seawolf Web site: www.seawolf.org.

Index

About the Author

Richard Knott writes from the perspective of both naval aviator and historian. He has logged several thousand pilot hours during more than thirty years of naval service. A former editor of *Naval Aviation News* magazine, he also headed the Office of Naval Aviation History and Publications before retiring in 1986.

Captain Knott holds a bachelor's and a master's degree and is a graduate of the Naval War College. He is the author of three books—*The American Flying Boat: An Illustrated History, Black Cat Raiders of World War Two,* and *A Heritage of Wings: An Illustrated History of Navy Aviation*—and numerous magazine articles on aviation history. A recipient of the Admiral Arthur W. Radford Award for Excellence in Naval Aviation History and Literature, and the Alfred Thayer Mahan Award for Literary Achievement, he was the National Air and Space Museum's Adjunct Ramsey Fellow for 1999.

Captain Knott and his wife live in Fairfax, Virginia.